Bernard H. Hamel
B.A. Universidad de Las Américas, México
M.A. University of California at Los Angeles
Ph. D. Universidad Autónoma de Madrid

WITHDRAWN

HAMEL'S BILINGUAL
DICTIONARY OF
LATIN AMERICAN SPANISH

DICCIONARIO BILINGÜE
DE AMERICANISMOS

D0022389

BILINGUAL BOOK PRESS

FIRST EDITION - 1996

BILINGUAL DICTIONARY OF LATIN AMERICAN SPANISH

Series director: Bernard H. Hamel

Published in the United States of America
by Bilingual Book Press, 10977 Santa Monica Blvd.,
Los Angeles, CA 90025.

ISBN 1-886835-03-9

Library of Congress Catalog Card Number: 95-94821

A mis hijos, Bernard y Carlos
(por orden alfabético). Porque sí.

Table of Contents

Abreviaciones y signos

adj.	Adjective	Adjectivo
adv.	Adverb	Adverbio
angl.	Anglicized word	Anglicismo
autom.	Automotive	Automóviles
biol.	Biology	Biología
bot.	Botany	Botánica
chem.	Chemistry	Química
cine	Cinema	Cinema
comm, com.	Commerce	Comercio
const.	Construction	Construcción
cost.	Sowing	Costura
culin.	Culinary	Culinario, cocina
dep.	Sport	Deportes
econ.	Economy	Economía
elect.	Electricity, electronics	Electricidad, electrónica
excl..	Exclamation	Exclamación
f.	Feminine	Femenino
ferro.	Railways	Ferrocarriles
fin.	Finance	Finanza
hum.	Humorous	Humorístico
interj.	Interjection	Interjección
jur.	Law, legal	Derecho, jurídico
m.	Masculine	Masculino
mech.	Mechanics, mechanical	Mecánica, mecánico
med.	Medicine	Medicina
mus.	Music	Música
naut.	Nautical	Náutica
min.	Mining	Minería
n.	Noun	Nombres, ustantivo
prep.	Preposition	Preposición
quim.	Chemistry	Química
rail.	Railways	Ferrocarriles
rel.	Religion	Religión
sew.	Sewing	Costura
v.	Verb	Verbo
zool.	Zoology	Zoología

INTRODUCTION

Although the selection in the present work is limited to words common to all, most or much of Latin America -excluded are those used exclusively in individual countries such as Argentina, Cuba, Chile, etc.-, once this limitation is established, it can be said that its content can be considered a fairly complete reference work on the subject, and as such can serve as a useful tool for teachers, translators and students of Spanish.

Initially students, through language learning texts and reading materials, are most often introduced to 'Castilian' Spanish, that is the Spanish spoken and written in Spain. This is not altogether unreasonable, given the rich and long cultural tradition of the mother country. In a sense it is the umbilical cord through which the cultural legacy of the old world is transmitted to the new.

In practice, however, the student soon finds Spain to be a distant land, that its people speak with a strange-sounding accent, and that they use words and expressions with which they are altogether unfamiliar (much in the same way that Spaniards must react in regards to Latin American Spanish). Even following a limited or extended stay in that country, the student, upon returning home, is likely to feel out of place and promptly revert to the Spanish as spoken in his immediate surroundings. Such as would occur to an American returning after a stay in England.

Knowledge of Latin American Spanish *is* therefore of utmost interest and importance. It is the Spanish that he is most likely to hear and need to speak. Undeniably, the prevailing Spanish-Speaking culture in this country is predominantly Latin American; the novels and poetry he will read, the persons he will meet, and the countries to which he may travel are more likely to be associated with Latin America than Spain.

Since our main interest in writing this book has centered around the language itself, it is more apt to include words of practical value rather than those of a scientific or encyclopedic nature (names of trees and plants, insects, animals, tribes, political parties, etc.). As such, it is more likely to appeal to translators than to scholars. We did, however, include words related to popular Latin American folklore: music, dress, typical dishes, customs, etc., since they are such an essential part of the daily life of the people, and since they so colorfully characterize Latin America. Omitted are words of obvious meaning: *Argentina, bolivianismo, paraguayo*, etc., and words considered 'anglicismos', since the use of these are not necessarily limited to Latin America, but is prevalent wherever Spanish is spoken. Also omitted are words referred to as 'barbarismos': *marqueta, braques*, etc.

This work is the second volume of a projected trilogy, the first of which was originally published in 1994[1]. The third volume will include words and expressions not included in the first two volumes and pertaining to individual countries of Latin America and thus concluding the trilogy.

Bernard H. Hamel
Los Angeles, California, 1995

---

[1] *Bilingual Dictionary of Mexican Spanish.* Bernard H. Hamel. Bilingual Book Press. 2nd Ed., 1996. ISBN 1-886835-05-5. 160 pags.

PRÓLOGO

Puede parecer temerario intentar un diccionario de americanismos, por añadidura bilingüe, dado la gran cantidad de voces que han surgido y siguen surgiendo del continente americano de habla hispana, como lo demuestran los varios diccionarios que se han escrito sobre este tema.

Por otra parte, entendemos que todo diccionario, y en especial los de esta índole, ha de ser relativamente completo para no resultar de reducida utilidad para el usuario. Por lo tanto, ante la imposibilidad inmediata de emprender tal empeño; es decir recoger en un solo tomo la mayoría de los americanismos existentes, hemos resuelto presentar la presente obra dentro de una trilogía, sin apartarnos del criterio de que debe ser completa en lo que abarca, cada una de las obras. Dicha trilogía consta de las siguientes obras: *Diccionario Bilingüe de Mexicanismos*[1], *Diccionario Bilingüe de Americanismos*. Vol. 1: Voces de uso general en toda o gran parte de Hispanoamérica, *Diccionario Bilingüe de Americanismos*. Vol. 2: Voces propias de determinados países de Hispanoamérica. Como se verá, el último tomo intenta recoger aquellas voces no incluidas en los dos anteriores tomos y cierra el círculo de nuestra obra.

Quisiéramos aclarar que nuestro interés al escribir esta obra ha sido más bien de carácter lingüístico o idiomático que informativo, científico o enciclopédico, ni pretende ser la nuestra, obra de erudición. Por lo tanto quedan excluidas palabras que no tengan valor semántico propio: nombres de árboles y plantas, insectos, animales, tribus indígenas, etc., palabras que a nuestro parecer abultan y entorpecen esta clase de obra. Dentro de esta categoría de palabras, nos hemos limitado a incluir aquellas de carácter folklórico que en su conjunto reflejan la particular idiosincrasia del pueblo hispanoamericano: bailes y canciones, platos típicos, vestimenta, costumbres, etc. Tampoco hemos creído conveniente incluir palabras de sentido obvio: *Argentina, paraguayo, bolivianismos*, etc., y anglicismos (salvo aquellos que han venido a sustituir la palabra castiza) por no considerar dichos anglicismos propiamente americanismos, ya que son de uso generalizado tanto en España como en Hispanoamérica (sin mencionar los Estados Unidos, por supuesto). Por motivos de orden práctico tampoco hemos incluido voces en desuso.

Bernard H. Hamel
Los Angeles, California, 1995

---

[1] *Bilingual Dictionary of Mexican Spanish*. Bernard H. Hamel. Bilingual Book Press. 2nd Ed., 1996. ISBN 1-886835-05-5. 160 pags.

A

A •A la mañana, A la tarde, A la noche. Por la mañana, por la tarde, por la noche. *In the morning, in the afternoon, in the evening.* || **2.** •A más...mayor... Cuanto más... mayor... *The more... the more...* ~A más esfuerzos, más rendimiento. Cuanto más esfuerzos, mayor rendimiento. *The more effort, the greater the result.* || **3.** •¿A POCO? (1) ¡No me diga! *Not really!, You don't say!* (2) Acaso, a lo mejor. ¿A POCO crees que...? ¿Acaso crees que...? *Do you really imagine that...?* (3) En caso de que. *In case that, in the instance that.* A POCO que pueda. En caso de que pueda. *If at all possible.* || **4.** •Al año, a la semana, a los pocos días. Un año, una semana, unos pocos días después. *A year, a week, a few days later.*

A DONDE. *adv.* Donde. *Where?* ~¿A DÓNDE está tu hermana? ¿Dónde está tu hermana? *Where is your sister?*

ABACORA. *n.f.* Especie de atún parecido al bonito. *Albacore (type of tuna, resembling the bonito).*

ABACORAR. v. (Acad.) Acaparar. *To monopolize, corner the market.*

ABADESA. *n.f.* Mujer que dirige un prostíbulo. *Madame, brothel keeper.*

ABAJAR. *v.* Bajar. *To lower.*

ABAJEÑO. *adj.* (Acad.) Procedente o relativo a las costas o tierras bajas. *Pertaining or coming from the coastland or lowland.* || **2.** *n.m.* (Acad.) Natural o procedente de las tierras o costas bajas. *Lowlander, coastal dweller.*

ABAJERO (variante de **abajeño**).

ABAJO. *adv.* Debajo. *Underneath.* ~ABAJO llevaba un vestido de seda. *Underneath she was wearing a silk dress.* || **2.** •ABAJO de. Debajo de. *Under.* ABAJO de la cama. *Under the bed.* || **3.** •El piso de ABAJO. *The floor below, the next floor down.* Note: Normally this expression means the bottom floor.

ABALEADOR. *n.m.* Pistolero, matón. *Gunman.*

ABALEAR. *v.* Tirotear. *To shoot off guns, fire in the air.* || **2.** (Acad.) Balear, disparar con bala sobre alguien o algo; herir o matar a balazos. *To fire, shoot at someone; to wound or kill with a gunshot.* || **3.** Fusilar, pasar por las armas. *To execute (by firing squad).*

ABALEO. *n.m.* Disparo, tiroteo. *Shooting.*

ABANDERADO (dep.). *n.m.* Juez de línea. *Linesman.*

ABANDERIZAR. *v.* Afiliarse en un bando, partido político. *To join a political party.*

ABANDONADO. *adj.* Dejado, descuidado en el aseo de su persona. *Slovenly, untidy.* || **2.** Pervertido. *Perverted.*

ABANDONO. *n.m.* Descuido. *Untidiness, disorder.*

ABANIQUEAR. *v.* Abanicar. *To fan.* || **2.** -se. *To fan oneself.*

ABARCAR. *v.* Acaparar mercaderías con fines de especulación. *To monopolize, stockpile, corner the market.*

ABARRAJADO. *adj.* Desvergonzado, descarado. *Shameless, insolent.*

ABARRAJAR. *v.* Tirar. *Hurl, throw.* || **2.** -se. Encanallarse, envilecerse. *To become corrupt or depraved.* || **3.** Tropezar, caer. *To slip, fall.*

ABARROTADOR. *n.m.* Persona que tiene tienda o despacho de abarrotes. *General store keeper.*

ABARROTAMIENTO. *n.m.* Efecto de **abarrotarse** un artículo de comercio. *Loss of* *value (product).*

ABARROTAR. *v.* Acaparar. *To monopolize, buy up.* || **2. -se.** Abaratarse una cosa por su excesiva abundancia. *To go down in price, to become a glut on the market.*

ABARROTE (variante de **abarrotería**). || **2. -s.** *n.m.* Comestibles, artículos de primera necesidad. *Groceries, food supply, provisions.*

ABARROTERÍA. *n.f.* Tienda de **abarrotes.** *Grocery store, general store.*

ABARROTERO. *n.m* Que tiene tienda de abarrotes. *Grocer, storekeeper.*

ABASTERO. *n.m.* Abastecedor de ganado. *Cattle-dealer.* || **2.** Abastecedor de comestibles. *Provision merchant.*

ABATANADO. *adj.* (Acad.) Dícese del tejido muy compacto o de mucho cuerpo. *Hardened, compressed, matted (fabric).*

ABATANAR. *v.* (Acad.) Desgastarse, apelmazarse un tejido por el uso o el lavado. *To become worn or matted due to wear or constant washing (fabric).*

ABEJERA. *n.f.* Colmena. *Beehive.*

ABERRACIÓN. *n.f.* Obstinación en un error. *Stubbornness, wrongheadedness, bullheadedness.* || **2.** Error de juicio inexplicable (angl.). *Aberration.*

ABETUNAR. *V.* Limpiar, lustrar. *To polish, clean.*

ABICHARSE. *v.* (Acad.) Agusanarse la fruta. *To become worm-eaten.* || **2.** (Acad.) Criar gusanos las heridas de una persona o animal. *To become worm-ridden (wound).*

ABIERTA. *n.f.* (Acad.) Abertura. *Opening.*

ABIERTO. *adj.* Liberal, pródigo. *Generous, open.* || **2.** Comprensivo, tolerante. *Understanding, tolerant.*

ABISMAL. *adj.* Profundo. *Abysmal.*

ABISMANTE. *adj.* Asombroso, extraordinario, pasmoso. *Amazing, astonishing.*

ABISMARSE. *v.* (Acad.) Quedarse sorprendido, asombrado, admirado. *To be amazed, astonished.*

ABIZCOCHADO. *adj.* Esponjoso, a ma-nera de un bizcocho. *Spongy.*

ABOCHORNADO. *adj.* Sonrojado. *Blushing.* || **2.** Avergonzado. *Embarrassed.*

ABOGADERAS. *n.f.* (Acad.) Argumentos capciosos. *Deceptive, misleading arguments, quibbling.*

ABOLSARSE. *v.* Fruncirse (ropa). *To bunch up (clothes).* || **2.** Formársele rodilleras a los pantalones por el uso. *To become baggy at the knees (trousers).*

ABOMBADO. *adj.* En mal estado (agua o alimento). *To be rotten, smell foul.* || **2.** (Acad.) Aturdido, atontado. *Bewildered, stunned, dazed.* || **3.** (Acad.) Tonto, falto o escaso de entendimiento, razón. *Silly, dopey.* ~¡No seas tan ABOMBADO! *Don't be such a dope!*

ABOMBARSE. *v.* Pudrirse (comida). *To rot, decompose; to smell bad (food).* || **2.** (Acad.) Achisparse, tomarse del vino. *To get tight.*

ABONERO. *n.m.* Que recoge abonos. *Tallyman, collector.*

ABONO. *n.m.* Tarjeta, cédula o billete en que consta que uno ha pagado un servicio, una diversión, etc., vale, bono. *Ticket, voucher, coupon.* || **2.** Depósito. *Down payment, deposit.*

ABORLONADO. *adj.* Se dice de las telas cuyo tejido aparece formado de cordoncillos, acanillado. *Ribbed, stripped (caused by a defect in weaving).*

ABORREGARSE. *v.* Abobarse. *To be silly, get silly.* || **2.** Volverse tonto, embrutecerse. *To become dull, slow or stupid.*

ABORRICARSE (variante de **aborregarse**).

ABRA. *n.f.* Hoja batiente de puerta o ventana. *Panel or leaf of a door.* || **2.** (Acad.) Espacio desmontado, claro en un bosque. *Clearing (in a wood), path (through the underbrush).*

ABRACAR. *v.* (Acad.) Abarcar, ceñir con los brazos, abrazar. *To hug, embrace.* || **2.** Abarcar, ceñir, rodear. *To cover, include, embrace.*

ABREBOCA. *adj.* Distraído. *Absent– minded.* || **2.** Aperitivo. *Appetizer.*

ABRELATA. *n.m.* Abrelatas. *Can opener.*

ABREVIAR. *v.* Acortar (el camino, los estudios). *To shorten.*

ABRIBOCA (variante de **abreboca**).

ABRIGADERO. *n.m.* Sitio o paraje donde acude la gente de mal vivir para ocultarse. *Lair, hideout.*

ABRILLANTADO. *adj.* Que brilla. *Shining.*

ABRILLANTAR. *v.* Glasear (fruta). *To glaze (fruit).*

ABRIR. *v.* Despejar (bosque). *To make a clearing in the woods.* || **2.** -se. (Acad.) Desistir de algo, volverse atrás, separarse de una compañía o negocio. *To back out, withdraw from a commitment.* || **3.** Abandonar un lugar disimulada y precipitadamente. *To leave stealthily and suddenly.* || **4.** En las carreras de caballo y autos, separarse involuntariamente de la línea que se sigue. *To swerve out.*

ABROCHADOR. *n.m.* Agrapador. *Stapler.*

ABROCHAR. *v.* Agrapar. *To staple together (papers).* || **2.** -se. *v.* Agarrarse para pelear cuerpo a cuerpo. *To struggle, wrestle.*

ABROGARSE. *v.* Arrogarse. *To assume, take upon oneself.*

ABRUMAR. *v.* Molestar. *To annoy, bother.*

ABSOLUTAMENTE. *adv.* De ninguna forma, en absoluto. *Not at all.*

ABUNDAR. *v.* •ABUNDAR en. Extenderse en consideraciones y razonamientos. *To go into great detail about something* || **2.** Ser una cosa frecuente o común. *To be common or frequent.* ~La traducción ABUNDA en errrores. *The translation is full of mistakes.*

ABUNDOSO. *adj.* Abundante. *Abundant.*

ABURRADO. *adj.* Parecido al burro. *Resembling a donkey, donkey-like.* || **2.** Embrutecido. *Made stupid, dull.*

ABURRARSE. *v.* Embrutecerse. *To become dull, stupid.*

ABURRICIÓN. *n.f.* Aversión, repugnancia, antipatía. *Revulsion, repugnance.*

ABURRIDO. *adj.* Harto. *Fed up.* ~Estoy ABURRIDO con los quehaceres de la casa. *I'm fed up with housework.*

ABUSADOR. *adj.* Confianzudo. *Cocksure, presumptuous.*

ABUSIVO. *adj.* Atrevido, descarado. *Said of someone who takes advantage.* ||**2.** Cruel, valentón. *Brute, bully.*

ACÁ. *adv.* Ultimamente, recientemente. *Lately, recently.* || **2.** (como demostrativo). Esta persona. *This person here.* ~ACÁ le contará. *He'll tell you about it.* ~ACÁ es mi señora. *And here is my wife.*

ACABADO. *adj.* Flaco. *Thin.*

ACABAR. *v.* Hablar mal de alguien. *To disparage, slander, speak ill of someone.* || **2.** -se. Envejecer. *To age, decline.* || **3.** Matarse, agotarse. *To wear oneself out.*

ACACITO. *adj.* Acá. *Here.*

ACADEMIA. *n.f.* •ACADEMIA de chóferes. *Driving school.*

ACALAMBRARSE. *v.* (Acad.) Contraerse los músculos a causa del calambre. *To get a cramp or cramps.*

ACAMASTRONARSE. *v.* Hacerse el camastrón; emplear astucia o maña. *To get crafty, become artful.*

ACÁPITE. *n.m.* (Acad.) Párrafo. *Paragraph.* || **2.** Sección. *Section.* || **3.** Encabezamiento. *Heading.* || **4.** Párrafo aparte. *Separate paragraph.*

ACARIÑAR. *v.* Acariciar. *To caress, to treat lovingly.*

ACARTONADO. *adj.* Enjuto. *Dried-up by age, withered.*

ACARTONARSE. Enflaquecer una persona, generalmente mayor de edad, hasta quedar enjuta. *To become withered with age.*

ACASERARSE. *v.* (Acad.) Hacerse parroquiano de una tienda. *To become a regular customer.*

ACATAR. *v.* Caer en cuenta, echar de ver. *To notice, realize, observe.*

ACCIDENTADO. *adj.* Jorobado. *Hunchbacked.*

ACCION. *n.f.* •ACCIONES son amores, no besos ni apachurrones. Obras son amores, que no buenas razones. *Actions speak louder than words.*

ACCIONAR. *v.* Iniciar un juicio. *To bring legal action against someone.*

ACECIDO. *n.m.* Acezo, jadeo. *Puffing, panting.*

ACEITADA. *n.f.* Lubrificación. *Oiling.*

ACEITERA. *n.f.* Vinagreras. *Cruet stand (for oil and vinegar).*

ACEITILLO. *n.m.* Aceite de tocador. *Cosmetic oil.*

ACEITUNO. *adj.* De color de aceituna verde. *Olive-colored.*

ACELERADA. *n.m.* Aceleración súbita. *Burst of acceleration.*

ACELERADO. *adj.* Nervioso. *Jumpy, nervous.* || **2.** Impaciente. *Impatient.*

ACELERARSE. *v.* Excitarse. *To get agitated, get jumpy, loose one's cool.* || **2.** Enloquecer. *To loose one's head.*

ACEQUIA. *v.* Arroyo. *Stream.* || **2.** Alcantarilla. *Sewer.*

ACERCARSE. *v.* Entablar. *To approach, open negotiations with someone.*

ACHACAR. *v.* Robar, hurtar. *Steal, rob, pilfer.* || **2.** Saquear. *Pillage, loot.*

ACHAJUANARSE. *v.* (Acad.) Sofocarse las bestias por trabajar mucho cuando hace demasiado calor o están muy gordas. *To get winded or tired (said of animals).*

ACHALAY. *Interj.* (Acad.) Interjección afectuosa o irónica que expresa admiración, ponderación y deseo. ¡Vaya!, ¡anda! *Well!*

ACHANTARSE. *v.* Detenerse. *To halt, stop.*

ACHAPLINARSE. *v.* Adoptar las peculiaridades características del actor Charles Chaplin. *To adopt mannerisms characteristic of Charles Chaplin.*

ACHATAMIENTO. *n.m.* Reducción o disminución del valor moral o intelectual de una institución o de una colectividad: *Loss of moral or intelectual fiber.* ~La dictadura produjo un ACHATAMIENTO en todos los órdenes de la vida nacional. *Dictatorship brought about a loss of moral and intelectual fiber at all levels of national life.*

ACHATARSE. *v.* Perder ánimo. *To loose heart, feel down.*

ACHICARSE. *v.* Rebajarse, humillarse. *To belittle oneself, minimize one's importance.*

ACHICHARRAR. *v.* Estrujar, aplastar, allanar una cosa. *To squash, crush, flatten.* || **2. -se.** Tostarse. *To roast.*

ACHICHARRONEAR (variante de **achicharrar**).

ACHINADO. *adj.* Que tiene la aparencia y algunas de las cualidades de los chinos. *Chinese-like.* || **2.** Vulgar, aplebeyado. *Common, coarse, vulgar.* || **3.** De tez amarilla. *Yellow-skinned.*

ACHINERÍA. *n.f.* Buhonería. *Peddling, canvassing.*

ACHIQUITAR. *v.* (Acad.) Achicar, empequeñecer. *To make smaller, reduce in size.*

ACHISPADO. *adj.* Ebrio. *Intoxicated, tipsy.*

ACHISPAR. *v.* Alegrar, animar, poner casi ebría a una persona. *To make someone merry or tipsy (with liquor).*

ACHOCLONARSE. *v.* Agolparse, apiñarse. *To crowd together.*

ACHOCOLATADO. *adj.* De color de chocolate. *Like chocolate, dark brown, chocolate-colored, tan.* || **2.** Relativo al chocolate. *Pertaining to chocolate.*

ACHOLADO. *adj.* Que tiene actidudes, modales o aparencia de cholo (meztizo de europeo y meztiza). *Like a mestizo or half-breed.* || **2.** Acobardado. *Cowed, intimidated.*

ACHOLADOR. *adj.* Que da vergüenza, avergonzante. *Abashing.*

ACHOLAR. *v.* Avergonzar. *To embarrass.* || **2.** Intimidar. *Scare.* || **3. -se.** Adquirir actitudes, modales o aparencia de cholo (meztizo de europeo y meztiza). *To adopt half-*

breed ways. || **4.** Acobardarse. *To be cowed.* || **5.** Avergonzarse. *To be abashed, become shy.* || **6.** Sonrojarse. *To blush.*

ACHOLO. *n.m.* Vergüenza. *Embarrassment.*

ACHUCHARRAR. *v.* (Acad.) Aplastar, estrujar. *To crush, crumple, squash.* || **2. -se.** Aplastarse. *To get squashed.*

ACHUCUTADO. *adj.* Abatido, marchito. *Gloomy, depressed.* || **2.** Marchito, falto de frescura, vigor y lozanía (como una flor). *Wilted.*

ACHUCUTARSE. *v.* Estar afligido. *To be or look dismayed.* || **2.** Deprimirse. *To be gloomy.* || **3.** Marchitarse. *To wilt.* || **4.** Ser tímido. *To be timid, shy.*

ACHUMADO. *adj.* Ebrio, borracho.*Drunk.*

ACHUMARSE. *v.* Embriagarse. *To get drunk.*

ACHUNCHAR. *v.* Avergonzar. *To shame, cause to blush.* || **2.** Intimidar, asustar. *To scare.* || **3. -se.** Avergonzarse. *To feel ashamed.* || **4.** Intimidarse. *To get scared.* || **5.** Sonrojarse. *To blush.*

ACHUPALLA. *n.f.* Piña, ananá. *Pineapple.*

ACHURA. *n.f.* Cualquier intestino o menudo de las reses, o todo otro pedazo de carne considerado como desperdicio. *Offal, innards, entrails, guts.*

ACHURAR. *v.* Sacar las entrañas a la res carneada. *To gut an animal.* || **2.** Herir o matar a tajos. *To cut to pieces.* || **3.** Sacar uno su parte en un despojo, saqueo o expoliación. *To benefit from a share-out, get something free.*

ACIGUATADO. *n.m.* Papanata, bobo.*Simple, dope, idiot.*

ACIGUATARSE. *v.* Envenenarse comiendo pescado **ciguato**. *To get fish poisoning.*

ACLARARSE. *v.* Purificarse, aclararse (líquidos). *To be clarified or purified (liquids).*

ACOCHAMBRAR. *v.* Ensuciar. *To dirty, soil.* || **2.** Manchar. *To stain.*

ACOCUYADO. *adj.* Achispado, alegre. *Tipsy, merry.*

ACOGOTAR. *v.* Agarrar. *To grab around the neck.* ~Te voy a ACOGOTAR. *I'm going to ring your neck.* || **2.** Poner en grave aprieto económico. *To have at one's mercy.*

ACOLCHONAR. *v.* (Acad.) Acolchar. *To quilt (fabric), pad (wall, door).*

ACOLITAR. *v.* (Acad.) Desempeñar las funciones de acólito. *To serve as an altar boy.*

ACOLLARAR. *v.* Unir. *To couple.* || **2. -se.** Unirse. *To get together.* || **3.** Confabularse. *To plot.* || **4.** Casarse. *To get married.*

ACOMEDIRSE. *v.* Aprestarse espontáneamente y graciosamente a hacer un servicio. *To offer to help.*

ACOMETIDO. *adj.* Oficioso, solícito, servicial. *Helpful, obliging.*

ACOMODAR. *v.* Proporcionar empleo por motivos ajenos a la preparación o competencia que uno tenga. *To procure someone a convenient job or position through personal influence rather than merit.* || **2.** Colocar. *To place, arrange.* ~ACOMODA tus juguetes en el armario. *Put your toys away in the cupboard.* ~Voy a ACOMODAR el equipaje en el coche. *I'm going to put the bags in the car.* || **3. -se.** Arreglarse. To fix, straighten. ~Se ACOMODÓ los anteojos. *He straightened his glasses.*

ACOMODO. *n.m* Empleo que se consigue por razones que excluyen la preparación o competencia. *Convenient job or position obtained through personal influence rather than merit.* || **2.** String-pulling. *Amiguismo.* || **3.** Soborno. *Bribe.*

ACOMPAÑADA. *n.f.* Amante. Concubina. *Lover, common-law wife.*

ACOMPAÑAMIENTO. *n.m.* Cortejo de boda, entierros, funerales, etc. *Funeral procession, wedding reception, etc.*

ACOMPLEJANTE. *adj.* Que da complejo. *That which gives a complex.* ~Es ACOMPLEJANTE ver alguien tocar así la guitarra. *It gives you a complex to see someone play the guitar that well.*

ACOPLADO. *n.m.* (Acad.) Vehículo destinado a ser remolcado por otro. *Trailer (vehicle)*.

ACOPLAR. *v.* (Acad.) Unir, agregar uno o varios vehículos a otro que los remolca. *To couple (up), join.* ‖ **2.** Unirse a otro u otras personas para acompañarlas. *To join the company of other people*.

ACORDONADO. *adj*. Flaco (animal). *Thin (animal)*.

ACORDONAR. *v.* Preparar un terreno para el cultivo en líneas rectas, como trazado a cordón. *To prepare for sowing*.

ACORTAR. *v.* Dejar de exagerar al hablar, ateniéndose a la verdad. *To tone down, attenuate*.

ACOSTAR. *v.* Dar a luz, parir. *To give birth.*

ACOSTUMBRARSE. *v.* •No se ACOSTUM-BRA. *It isn't customary or usual*. Aquí no se ACOSTUMBRA decir eso. *People don't say that here.*

ACOTEJAR. *v.* (Acad.) Arreglar, colocar objetos ordenadamente, acomodar.*Arrange, put in order*.

ACREENCIA. *n.f.* (Acad.) Crédito, deuda que uno tiene a su favor. *Credit balance.*

ACRÍLICO. *n.m.* Plexiglas (para techos). *Plexiglas.*

ACRIOLLADO. *adj*. Extranjero que se acomoda a las costumbres del país. *Foreigner who adapt himself to the customs of a country.*

ACRIOLLARSE. (Acad.) Adaptarse un extranjero a los usos y costumbres de la gente de un país hispanohablante donde vive. *To take on the habits of a country.*

ACTA. *n.f.* Ley, disposición. *Act, law.* ‖ **2.** Acta orgánica. *Constitution.*

ACTIVARSE. *v.* Tomar medidas enérgicas (obreros, disidentes). *To take active steps.*

ACTIVISMO. *n.m.* Actividad política. *Political activity.*

ACTIVISTA. *n.m.* Activista político. *Political activist.*

ACTUACIÓN. *n.f.* Figuración, papel, conducta, eficacia de una persona o grupo en las funciones que le son propias.*Role, handling, performance.*

ACUATIZAR. *v.* Descender un hidroavión sobre la superficie del agua. *To come down or land on water.*

ACUILMARSE. *v.* Entristecerse, amustiarse. *To get depressed, to loose heart or courage; to grieve.*

ACULLICAR. *v.* Mascar coca. *To chew coca leaves.*

ACUSETE. *n.m.* (Acad.) Acusón, soplón (principalmente entre escolares). *Telltale, sneak (particularly among students).*

ADEFESIERO. *adj*. Disparatado. *Nonsensical.*

ADELANTE. *adv.* •ADELANTE de. Delante de. *Before, in front of.*

ADELANTO. *n.m.* Llegar con un ADELANTO de 15 minutos. *To arrive 15 minutes early.*

ADENTRO. *adv.* •ADENTRO de. Dentro de. *In, inside.*

ADEPTO. *n.m.* Adicto (droga). *Drug addict.*

ADEVERAS. adj. •De veras. *Really, truly.*

ADICIÓN. *n.f.* Cuenta (hotel, restaurante). *Bill, check.*

ADIOSITO. *interj*. Hasta luego. *Good bye.*

ADOLORIDO. *adj*. Dolorido.*Sore, tender, aching; distressed.*

ADOROTE. *n.m.* Carretilla. *Wheel-barrow.*

ADOSAR. *v.* Añadir, asegurándola, una cosa con otra. *To join firmly.* ‖ **2.** Adjuntar, acompañar (en una carta). *To attach, enclose (with a letter).*

ADUANAL. *adj*. (Acad.) Aduanero. *Custom (before an adj.).*

ADUAR. *n.m.* (Acad.) Ranchería de indios. *Indian settlement.*

ADULETE. *n.m.* (Acad.) Adulón. *Flatterer.*

ADULONERÍA. *n.f.* Adulación. *Flattering, fawning.*

ADVOCAR. *v.* Abogar. *To advocate.*

AEROMOZA. *n.f.* Azafata. *Stewardess, air hostess, flight attendant.*

AEROMOZO. *n.m.* Auxiliar de vuelo.

Flight attendant.

AEROPOSTA. *n.f.* Correo aéreo. *Airmail.*

AFANAR. *v.* Empujar. *To hustle, jostle.*

AFAROLADO. *adj.* Agitado, emocionado. *Excited, worked up.*

AFAROLARSE. *v.* Poner nervioso, agitarse. *To get excited, get worked up.*

AFECTAR. *v.* Lastimar, perjudicar, dañar. *To hurt, damage, harm.* || **2.** Hablando de forma o figura, tomar, tener. *To take on, assume.* || **3.** Destinar fondos. *To set aside for, devote to (money).* || **4.** -se. Contraer una enfermedad. *To fall ill, contract an illness.*

AFECTUOSAMENTE. *adj.* Cordialmente, cariñosamente (en carta). *Yours affectionately (in letter).*

AFFAIRE, AFFAIR. *n.m.* Relación amorosa. *Affair.*

AFIANZADO, DA. *n.m/f.* Novio(a). *Sweetheart, boyfriend (girlfriend).* || **2.** Prometido(a). *Fiancé(e).*

AFICHE. *n.m.* Cartel. *Poster*

AFIEBRARSE. *v.* Agarrar, coger una fiebre. *To become feverish.*

AFILADOR, RA. *n.m/f.* (Acad.) Piedra para afilar. *Whetstone, hone*

AFLATARSE. *v.* Estar triste, afligirse. *To be sad, gloomy.*

AFLICTIVO. *adj.* Penoso, doloroso. *Distressing, grievous.*

AFLIGENTE. *adj.* Que causa angustia. *Distressing, upsetting.*

AFLIGIR. *v.* Causar dolor o molestias. *To pain, distress.* || **2.** Golpear. *To hit, beat.* || **3.** -se. Mortificarse. *Feel ashamed, be embarrassed.*

AFLOJAR. *v.* Entregarse, soltar del dinero. *To pay up, cough up.* || **2.** Soltar, ceder. *To let go.* || **3.** Acceder, consentir en algo que antes se negaba. *To give in, submit.* || **4.** Hacer el rodaje de (motor). *To run in.* || **5.** -se. Dejar de actuar con vigor, energía o dedicación. *To slacken, weaken, loose interest in something.*

AFLUS. *adj.* Sin dinero. *Broke, flat.*

AFLUXIONARSE. *v.* Coger un resfríado. *To catch a cold.*

AFRAILADO. *adj.* Que se asemeja a los frailes. *Acting like or resembling a priest.* || **2.** Beato. *Church-goer.*

AFRECHO. *n.m.* Serrín. *Sawdust.*

AFRONEGRISMO. *n.m.* Voz del español tomada de una lengua de África. *Word borrowed from an African language.*

AFUERA. *adv.* Fuera. *Outside.* || **2.** •AFUERA de. *Outside of.*

AFUEREÑO. *adj.* Foráneo, extraño. *Foreign, strange.* || **2.** Que viene de fuera. *From elsewhere, from outside.* || **3.** *n.m.* (Acad.) Forastero, que es o viene de afuera. *Stranger, foreigner, outsider.* || **4.** En los establecimientos de campo se dice del trabajador que vive fuera. *Itinerant worker, casual worker.*

AFUETAR. *v.* Azotar, dar o castigar con el fuete. *To whip, beat.*

AFUSILAR. *v.* Fusilar. *To shoot, execute by firing squad.*

AGACHADO. *n.m.* Holgazán, vagabundo. *Down-and-out, bum.*

AGACHARSE. *v.* Ceder, someterse. *To give in, submit.* || **2.** Prepararse. *To get ready.*

AGACHÓN. *n.m.* Consentidor, sumiso. *Weak-willed, submissive.*

AGALLA. *n.f.* •Tener AGALLAS. || **1.** Ser glotón. *To be greedy.* || **2.** Ser descarado, desvergonzado. *To be shameless, to have the nerve or gall to + inf.* ~¡Hay que tener AGALLAS!. *What gall!* || **3.** Ser osado, temerario. *To have guts or courage.*

AGALLEGADO. *adj.* Persona que aunque nacida en Hispanoamérica habla como español. *Said of a person who although born in Latin America speaks Spanish like a Spaniard.*

AGALLÓN. *n.m.* (Acad.) Inflamación de las amígdalas; anginas. Tonsilitis. *Tonsillitis.*

AGALLUDO. *adj.* (Acad.) Dícese de la persona animosa, resuelta, valiente. *Daring, bold.* || **2.** (Acad.) Ambicioso, avariento. *Greedy.*

AGARRADA. *n.f.* Riña. *Row, argument.* ǁ
2. Pelea. *Scrap, brawl.*

AGARRADERA. *n.f.* Asa, mango, agarradero (de una taza, olla). *Handle, grip, holder.* ǁ **2.** Correa (autobus, tren). *Strap, handgrip (bus, train).* ǁ **3.** Cordón (cortina). *Cord (curtain).* ǁ **4.** Paño. *Pot holder.* ǁ **5.** Guante. *Oven glove.* ǁ **5.** •Tener buenas AGARRADERAS. Poder contar con valiosas influencias y relaciones. *To have pull, have friends in the right places.*

AGARRAR. *v.* Coger (se evita emplear esta palabra en gran parte de Hispanoamérica por ser sinónimo de «copular»). *To take, pick up.* AGARRAR un autobús. Coger un autobús. *To catch a bus.* AGARRAR una flor. Coger una flor. *To pick a flower.* AGARRAR un resfriado. Coger un resfriado. *To catch a cold.* ǁ **2.** •AGARRAR para. Dirigirse a, ir rumbo a. *To set out for, head for.* ǁ **3.** •AGARRAR por. Tomar en dirección a. *Take (direction).* ~AGARRE por esta calle. *Take this street.* ǁ **4.** Pescar, atrapar. *To catch.* ~Si te AGARRO te acogoto. *If I catch you I'll break your neck.* ǁ •AGARRAR y... Actuar de forma inesperada. *To act rashly.* ~Un buen día AGARRA y me dice que no me quiere y se va. *One fine day she decides she no longer loves me and leaves.*

AGARRE. *n.m.* Influencia (con personas conocidas). *Influence, pull.* ǁ **2.** Agarro. *Hold, grasp.*

AGARRÓN. *n.m.* Tirón, sacudida fuerte. *Jerk, pull, tug.* ǁ **2.** Altercado, riña o pendencia. *Quarrel, dispute.* ǁ **3.** Pelea. *Scrap, fight.*

AGAUCHADO. *adj.* (Acad.) Que imita o se parece en su porte o maneras al gaucho. *Like a gaucho.*

AGAUCHAR. *v.* Tomar el aspecto, los modales y las costumbres propias del gaucho. *To imitate or dress like a gaucho.*

AGENTE. *n.m.* Empleado público. *Public service employee.*

AGILITAR. *v.* Activar. *Activate, set in motion.*

AGIOTISTA. *n.m.* Usurero, especulador. *Shark (coll.).*

AGONIOSO. *adj.* Egoísta. *Selfish.* ǁ **2.** Fastidioso. *Bothersome.* ~Es tan AGONIOSO. *He's such a pest.*

AGORA. *adv.* Ahora. *Now.*

AGOTADO. *adj.* Acabado, concluido, inoperable. *Dead, exhausted, drained (battery).* ~La pila está AGOTADA. La pila esta acabada. *The battery is dead.*

AGRADAR. *v.* Gustarle a uno. *To please, be pleasing.* ~Le AGRADA la carne? *Do you like meat?*

AGRADECIDO. *adj.* •Muy AGRADECIDO. Muchas gracias. *Thank you very much.*

AGRADO. *n.m.* •Tengo el AGRADO de informarle que.... Tengo el placer de informarle que... *I have the pleasure to inform you that...*

AGRANDAMIENTO. *n.m.* Engrandecimiento. *Aggrandizement.*

AGRANDARSE. *v.* Enfrentar un peligro, normalmente con éxito. *To face up to a challenge or a dangerous situation, usually with success.*

AGREGADO. *n.m.* Persona o cosa que de improviso se incorpora a un grupo formado. *Newcomer.* ǁ **2.** Cosa que de improviso se incorpora a una colección. *Thing newly added to a collection.* ǁ **3.** (Acad.) Persona que ocupa una cosa o propriedad ajena, generalmente rural, a cambio de pequeños trabajos, pagando un arrendamiento, o gratuitamente. *Sharecropper, tenant farmer.*

AGREMIACIÓN. *n.f.* Sindicato. *Union, labor union.*

AGREMIAR. *v.* To unionize. *Sindicar.* ǁ **2.** -se. Formar un sindicato. *To form a union.*

AGRICULTURAL (angl.). *adj.* Agrícola. *Agricultural.*

AGRIERA. *n.f.* Acidez de estómago. *Heartburn.*

AGRINGADO. *adj.* (Acad.) Que tiene aspecto o costumbres de **gringo**. *Americanized.*

AGRINGARSE. *v.* (Acad.) Tomar aspecto o costumbres de gringo. *To adopt North American ways and customs.*

AGRIPADO. *adj.* Tener gripe. *To have the flu.*

AGRIURA. *n.f.* Calidad de agrio, agrura. *Sourness, tartness.*

AGUA. *n.f.* •Agua gruesa. Agua no potable. *Hard water.* || **2.** Jugo. *Fruit juice.* Agua de pera. *Pear juice.* || **3.** •Estar uno como agua para chocolate. Estar hecho uno una furia. *To be hopping mad, to be hot under the collar.*

AGUACATE. *n.m.* Persona torpe y poco animosa. *Weakling, milksop.*

AGUACHENTO. *adj.* (Acad.) Dícese de la fruta u otro alimento insípido por exceso de agua. *Watery, moist, sodden.*

AGUADA. *n.f.* Abrevadero. *Water trough, watering place.*

AGUADO. *adj.* (Acad.) Débil, desfallecido, flojo. *Weak, simpering.* || **2.** Dícese de las cosas blandas y sin constancia. *Weak, watered down.*

AGUAITADA. *n.f.* Mirada. *Look, glance.* || **2.** •Echar una aguaitada. *To take a look at, watch, observe.*

AGUAITADOR. *adj.* Que observa. *Watching, observing.* || **2.** *n.m.* Persona que observa, mira. *Observer, watcher.*

AGUAITAMIENTO. *n.m.* Mirada, vigilancia. *Watching, observing; look.*

AGUAITAR. *v.* Vigilar. *To watch, keep an eye on.* || **2.** Espiar. *To spy on.* || **3.** Acechar. *To lie in wait for.* || **4.** Mirar. *To look, watch.* ~Aguaitar por la ventana. *To look out of the window.*

AGUAJE. *n.m.* (Acad.) Aguacero. *Heavy shower, downpour.*

AGUAMANIL. *n.m.* Fregadero. *Sink.*

AGUAMIEL. *n.m.* (Acad.) La preparada con la caña de azúcar o papelón. *Cane sugar and water.*

AGUANTADERAS. *n.f.* •Tener aguantaderas. Ser muy tolerante. *To be very patient, tolerant.*

AGUANTADOR. *adj.* •Ser aguantador. Tener paciencia. *To be patient, enduring.* || **2.** Resistente (ropa, tela). *Hard-wearing, long wearing, tough.*

AGUANTARSE. *v.* Callarse. *To keep one's mouth shut.* || **2.** Aguantarse de hacer algo, contenerse. *To hold back from doing something, control, restrain oneself.* ~¡Aguántate! *Calm down, hang on a minute, take it easy!* ~Tendrá que aguantarse. *He'll just have to put up with it.*

AGUARRAPARSE. *v.* (Acad.) Tomar calidad o sabor de guarapo la caña de azúcar, la fruta o un líquido. *To acquire the flavor of guarapo (sugar cane juice).*

AGUASARSE. *v.* Tomar los modales y costumbres del **guaso**. *To become countryfied, take on rural customs.*

AGUATERO. *n.m.* Aguador. *Water-carrier, water-seller.*

AGUAYO. *n.m.* (Acad.) Lienzo fuerte. *Strong cloth.*

AGÜEITAR (variante de **aguaitar**).

AGÜERO. *n.m.* Adivino, agorero. *Fortune-teller.*

AGUILILLA (variante de **aguilillo**).

AGUILILLO. *n.m.* Caballo de paso veloz. *Fast horse.*

AGUINALDO. *n.m.* Villancico que se canta en las fiestas de Navidad. *Christmas carol.* || **2.** Paga extra que se paga en Navidad. *Extra month's salary paid at Christmas.*

AGUJA. *n.f.* •Aguja de arria. Aguja de enjalmar que sirve para coser aparejos, costales, etc. *Pack needle.* || **2.** •Aguja de tejer. Aguja de hacer calceta o punto. *Knitting-needle.* || **3.** •Aguja de tranquera. Cada uno de los maderos clavados en tierra para formar una tranquera. *Upright, stake, post forming a fence or barricade, fencepost.*

AGUJETERO. *n.m.* (Acad.) Cañuto para guardar las agujas. *Pincushion, needlecase.*

AGUZADO. *adj.* Astuto, hábil. *Sharp, on the ball.*

AHÍ. *adv.* Más o menos. *So-so.* ~¿Cómo está tu madre? Ahí anda. *So-so.*

AHIJUNA. *interj.* Interjección que expresa diversos sentimientos, especialmente admiración o ira. *Interjection expressing admi-*

ration or surprise.

AHOGADO. *n.m.* (Acad.) Rehogado o estofado, hecho de diversas formas según el país. *Stew.* || **2.** (Acad.) Salsa con que se rehoga un alimento. *Stewing sauce.*

AHOGO. *n.m.* (Acad.) Asma. *Asthma.*

AHORA. *adv.* •Aʜᴏʀᴀ que. Tan pronto como. *As soon as.*

AHORITITA. *adv.* (Acad.) Ahora, ahora mismo. *Right now, this very minute.*

AHUESARSE. *v.* (Acad.) Quedarse inútil o sin prestigio una persona o cosa. *To go out of style, become passé.* || **2.** (Acad.) Quedarse una mercancía sin vender. *To become unsalable (due to damage or being out of fashion).* || **3.** Enflaquecer. *To loose weight, become bony.*

AHUEVADO. *adj.* (Acad.) Acobardado, atontado. *Person who lacks back bone.*

AHUIZOTE. *n.m.* (Acad.) Agüero, brujería. *Augury, witchcraft.*

AINDIADO. *adj.* De tipo y color de indio. *Indian-like, Indian-looking, dark-skinned.*

AIRECITO. *n.m.* Vientecito. *Breeze, gentle wind.*

AJEAR. *v.* (Acad.) Proferir ajos o palabrotas. *To swear, cuss.*

AJESUITADO. *adj.* Astuto. *Crafty.*

AJÍ. *n.m.* Pimiento. *Chili, red pepper.* || **2.** Salsa. *Chile sauce.* || **3.** •Ponerse como un ᴀᴊɪ́ picante. *To get furious.* || **4.** •Soltar (echar) ᴀᴊɪ́ y cebollas. *To cuss.*

AJIACO. *n.m.* (Acad.) Guisado de caldo y carne, patadas picadas, cebolla y ají picante; los ingredientes varían de país a país. *Stew made of vegetables, meat and chile.*

AJILAR. *v.* Dirigirse hacia un lugar determinado. *To go to a specific place.*

AJÓ. *interj.* Palabra que se emplea para animar a hablar a los niños. *Word used to encourage children to begin to speak.*

AJOTAR. *v.* (Acad.) Azuzar, incitar. *To tease, incite (a dog).*

AJUSTAR. *v.* Atacar a uno los dolores o una enfermedad. *To catch, come down with* an illness. || **2.** (Acad.) Cumplir, completar. *To turn (age).* ~Tomás ᴀᴊᴜsᴛó catorce años. *Tom just turned fourteen.* || **3.** (Acad.) Contratar a destajo. *To contract by the job.*

AJUSTÓN. *n.m.* Castigo, mal trato. *Punishment, ill treatment.* || **2.** Revisión, ajuste (aut.) *Overhaul.*

ALAMBIQUE. *n.m.* (Acad.) Fábrica de aguardiente. *Distillery.*

ALAMBIQUERO. *n.m.* (Acad.) Persona que tiene un **alambique**. *Owner or manager of a distillery.*

ALAMBRAR. *v.* Poner alambrados. *To fence with wire.*

ALAMBRITO. *n.m.* Persona alta y delgada. *Tall thin person.*

ALAR. *n.m.* Acera. *Pavement, sidewalk.*

ALBARDA. *n.f.* (Acad.) Especie de silla de montar, de cuero crudo o curtido. *Saddle.*

ALBOROTO. *n.m.* (Acad.) Rosetas de maíz o maicillo con azúcar o miel (palomita de maíz). *Popcorn.*

ALCALDE. *n.m.* Alcahuete, chulo. *Procurer, pimp.*

ALCANCÍA. *n.f.* (Acad.) Cepillo para limosnas o donativos. *Alm box, collection box, poor box.* || **2.** Hucha. *Piggy bank.*

ALCANFOR. *n.m.* Alcahuete, chulo. *Procurer, pimp.*

ALCANFORADO (variante de **alcanfor**).

ALCANFORARSE. *v.* Evaporarse, desaparecer, perderse una cosa. *Vanish, disappear.*

ALCANZAR. *v.* •¿A cuánto ᴀʟᴄᴀɴᴢᴀ? *How much does it come to?* || **2.** Pasar, dar. *To hand over, to pass, to give.* ~Me ᴀʟᴄᴀɴᴢᴀ la sal, por favor. *Will you please pass the salt.*

ALCUZA. *n.f.* Vinagreras, aceitera, angarillas para aceite y vinagre. *Cruet, cruet stand.*

ALEBRESTAR. *v.* Emocionar. *To excite, stimulate.* || **2.** -se. *v.* (Acad.) Alterarse, agitarse. *To get distressed, become agitated.*

ALECHADO. *adj.* Parecido a la leche. *Milky, like milk.* || **2.** Mezclado con un poco de leche. *Mixed with milk.*

ALEGADOR. *adj.* (Acad.) Discutidor, amigo de disputas. *Argumentative.*

ALEGAR. *v.* (Acad.) Disputar, altercar. *To argue against, dispute.* || **2.** Discutir. *To argue, quarrel.* || **3.** Protestar. *To complain loudly, kick up a fuss, gripe.*

ALEGATO. *n.f.* (Acad.) Disputa, discusión. *Argument, fight.*

ALEGRÓN. *adj.* Calamocano, alegre a causa de la bebida. *Tipsy.* || **2.** Muy alegre. *Very gay, merry or cheerful.* || **3.** Enamoradizo, coquetón. *Flirtatious.*

ALEGRONA. *n.f.* Prostituta. *Prostitute.*

ALELUYA. *n.m.* Excusa frívola. *Frivolous or flimsy excuse.*

ALENTADO. *adj.* (Acad.) Dícese de la persona que ha mejorado o se ha restablecido de una enfermedad. *Healthy, well again.*

ALENTARSE. *v.* (Acad.) Mejorar, convalecer o restablecerse de una enfermedad. *To get well.*

ALEONAR. *v.* Alborotar (generalmente con fines de diversión). *To stir up, agitate (generally for fun or through enthusiasm).*

ALEVINO. *n.m.* Pez recién nacido criado para poblar ríos, arroyos y estanques. *Young fish, fry (for restocking rivers, etc.).*

ALFA. n.f. (Acad.) Alfalfa. *Lucerne, alfalfa.*

ALFAJOR. *n.m.* (Acad.) Golosina compuesta de dos o más piezas de masa relativamente fina, adheridas una a otra con dulce. *Pastry filled with sweet filling.*

ALFALFAR. *v.* (Acad.) Sembrar de alfalfa un terreno. *To sow with alfalfa.*

ALFERAZGO. *n.m.* Fiesta religiosa que costean una o más personas. *Religious festival paid for by one or more persons.*

ALFÉREZ. *n.m.* Persona que costea los gastos de una fiesta y tiene derecho en encabezar la procesión correspondiente. *Official standard bearer in processions.* || **2.** Persona elegida para pagar los gastos de una fiesta, baile, etc. *Person chosen to pay the expenses of a ball, party, etc.*

ALFILER. *n.m.* (Acad.) •ALFILER de gan-

cho. Imperdible. *Safety-pin.*

ALFOMBRADO. *adj.* Enmoquetado. *Carpeted.*

ALGOTRO. *adj.* (Acad.). Algún otro. *Some other...*

ALHAJA. *adj.* (Acad.) Bonito, agradable. *Treasure, gem (person).*

ALHAJERO. *n.m.* Joyero. *Jewel case.*

ALHARAQUERO. (Acad.) Alharaquiento. *Demonstrative, highly emotional.*

ALIANZA. *n.f.* Anillo de bodas. *Wedding ring.*

ALILAYA. *n.f.* Excusa frívola. *Frivolous or flimsy excuse.*

ALINDERAR. *v.* (Acad.) Señalar o marcar los límites de un terreno. *To mark out the boundaries of a plot of land.*

ALIPEGARSE. *v.* (Acad.) Juntarse una o varias personas de manera inoportuna o sin ser invitadas. *To join in uninvited.*

ALISTARSE. *v.* Vestirse, arreglarse para salir. *To get dressed, get ready to go out.*

ALLACITO. *adv.* Allí. *Over there.*

ALLANAMIENTO. *n.m.* (Acad.) Registro policial de un domicilio. *Raid, search (police).* ~La policía hizo varios ALLANAMIENTOS. *The police carried out various raids.* || 2. •Orden de ALLANAMIENTO. Orden de registro. *Search warrant.*

ALLANAR. *v.* (Acad.) Registrar un domicilio con mandamiento judicial. *To carry out a raid (with a warrant).*

ALMA. *n.f.* •Sacar el ALMA. Matarse trabajando. *To work one's fingers to the bone.* || **2.** •ALMA Mater. (angl.). La universidad donde ha estudiado uno. *Alma mater, school or college that one attended.*

ALMACÉN. *n.m.* (Acad.) Tienda donde se venden varios artículos domésticos de primera necesidad. *Grocery store.*

ALMACENERO. *n.m.* Mozo que trabaja en un almacén. *Shopkeeper.*

ALMACENISTA (variante de **almacenero**).

ALMACIGADO. *adj.* Se dice del color cobrizo subido del ganado.*Bay-colored cattle.*

ALMAREARSE. *v.* Marearse. *To get dizzy.*

ALMIBAR. *n.m.* •ALMÍBAR de pelo. Almíbar espeso. *Heavy syrup.*

ALMOFRÉ. *n.m.* Funda de la cama de camino. *Sleeping bag, bedroll.*

ALMOFREZ. (variante de **almofré**).

ALMOHADILLA. *n.f.* Acerico. *Pincushion.*

ALMORZADA. *n.f.* (Acad.) Almuerzo copioso y agradable. *Generous and excellent meal.*

ALÓ. *interj.* ¿Hola? (contestando al teléfono). *Hello? (answering the telephone).*

ALOCAR. *v.* Gustarle en extremo una cosa a alguien, enloquecerse por una cosa. *To drive crazy with pleasure.* ~Me ALOCAN las pizzas. *I'm crazy about pizza*

ALOJA. *n.f.* (Acad.) Bebida fermentada hecha de algarroba o maíz y agua. *Kind of beer made from corn or carob bean pods.*

ALOJADO. *n.m.* (Acad.) Huésped en casa ajena. *Guest, lodger.*

ALÓN. *adj.* (Acad.) De ala grande. Dícese especialmente del sombrero. *Wide-brimmed (hat).*

ALPECHÍN. *n.m.* Jugo de la cáscara de las frutas cítricas y todo otro jugo vegetal acre. *Tart juice squeezed from some citric fruits.*

ALPISTE. *n.m.* Dinero. *Money.*

ALTILLO. *n.m.* Desván. *Attic.*

ALTIPLANO. *n.m.* Altiplanicie. *High Andean plateau.*

ALTO. *n.m.* (Acad.) Montón, gran cantidad de cosas. *Heap, pile.*

ALTOPARLANTE. *n.m.* (Acad.) Altavoz. *Loudspeaker.*

ALTOZANO. *n.m.* (Acad.) Atrio de una iglesia. *Porch of a church.*

ALUMNADO. *n.m.* El conjunto de los alumnos de un establecimiento de enseñanza. *Student body.*

ALUZAR. *v.* (Acad.) Alumbrar, llenar de luz y claridad. *To light, illuminate.*

ALVERJA. *n.f.* Guisante. *Pea.*

ALZA. *n.f.* •En ALZA. Prosperar, andarle bien en los negocios.*Rising, prosperous.* ‖ **2.** Disfrutar de una buena reputación. *To have a good name.*

ALZADO. *adj.* (Acad.) Dícese de la persona engreída, soberbia e insolente.*Vain, stuck up.* ‖ **2.** Insolente, malcriado. *Insolent, spoiled.* ‖ **3.** (Acad) Dícese de los animales domésticos que se hacen montaraces. *Untamed, wild (animal).* ‖ **4.** En celo. *In heat (animal).*

ALZAR. *v.* Recoger, levantar. *To pick up.* ‖ **2. -se.** Fugarse (animal). *To run away (animal).* ‖ **3.** •ALZARSE con algo. Robar.*To steal, make off with.*

AMA. *n.f.* •AMA de brazos. Niñera. *Nurse maid, nanny.* ‖ **2.** •AMA de cría. Nodriza. *Wet-nurse.*

AMACHINADO. *adj.* Amancebado.*Living together out of wedlock.*

AMACHINARSE. *v.* (Acad.) Amancebarse. *To set up house together, cohabit.*

AMACHORRARSE. *v.* (Acad.) Hacerse machorra una hembra o planta.*To turn steril.*

AMADRINAR. *v.* (Acad.) Acostumbrar al ganado caballar a que vaya en tropilla detrás de la yegua madrina.*To train horses to follow a leader.*

AMAGAMIENTO. *n.m.* (Acad.) Quebrada poca profunda. *Narrow gorge.*

AMALAYA. *interj.* ¡Ojalá! *God grant!, I wish!*

AMALAYAR. *v.* (Acad.) Desear vivamente una cosa. *To covet, long for.* ‖ **2.** (Acad.) Proferir la interjección ¡**Amalaya**! *To wish deeply for something to happen.*

AMANECER. *v.* •¿Cómo AMANECIÓ? Buenos días. *Good morning. How are you this morning?* ‖ **2.** (Acad.) Pasar la noche en vela. *To stay up all night.* ~AMANECIÓ bailando. Estuvo bailando toda la noche. *He danced all night.*

AMANERADO. *adj.* Excesivamente cortés. *Excessively courteous.*

AMANSADOR. *n.m.* (Acad.) Domador de caballos. *Horse breaker.*

AMAÑARSE. *v.* (Acad.) Unirse en concubinato. *To live together.*

AMAÑO. *n.m.* (Acad.) Amancebamiento, concubinato. *Cohabitation.*

AMARCHANTARSE. *v.* Hacerse cliente asiduo de cierto lugar. *To become a regular customer of.*

AMARGOSO. *adj.* Amargo. *Bitter.*

AMARRA. *n.f.* Amarradura, atadura. *Rope.*

AMARRADO. *adj.* Mezquino, miserable. *Mean, stingy.*

AMARRAR. *v.* Atar. *To tie (shoes), tie up (package).* || **2.** -se. Atarse. *To tie.* ~Todavía no ha aprendido a AMARRARSE los zapatos. *He hasn't yet learned how to tie his shoes.* || **3.** (Acad.) •AMARRÁRSELA. Embriagarse. *To get drunk.* || **4.** (Acad.) Concertar o pactar. *To arrange, agree on, negotiate.* || **5.** (Acad.) Casarse, contraer matrimonio. *To get married.*

AMARRETAS (variante de **amarrado**).

AMARRETE (variante de **amarrado**).

AMASANDERO. *n.m.* (Acad.) Persona que amasa la harina para hacer el pan. *Bakery worker.*

AMASÍA. *n.m.* Concubina. *Common-law wife.*

AMASIATO. *n.m.* (Acad.) Concubinato. *Common-law marriage.*

AMBIENTADO. *adj.* Climatizado. *Air conditioned.*

AMBIENTE. *n.m.* (Acad.) Habitación, aposento, cámara. *Room.* ~Un piso de cuatro AMBIENTES. *A four room flat.*

AMELCOCHARSE. *v.* (Acad.) Reblandecerse. *To become soft.* || **2.** (Acad.) (fig.) Acaramelarse, derretirse amorosamente, mostrarse uno extraordinariamente meloso o dulzón. *To fall in love; to become sentimental.*

AMERICANO. *adj.* •Ir o pagar a la AMERICANA. *To go Dutch.*

AMERITADO. *adj.* Merecedor. *Worthy,* deserving.

AMERITAR. *v.* (Acad.) Dar méritos. *To give credit.* || **2.** (Acad.) Merecer. *To deserve, warrant.* ~Un problema que AMERITA un cuidadoso examen. *A problem which deserves (warrants) close scrutiny.*

AMIGAZO. *n.m.* Gran amigo. *Close friend.*

AMIGUERO. *adj.* (Acad.) Dícese de la persona que entabla amistades fácilmente. *Friendly, sociable.*

AMOBLAR. *v.* Amueblar. *To furnish.*

AMOHOSARSE. *v.* (Acad.) Enmohecerse. *To become moldy.*

AMOLADERA. *n.f.* Tipo pesado. *Pest, nuisance.*

AMONEDADO. *adj.* Adinerado. *Rich, well-off.*

AMORATADO. *adj.* Que tiene moretones como consecuencia de golpes o caídas. *Bruised, black and blue.*

AMORATARSE. *v.* Ponerse de color morado o llenarse de moretones. *To turn black and blue.*

AMORIÑARSE. *v.* Entristecerse. *To become sullen and sad.*

AMOROSO. *adj.* Encantador. *Charming.*

AMOSTAZARSE. *v.* (Acad.) Avergonzarse. *To become embarrassed or confused.*

AMPARAR. *v.* Reconocer la autoridad a una persona el derecho de explotar una mina. *To acquire the right to work in a mine.*

AMPÁYAR (angl.). *n.m.* Árbitro, el que dirige un partido de béisbol. *Umpire.*

AMPLIADO. *n.m.* Reunión política. *Political meeting.*

AMPLIFICACIÓN (phot.). *n.f.* Ampliación, reproducción de tamaño mayor de una fotografía. *Enlargement.*

AMPLIFICAR (phot.). Ampliar. *To enlarge.*

AMUCHAR. *v.* (Acad.) Aumentar el número o la cantidad. *To multiply, grow.*

AMURRARSE. *v.* Entristecerse. *To become sad, get depressed, feel low.*

ANANÁ. *n.m.* Piña. *Pineapple.*

ANARQUIZAR. *v.* Causar o introducir desorden, desunión o rebeldía. *To produce anarchy, cause disorder.*

ANCAS. *n.f.* Trasero. *Backside, behind.* ~Le dieron una patada en las ANCAS. *They kicked him in the behind.*

ANCESTRO (angl.). *n.m.* Antepasado, progenitor. *Ancestor.* || **2.** Linaje. *Ancestry.*

ANCHETA. *n.f.* Ganga, buen negocio sin mucho esfuerzo. *Bargain, good deal.* || **2.** (Acad.) Cosa inoportuna o sin importancia que revela desfachatez o descaro. *Silliness, foolishness.*

ANDADA. *n.f.* Caminata. *Stroll, walk.*

ANDANCIA. *n.f.* Enfermedad, epidémica leve. *Light epidemic illness.* || **2.** (Acad.) Andanza, buena o mala suerte. *Fortune, fate.*

ANDAR. *v.* •ANDAR a (en), *To ride (a horse, bicycle).* ~No sé ANDAR a caballo, en bicicleta. *I do not know how to ride a horse, a bicycle.* ~ANDUVIMOS en bicicleta todo el día. *We went cycling all day.* || **2.** •¡ÁNDATE de aquí! *Get out of here!* || **3.** •¡ÁNDATE luego! *Get a move on!*

ANDÉN. *n.m.* Bancal o terraza para cultivos (son famosas las de origen incaico). *Cultivation terraces (in the Andes).*

ANDENERÍA. *n.f.* (Acad.) Conjunto de andenes o bancales. *Group of cultivation terraces (in the Andes).*

ANDINISMO. *n.m.* (Acad.) Deporte que consiste en la ascención a los Andes y a otras montañas altas. *Mountain climbing.*

ANDINISTA. *n.m.* Persona que practica el andanismo. *Mountain climber in the Andes.*

ANDÓN. *adj.* (Acad.) Que anda mucho. Se dice de las caballerías. Andador. *Fast, fast-walking (horse).*

ÁNFORA. *n.f.* Urna para votaciones. *Ballot box.*

ANFRACTUOSIDADES. *n.m.* Desigualdades, quebraduras. *Rough places in the ground.*

ANGARILLAS. *n.f.* Carretilla. *Hand-barrow.*

ANGAS. *n.f.* Por ANGAS o por mangas. Por una causa u otra. *By hook or by crook, one way or another.*

ANGELITO. *n.m.* Criatura recién fallecida. *Dead child.*

ANGELOTE. *n.m.* Buena persona. *Decent person.*

ANGURRIA. *n.f.* (Acad.) Hambre insaciable. *Inordinate appetite.* || **2.** Codicia, egoísmo. *Greed, avarice.* || **3.** (Acad.) Deseo vehemente o insaciable. *Overwhelming desire.*

ANGURRIENTO. *adj.* (Acad.) Ávido, codicioso, hambriento. *Greedy, avaricious.*

ANIMADO. *adj.* Mejorado, dicho de los convalecientes. *Recovering, improving.*

ANIMADOR. *adj.* (Acad.) Persona que tiene como profesión organizar fiestas o reuniones y mantener el interés de los concurrentes. *Master of ceremonies.*

ANIMALADA. *n.f.* Rebaño. *Group, herd of animals.*

ANIMALAJE (variante de **animalada**).

ANIMALIZARSE. *v.* Volverse torpe o brutal como un ser irracional. *To become brutalized.*

ANIQUILAR. *v.* Matar. *To kill.*

ANOTACIÓN. *n.f.* Gol. *Goal (soccer), touchdown (football), point (basketball).*

ANOTADOR. *n.m.* Tarjeta en que se lleva el tanteo, marcador. *Scorecard.* || **2.** Jugador que marca un goal. *Scorer.*

ANOTAR. *v.* Marcar un gol. *To score a goal.*

ANSINA (barb.). *adj.* Así. *In this way, thus.*

ANTA. *n.f.* Tapir. *Tapir.*

ANTECOMEDOR. *n.m.* Pieza contigua al comedor. *Room adjoining the dining room.*

ANTEOJOS. *n.m.* Gafas, lentes. *Glasses.*

ANTICIPACIÓN. *n.f.* Con ANTICIPACIÓN. Por adelantado. *In advance, beforehand.*

ANTICIPAR (angl.). *v.* Prever. *Anticipate.*

ANTICLINAL. *adj.* Línea imaginaria de separación de las vertientes de las aguas. *Watershed.*

ANTIDESLIZANTE. *adj.* Dispositivo en los neumáticos que impide que el coche patine. *Non-skid (tire).*

ANTIER. *adv.* Anteayer. *Yesterday.*

ANTIFRIS (angl.). *n.m.* Anticongelante. *Antifreeze (solution).*

ANTIPASTO. *n.m.* Entremes. *Hors d'oeuvre.*

ANTIPATIZAR. *v.* (Acad.) Sentir antipatía contra algo o alguien. *To dislike someone.*

ANTISUDORIAL. *n.m.* Substancia que evita o reduce el sudor excesivo (Se emplea también como adjetivo). *Deodorant (also used as an adjective).*

APACHETA. *n.f.* Altar rústico en el camino. *Wayside shrine.*

APAGOZO. *adj.* Apagadizo. *Slow to burn, difficult to ignite.*

APALABREAR. *v.* Apalabrar. *To agree to.*

APAÑAR. *v.* (Acad.) Encubrir, ocultar o proteger a alguien. *To cover up for someone.*

APARRAGARSE. *v.* Achaparrarse. *To remain stunted.*

APARTAMENTO. *n.m.* Departamento. *Apartment.*

APARTE. *n.m.* (Acad.) Separación que se hace en un rodeo, de cierto número de cabezas de ganado. *Penning, corralling.*

APELATIVO. *n.m.* Apellido. *Family name.*

APENADO. *adj.* Avergonzado. *Ashamed, embarrassed.*

APENARSE. *v.* Avergonzarse. *To feel ashamed, to feel embarrassed.* ‖ **2.** Dar pena. ~Me APENO que su esposa no se sienta mejor. *I'm sorry (I'm sad) that your wife does not feel better.*

APENAS. *conj.* En cuanto. *As soon as.* ~Le llamo APENAS llegue. *I'll call you as soon as he comes in.*

APENSIONADO. *adj.* Triste, afligido. *Sad, Depressed, grieved.*

APENSIONARSE. *v.* (Acad.). Entristecerse, apesadumbrarse, *To become sad, get depressed.*

APERAR. (Acad.) Proveer, abastecer de ins-

trumentos, herramientas o bastimentos. *To provide with clothes, food or tools.*

APERO. *n.m.* (Acad.) Recado de montar más lujoso que el común, propio de la gente del campo. *Harness, trappings, riding gear.*

APERREAR. *v.* Insistir. *Insist.*

APERREO. *n.m.* Molestia. *Nuisance.*

APESTADO. *adj.* Maloliente. *Foul-smelling, stinking.* ‖ **2.** Que tiene la peste. *Plague-ridden.*

APESTARSE. *v.* Enfriarse. *To catch a cold, catch the flu.*

APETITO. *n.m.* •¿Tiene Ud. APETITO? ¿Tiene Usted hambre? *Are you hungry?*

APILONAR. *v.* Apilar. *To heap up, pile up.*

APIMPLADO. *adj.* Ebrio. *Tight, tipsy.*

APIR (variante de **apiri**).

APIRI. *n.m.* (Acad.) Operario que transporta el mineral en las minas. *Mine worker.*

APLANACALLES. *n.m.* Vago, holgazán. *Idler, loafer.*

APLANADORA. *n.f.* Apisonadera. *Steamroller.*

APLANCHAR. Planchar. *To iron.*

APLAZAR. *v.* (Acad.) Suspender a un examinando. *To fail, flunk .*

APLICACIÓN (angl.). *n.f.* •Enviar una APLICACIÓN. Enviar una solicitud (de trabajo, etc.). *To send in one's aplication.*

APOLISMAR. *v.* Magullar, estropear. *To ruin, destroy.* ‖ **2.** Consumirse, desmedrarse. *To grow weak, weaken.*

APOLOGÍA. *n.f.* Elogio, panegírico. *Eulogy, panegyric.*

APORREAR. *v.* Golpear. *To beat, bash, club.* ‖ **2.** Aplastar. *To crush completely (in an argument).*

APORTE. *n.m.* Aportación. *Contribution.*

APOZARSE. *v.* Estancarse las aguas, formando **pozas**. *To become stagnant; to form a pool.*

APRECIAR. *v.* Darse cuenta de. *To realize.* ‖ **2.** Realzar. *To add value to, enhance, improve.* ‖ **3.** Agradecer (angl.). *To be* grateful for, appreciate.

APRETAR. *v.* Esforzarse. *To make an extra or special effort.*

APROCHES (angl.). *n.m.* Proximidad, entrada, vía de acceso, cercanías. *Approaches (city).*

APROPIAR (angl). *v.* Consignar, adjudicar. *To appropriate funds.*

APUNAMIENTO. *n.m.* Malestar que produce la alta altura. *Altitude or mountain sickness.*

APUNARSE. *v.* Contraer o padecer el malestar que produce la alta altura de la montaña. *To get altitude sickness or soroche.*

APUNTAR. *v.* Empezar a germinar las plantas. *To sprout, appear, show.* ||**2.** Prometer los sembrados cosechas abundantes. ~El maíz APUNTA bien este año. *The corn is coming along nicely this year.* ||**3.** -se. Apostar. *To bet, place bets.*

APUNTE. *n.m.* Apuesta. *Bet.* || **2.** Sketch (teat.). *Sketch (theat.)*

APUÑALEAR. *v.* Apuñalar. *To stab, to knife.*

APUÑAR. *v.* (Acad.) Heñir. *To knead (as dough).*

APURADAMENTE. *adj.* De prisa. *Hurriedly.*

APURADO. *adj.* Apresurado. *Hurried, rushed.* || **2.** •Estar APURADO. Tener prisa. *To be in a hurry.*

APURAR. *v.* Apresurar. *To hurry, rush.* ~No me APURES. *Don't rush me.* || **2.** -se. Apresurarse. *To hurry up, get a move on.*

APURO. *n.m.* Prisa. *Haste, hurry, rush.* ||**2.** •Tener APURO. Tener prisa. *To be in a hurry.*

APURÓN. *n.m.* (Acad.) Gran apresuramiento. *Great haste, great hurry.*

AQUEJUMBRASE. *v.* Quejarse, lamentarse. *To groan, grumble.*

ARA. *n.m.* Papagayo. *Parrot.*

ARABLE. *adj.* Se dice del terreno cultivable. *Arable.*

ARANDELA. *n.f.* (Acad.) Chorrera y vuel-tas de la camisola. *Dress or shirt ruffles, frill.*

ARAÑA. *n.f.* Carruage ligero y pequeño. *Light carriage.* || **2.** Prostituta. *Prostitute.*

ARCHIVADO. *adj.* Estar fuera de moda, en desuso. *Out-of-date, old-fashioned.*

ARCHIVAR. *v.* Dejar de usar una cosa. *To take out of circulation.*

ARCHIVISTA. *n.m.* Archivero. *Archivist.*

ARCO. *n.m.* Portería, meta (dep.). *Goal (sp.).*

ARDER. *v.* Escocerle a uno algo. *To sting, cause to smart.* || **2.** •Está que ARDE. Estar en un punto de excitación grande. *It's at the breaking point, things are pretty hot.* ~La reunión está que ARDE. *The meeting is at a breaking point.*

ARDIDO. *adj.* (Acad.) Irritado, enojado, ofendido. *Cross, angry.*

ARDIL. *n.m.* (Acad.) Ardid, artificio empleado con maña. *Trick, ruse.*

ARDILLA. *n.m.* Listo para los negocios. *Clever businessman, go-getter (in business).* || **2.** Persona de quien no se puede fiar. *Untrustworthy person.*

ARDILOSO. *adj.* (Acad.) Ardidoso. *Crafty, wily.*

AREPA. *n.f.* Especie de torta hecha de harina de maíz. *Cornmeal griddlecake.*

AREPERA. *n.f.* Mujer que vende **arepas.** *Arepa seller.* || **2.** Sartén para preparar **arepas.** *Pan for making arepa.* || **3.** Lesbiana. *Lesbian.*

ARETES. *n.m.* Pendientes. *Earrings.*

ARGOLLA. *n.f.* Anillo, sortija. *Ring.* || **2.** •ARGOLLA de novios. Anillo de compromiso. *Engagement ring.* ||**3.** •ARGOLLA de boda, de matrimonio. Alianza, anillo de boda. *Wedding ring.*

ARGÜENDE. *n.m.* Discusión. *Argument.*

ARGUMENTO. *n.m.* Discusión. *Argument, quarrel.*

ARISCO. *adj.* Que rehuye el trato social. *Reserved.*

ARMA. *n.m.* •Ser de ARMAS tomar. Ser de llevar armas. *To be bold, determined.*

ARMADA. *n.f.* (Acad.) Forma en que se dispone el lasso. *Circular shape of lassos coiled for throwing.*

ARMADO. *adj.* Terco. *Stubborn.*

ARMADOR. *n.m.* Chaleco. *Waistcoat.* || **2.** Percha. *Coat hanger.*

ARMADURÍA. *n.f.* Planta de montaje de coches. *Car assembly plant.*

ARMARSE. *v.* Mejorar de fortuna. *To get what one wants.* || **2.** Enriquecerse. *To strike it rich.*

ARMAZÓN. *n.f.* Estantes, anaqueles. *Shelves, shelving.*

ARNERO. *n.m.* Colador. *Sieve.*

ARO. *n.m.* (Acad.) Arete, zarcillo. *Earring.* || **2.** Anillo de boda. *Wedding ring.* || **3.** •Pasar a uno por el ARO. (Acad.) Ejecutar, vencido por fuerza o maña, lo que no quería. *To play tricks on someone.*

AROMATIZADOR. *n.m.* Pulverizador. *Spray.*

ARPAR. *v.* Robar, hurtar. *To steal, pilfer.*

ARPIR. *n.m.* Peón de minas. *Mine hand.*

ARQUEAR. *v.* Hacer el balance de contabilidad. *To check, check the content of.*

ARQUERO. *n.m.* Portero. *Goalkeeper.*

ARRABAL. *n.m.* Barrio bajo. *Slums, slum quarter.*

ARRAIGAR. *v.* Notificar judicialmente a una persona que no debe alejarse de la población bajo cierta pena. *To put someone under a restriction order, to confine someone to the town limits, to put under partial arrest.*

ARRANCADA. *n.f.* Partida o salida impetuosa. *Sudden dash, escape attempt.*

ARRANCAR. *v.* Huir, retirarse. *To escape, run off.* || **2.** Partir, salir corriendo con mucho ímpetu. *To start running, break into a run.* || **3.** Poner en marcha el motor de un automóvil. *To start a motor.* || **4.** (Acad.) Morirse. *To die, kick the bucket (coll.).*

ARRANCHAR. *v.* (Acad.) Quitar violentamente algo a alguien. *To seize, snatch, take.*

ARRANQUE. *n.m.* •Estar en el ARRANQUE.

(Acad.) Estar arruinado, sin un céntimo. *To be broke.*

ARRASTRADO. *adj.* Servil. *Servile.*

¡ARRE! *interj.* ¡Dése prisa! *Hurry up!*

ARREADA. *n.f.* (Acad.) Robo de ganado. *Rustling, cattle-thieving.*

ARREADO. *adj.* (Acad.) Flojo o cansado para el trabajo. *Slow, sluggish, lazy.*

ARREADOR. *n.m.* (Acad.) Látigo de mango corto y lonja larga, destinada a arrear. *Small whip for driving or herding cattle.*

ARREAR. *v.* Conducir (gente). *To hurry along, urge on.* || **2.** •ARREAR con. Llevarse. *To carry off.* || **3.** (Acad.) Llevarse violenta o furtivamente ganado ajeno. *To steal, rustle.*

ARRECHAR. *v.* Excitarse sexualmente (vulg.). *To arouse, excite, turn on.* || **2.** Enojar, fastidiar. *To irritate, bother; to bug (colloq.).* || **3.** -**se.** Excitarse sexualmente. *To get sexually aroused, excited (person), to be in heat (animal).* || **4.** Enojarse. *To get furious.* || **5.** (Acad.) Sobrar animación y brío. *To become lively or animated.*

ARRECHERA. *n.f.* Excitación sexual. *Sexual arousal, excitement.* || **2.** Enojo. *Bad temper.*

ARRECHO. *n.m&f.* Sexualmente excitado. *Sexually aroused.* || **2.** Enojado. *Furious, mad.*

ARRECIRSE. *v.* Estar muerto de frío. *To be frozen stiff.*

ARREDOMADO. *adj.* Astuto. *Sly, artful.*

ARREGLADO. *adj.* Amañado. *Fixed, rigged.*

ARREGLAR. *v.* Capar a los gatos. *To castrate (cat).* || **2.** -**se.** *v.* Prepararse. *To get ready.* ~Ya es hora de ARREGLARSE. Ya es tiempo de prepararse. *It's time to get ready.* || **3.** Tener suerte. *To have a stroke of luck.*

ARRENQUÍN. *n.m.* Ayudante. *Helper, assistant.* || **2.** (Acad.) Persona que no se separa de otra para ayudarla y acompañarla. *Person in constant company of another.* ||**3.** Sirviente leal. *Devoted servant.* || **4.** (Acad.) Animal que guía la recua. *Leading animal* *of a mule train.*

ARREO. *n.m.* Rebaño, manada. *Drove or herd of cattle.* || **2.** Recorrido. *Drive.*

ARREQUINTAR. *v.* (Acad.) Apretar fuertemente con cuerda o vendaje. *To tighten with a cord or bandage.*

ARRÍA. *n.f.* Recua de animales de carga que marcha en fila atados uno a otro. *Mule train.*

ARRIBA. *adv.* Encima de. *On top of.*

ARRIBEÑO. *adj.* (Acad.) Aplícase por los habitantes de las costas, al que procede de las tierras altas. *Highlander.*

ARRIESGAR. *v.* •El que no ARRIESGA no gana. El que no se arriesga no pasa la mar. *Nothing ventured, nothing gained.*

ARRIMADO. *n.m.* (Acad.) Persona que vive en casa ajena, a costa o ámparo de su dueño. *Unwelcomed guest; scrounger, freeloader.*

ARRIMARSE. *v.* Vivir a cuesta de otro. *To sponge.*

ARRINQUÍN (variante de **arrenquín**).

ARRISCADO. *adj.* (Acad.) Remangado, respingado, vuelto hacia arriba. *Turned up.*

ARRISCAR. *v.* Llegar, alcanzar. *To amount to.*

ARROJAR. *v.* Vomitar. *Vomit.*

ARROLLADO. *n.m.* (Acad.) Carne de vaca o puerco que, cocida y aderezada, se acomoda en rollo formado de la piel cocida del mismo animal. *Rolled beef or pork.*

ARROLLAR. *v.* Mecer (a un niño). *To rock (a child).*

ARROPE. *n.m.* Dulce de tuna, algarrobillo y otros frutos. *Sweet made of fruits.*

ARRORRÓ. *n.m.* Nana, tonada que se canta al niño pequeño para hacerle dormir. *Lullaby.*

ARROYO. *n.m.* (Acad.) Río navegable de poca extensión. *Small navigable river.*

ARROZ. *n.m.* •Este ARROZ ya se coció. Ya cayó el chivo en el lazo. *It's in the bag.*

ARRUINADO. *adj.* (Acad.) Enclenque, enfermizo. *Sickly, stunted.*

ARRUINAR. *v.* Desvirgar. *Deflower.*

ARVEJA. *n.f.* (Acad.) Guisante. *Green pea.*

ARVEJAL. *n.m.* Terreno plantado de arvejas. *Green pea garden.*

ASADO. *adj.* Enojado, enfadado. *Cross, angry.* || **2.** Carne asada a la parrilla. *Barbecued meat.* || **3.** Reunión en que se sirve carne asada a la parrilla. *Barbecue get-together.*

ASCENDENCIA (angl.). *n.f.* Predominio moral o influencia que una persona ejerce sobre otra. *Ascendancy, hold, influence.*

ASCO. *n.m.* •Sin ASCO. (Acad.) Con decisión, sin escrúpulos. *With determination.*

ASEGÚN (barb.). *adv., prep.* Según. *According to.*

ASENTADO. *adj.* Maduro, juicioso. *Mature, sensible.*

ASENTARSE. *v.* Adquirir madurez. *To settle down.*

ASERRÍN. *n.m.* Serrín. *Sawdust.*

ASERRUCHAR. *v.* (Acad.) Cortar o dividir con serrucho la madera u otra cosa. *To saw, cut with a handsaw.*

ASESORATO. *n.m.* Acto de asesorar. *Advising.* || **2.** Oficina del asesor. *Consultant's office.*

ASÍ. *conj.* Aunque. *Even if.* ~Así se esté muriendo de dolor. *Even though he may be dying of pain.*

ASIENTO. *n.m.* (Acad.) Territorio y población de las minas. *Mining town.*

ASIGNATORIO. *n.m.* (Acad.) Persona a quien se asigna la herencia o legado. *Heir, legatee, beneficiary.*

ASILAR. *v.* Otorgar asilo político. *To give political asylum to.*

ASIMILADO. *n.m.* Persona que ejerce su profesión en el ámbito del ejército. *Professional person attached to the army.* || **2.** •Médico ASIMILADO. *Medical doctor.*

ASÍSMICO. *adj.* A prueba de terremotos. *Earthquake proof.* Construcción ASÍSMICA. *Earthquake resistant building.*

ASNEAR. v. Hacer tonterías. *To act the fool, do something silly.* || **2.** Ser torpe. *To be clumsy.*

ASOCIO. n.m. (Acad.) Compañía, colaboración, asociación. *Association, company.* || **2.** •En ASOCIO con. *In association with.*

ASOLEADA. n.f. Insolación. *Sunstroke, insolation.* || **2.** Acción de orear, o airear (ropa). *Airing in the sun (clothes).*

ASOLEADO. adj. Tonto, torpe. *Dumb, stupid, foolish.*

ASOLEARSE. v. Tomar el sol. *To sunbathe.*

ASORROCHARSE. v. Contraer la enfermedad del SOROCHE o mal de montaña. *To get, or suffer from altitude sickness.* || **2.** Ruborizarse. *To blush.*

ASPIRAR. v. Pasar la aspiradora. *To vacuum.*

ASTABANDERA (asta bandera en la Argentina). n.f. Asta para izar la bandera. *Flagstaff, flagpole.*

ASUMIR. v. Suponer. *To assume.*

ATACARSE. v. Atracarse. *To stuff oneself.*

ATAJAR. Coger al vuelo. *To catch, catch in flight.* ATAJAR la pelota. *To catch the ball.* || **2.** Contener una persona por la fuerza. *To hold someone back, stop a fight.* ||**3.** •ATAJAR un golpe. Parar, desviar golpes. *To parry a blow.*

ATARRAGARSE. v. (Acad.) Atracarse, atiborrarse de comida. *To eat excessively, to stuff oneself.*

ATASCARSE. v. Enfermar por obstrucción del tubo digestivo. *To have an internal blockage.* ||**2.** •ATÁSCATE ahora que hay lodo. Aprovecha gaviota, que no hay otra. *Gather ye rosebuds while ye may.*

ATENCIOSO (barb.). Atento. *Attentive.*

ATENDER (angl.). v. Asistir. *To attend, be present at.* || **2. -se.** •ATENDERSE con. Tener trato con. *To see someone professionally.* ~¿Con qué médico se ATIENDE Ud.? *Who is your doctor?*

ATENUANTE (jur.). n.m. Disculpa. *Excuse, plea.*

ATESAR (barb.). v. Atiesar. *To stiffen, stiffen up.*

ATINGENCIA. n.f. (Acad.) Relación, conexión, correspondencia. *Connection, relation, bearing.* || **2.** Reflexión, observación. *Remark, observation.*

ATINGIR. v.Tener relación una cosa con otra. *To concern, bear on, relate to.* || **2.** (Acad.) Afligir, oprimir, tiranizar. *To oppress.*

ATISBADERO. n.m. Mirilla. *Peephole.*

ATMÓSFERA. n.f. Buen acogida social. *To have social standing, stand well with everyone.*

ATOCAR (barb.). v. Tocar. *To touch.*

ATOL (variante de **atole**).

ATOLE. n.m. Bebida hecha de harina de maíz disuelta en agua o leche. *Drink made of corn flour.* || **2.** •Más vale ATOLE con risas que chocolate con lágrimas. Contigo pan y cebolla. *I'll go through thick and thin with you.*

ATOLERÍA. n.f. Lugar donde se hace o vende **atole**. *Place where **atole** is made or sold.*

ATOLLADERO. n.m. Apuro. *Predicament.* || **2,** •Estar metido en un ATOLLADERO. *To be in a fix or jam.*

ATOMÍA. n.f. Salvajada, mala acción. *Evil deed, savage act.*

ATORAR. v. Tapar, obstruir (cañería). *To block, block up.* || **2. -se.** Atragantarse. *To choke.* || **3.** Obstruirse, taparse (cañería). *To get blocked .* || **4.** Atascarse (puerta, cajón). *To jam.* || **5.** Detenerse una cosa. *To become stuck.* ~Se le ATORÓ la comida en la garganta. *The food became stuck in his throat.*

ATORNILLADOR. n.m. Destornillador. *Screwdriver.*

ATORNILLAR. v. Molestar, importunar, fastidiar. *To disturb, bother, pester, harass.*

ATORO. n.m. Destrucción. *Destruction.*

ATRACADA. n.m. (Acad.) Atracón. *Surfeit, excess.*

ATRÁS. prep. •ATRÁS de. Detrás de. *Behind.*

ATRASARSE. *v*. Sufrir menoscabo financiero. *To suffer a setback.*

ATRASO. *n.m.* Menstruación. *To have a period.*

ATRAVESADA. *n.m.* Acción de atravesar. *Crossing, passage.*

ATRAVESAR. *v*. Acaparar. *Monopolize, corner the market.* || **2.** Toparse con. *To bump into someone.* ~Se ATRAVESARON en la calle. *They bumped into each other in the street.*

ATRENZO. *n.m.* (Acad.) Conflicto, apuro, dificultad. *Trouble, difficulty.* || **2.** •Estar en un ATRENZO. Estar en un apuro. *To be in trouble.*

ATRINCAR. *v*. (Acad.) Trincar, sujetar, asegurar con cuerdas y lazos. *To tie up tightly.* || **2.** (Acad.) Apretar. *To tighten.*

ATROPELLAR. *v*. Hacer el amor a una mujer. *To make love to.* || **2.** Ultrajar. *To seduce, dishonor.*

AUDICIÓN. Revisión contable, auditoría. *Audit.*

AUDÍFONO. *n.m.* Tubo auricular del teléfono. *Earpiece, receiver.*

AUREOLAR. *v*. Honrar, glorificar a una persona. *To praise, extol the virtues of.*

AUSPICIAR. *v*. Favorecer, patrocinar, amparar. *To back, sponsor, support.* || **2.** Desear éxito. *To wish good luck to.*

AUSPICIOS. *n.m.* Patronato. *Auspices, patronage.*

AUTAZO. *n.m.* Robo de coche. *Theft of a car.*

AUTERO. *n.m.* Ladrón de coches. *Car thief.*

AUTO. *n.m.* Coche. *Car.*

AUTOCARRIL. *n.m.* Automotor, autorriel. *Railway car.*

AUTOMEDONTE (hum.). *n.m.* Cochero. *Coachman, driver.*

AUTOMOTOR. *n.m.* Relativo al automóvil. *Relative to cars.*

AUXILIAR (Dep.). *n.m.* •AUXILIAR técnico. Entrenador auxiliar. *Co-trainer.*

AUYAMA. *n.f.* Calabaza o zapallo. *Gourd, pumpkin.*

AVALUACIÓN. *n.f.* Valoración. *Valuation, appraisal.*

AVALUAR. *v*. Valorar. *Appraise, value.*

AVARIOSIS. *n.f.* Sífilis. *Syphilis.*

AVENTAR. *v*. Tirar. *To throw, throw out.* || **2.** -se. Tirarse. *To throw oneself, to jump, dive.*

AVENTON. *n.m.* (Acad.) Empujón. *Push, shove.*

AVESTRUZ. *n.m.* Tonto, imbécil. *Idiot, dimwit.*

AVIADOR. *n.m.* Prestamista o inversor en trabajos de minas, ganado o agricultura. *Supplier or financier of miners or farmers.*

AVIAR. *v*. Prestar dinero o efectos a labrador, ganadero o minero. *To equip or supply farmers or miners with equipment or money.* || **2.** Proveer de alimentos para el camino a quien va a viajar. *To provide with food for a journey.*

AVIATORIO. *adj.* Accidente AVIATORIO. Accidente de avión. *Air crash, plane crash.*

AVÍO. *n.m.* Préstamo que se hace al minero, agricultor o ganadero. *Loan to a farmer or miner.*

AVISAR. *v*. Dar parte. *To inform, report.*

AVISO. *n.m.* Anuncio. *Advertisement.*

AVISPADO. *adj.* Nervioso. *Jumpy, nervous.*

AVISPARSE. *v*. Espantarse, alarmarse. *To become concerned, get alarmed.*

AVIVAR. *v*. Avisar, advertir. *To warn, alert.* || **2.** Despabilarse. *To wise up.*

AVIVATO. *n.m&f.* Oportunista, vivo. *Sharp, smoth operator.*

AYUDA. *n.f.* Laxante. *Laxative.*

AZAFATE. *n.m.* Bandeja. *Tray.* || **2.** Jofaina. *Washbasin.*

AZAREARSE. *v*. (Acad.) Turbarse, avergonzarse. *To get flustered, rattled, embarrassed or confused.*

AZORO. *n.m.* Azoramiento. *Embarrassment.*

AZOTERA. *n.f.* Paliza. *Beating, thrashing.*

AZUCARARSE. *v.* Cristalizarse el almíbar de las conservas. *To crystallize, turn sugary (syrup in preserves).*

AZUCARERA. *n.f.* Recipiente para azúcar. *Sugar bowl.*

AZULEJO. *adj.* (Acad.) Azulado, que tira a azul. *Bluish.*

AZULOSO. *adj.* Azulino. *Bluish.*

B

BABOSADA. *n.f.* Tontería, bobada. *Drivel, rubbish, nonsense.* ~Son puras BABOSADAS. *Its all rubbish.*

BABOSO. *adj.* Tonto, bobo (persona), ridículo (libro, espectáculo). *Foolish, stupid, dim (person), ridiculous (book, show).* ‖ **2.** *n.m.* Tonto, bobo. *Foolish, stupid person.*

BABY. *n.m&f.* Niño pequeño. *Baby.*

BACENICA. *n.f.* Bacinica. *Small chamberpot.*

BACENILLA (variante de **bacenica**).

BACHICHA. *n.m.* (Acad.) Apodo con que se designaba al italiano (pey.). *Dago, wop (derog.).*

BACINETE. *n.m.* Taza de lavabo. *Lavatory pan.*

BADULAQUE. *n.m.* Bribón, embustero, pícaro. *Rogue.*

BAGAJE. *n.m.* Equipaje. *Luggage, baggage.*

BAGAZO. *n.m.* Cáscara de la caña de azúcar. *Husks of sugar cane.*

BAGRE. *n.m.* Mujer fea. *Ugly woman, old bag (coll.).* ‖ **2.** Persona antipática. *Unpleasant person.* ‖ **3.** Pez abundante en América, de carne amarilla y con pocas espinas. *Catfish.*

BAGUAL. *n.m.* Potro a medio domar. *Wild, untamed horse.* ‖ **2.** Individuo torpe y grosero. *Lout, uncouth person.* ‖ **3.** *adj.* Se dice del individuo torpe y grosero. *Ill-mannered, unsociable.*

BAILADA. *n.f.* Baile. *Dance, dancing.*

BAILE. *n.m.* •BAILE de medio pelo. Baile al que acude personas de escasa posición social. *Village dance.* ‖ **2.** •BAILE de fantasía. Baile de disfraces. *Masked ball.*

BAILECITO. *n.m.* Baile popular. *Folk dance.*

BAILONGO. *n.m.* Baile pobre pero alegre. *Local dance.*

BAJANTE. *n.f.* (Acad.) Descenso del nivel de las aguas. *Low tide.*

BAJAREQUE. *n.m.* (Acad.) Pared de palos entretejidos con cañas y barro. *Mud wall.* ‖ **2.** Choza. *Hut.*

BAJATIVO. *n.m.* (Acad.) Copa de algún licor que se toma despúes de las comidas. *Digestive.*

BAJERA. *n.f.* (Acad.) Cada una de las hojas inferiores de la planta del tabaco, que son de mala calidad. *Lower leaves of the tobacco plant.* ‖ **2.** Tabaco de inferior calidad. *Rough or inferior tobacco.*

BAJIAL. *n.m.* Terreno bajo y anegadizo. *Lowlands; flats, floodplain.*

BAJÍO. *n.m.* Terreno bajo. *Lowland.* ‖ **2.** Dar en un BAJÍO. Tropezar en un grave inconveniente. *To come across a serious difficulty, get stuck.*

BALA. *n.f.* Ni a BALA. De ninguna manera. *By no means, not on any account.* ~Ni a BALA se da por entendido. *There is no way he will take a hint.* ‖ **2.** •Lanzamiento de BALA expansiva. Lanzamiento de peso. *Shot put.*

BALACA. *n.f.* Fanfarronada. *Boast, boasting.*

BALACERA. *n.f.* (Acad.) Tiroteo. *Shooting.* ‖ **2.** Enfrentamiento. *Shoot-out.* ~Se armó una BALECERA entre la policía y los asaltantes. *There was a shoot-out between the police and the bank robbers.* ‖ **3.** Lluvia de balas. *Hail of bullets.*

BALANCE (angl.). *n.m.* Saldo. *Balance.*

BALANZA. *n.f.* Balancín de voltinero. *Acrobat's balancing pole.*

BALAY. *n.m.* (Acad,) Cesta de nimbre o de

carrizo. *Wicker basket.*

BALAZO. *n.m.* No me entra ni a BALAZOS. *No lo aguanto. I can't stand him.*

BALCONEARSE. *v.* Ponerse en evidencia. *To make a fool of oneself.*

BALDE. *n.m.* •BALDE de la basura. Cubo de la basura. *Trash-can.* ‖ **2.** •Ni en BALDE. De ninguna manera. *Not on your life!, no way! (coll.).*

BALDÍO. *n.m.* (Acad.) Solar, terreno urbano sin edificar. *Piece or plot of land, vacant lot.*

BALDOSA. *n.f.* Lápida. *Tombstone.*

BALDOSADO. *n.m.* Embaldosado. *Tiled floor.*

BALEADO. *n.m&f.* Persona que ha sido **baleado** (ver **balear**). *Shooting victim.*

BALEAR. *v.* (Acad.). Tirotear, disparar balas sobre alguien o algo. *To shoot at.* ‖ **2.** Matar. *To shoot down, shoot dead.* ~Murió BALEADO. *He was shot dead.* ‖ **3.** Estafar. *To cheat, swindle.* ‖ **4. -se.** Tirotearse. *To shoot at each other.*

BALEO. *n.m.* (Acad.) Acción y efecto de balear, disparar balas; tiroteo. *Shooting.*

BALERO. *n.m.* (Acad.) Boliche, juego de niños. *Cup-and-ball toy.*

BALNARIO. *n.m.* Punto de veraneo. *Seaside resort.*

BALÓN. *n.m.* (Acad.) Bombona de metal para gases. *Drum, cannister.*

BALSA. *n.f.* •Madera de BALSA. *Balsa wood.* ‖ **2.** •BALSA de aceite. Lugar o persona serena, apacible. *Quiet, tranquil place or person.*

BALUARTE. *n.m.* Artificio en forma de embudo para coger peces. *Funnel-shaped device used to catch fish.*

BALUMBA. *n.f.* Alboroto. *Noise, uproar.*

BALURDO. *adj.* Ostentoso. *Flashy.*

BAMBOLLA. *n.f.* Charla, conversación ligera. *Idle talk, chatter.*

BANANA. *n.f.* Plátano. *Banana (fruit).* ‖ **2.** Banano. *Banana tree.*

BANANAL. *n.m.* (Acad.) Conjunto de plá-tanos que crecen en un lugar. *Banana plantation.*

BANANAR (variante de **bananal**).

BANANERO. *n.m.* Banano. *Banana tree.* ‖ **2.. *adj.* •Plantación BANANERA. *Banana plantation.* Compañía BANANERA. *Banana company.*

BANANO. *n.m.* Bananero. *Banana tree.* ‖ **2.** Plátano. *Banana (fruit).*

BANCA. *n.f.* (Acad.) Banco, asiento. *Bench, seat.* ‖ **2.** •Hizo quebrar la BANCA. *She broke the bank.*

BANCADA. *n.f.* (Acad.) Conjunto de los legisladores de un mismo partido. *Political group.*

BANDA. *n.f.* (Acad.) Correa del ventilador del coche. *Fan belt (car).* ‖ **2.** Faja que se usa a modo de cinturón. *Sash used as a belt.*

BANDALAJE. *n.m.* Bandolerismo. *Banditry.*

BANDEAR. *v.* (Acad.) Atravesar, pasar de parte a parte; taladrar. *To drill (through).* ‖ **2.** (Acad.) Cruzar el río de una banda a otra. *To cross a river.*

BANDEJA. *n.f.* Platón. *Large serving dish, bowl.*

BANDERILLA. *n.f.* Estafa. *Swindle.*

BANDERILLAZO (variante de **banderilla**).

BANGAÑA (variante de **bangaño**).

BANGAÑO. *n.m.* Fruto de una calabaza. *Pumpkin, gourd.* ‖ **2.** Vasija hecha con este fruto. *Vessel made from a gourd.*

BANIATAL. *n.m.* Field of sweet potatoes. *Plantío de batata.*

BANQUETERO. *n.m.* Encargado del servicio de comida y bebida en fiestas, etc. *Caterer.*

BANTAM. *n.f.* Persona pequeña y movediza. *Small restless person.*

BANYO. *n.m.* Banjo. *Banjo.*

BAÑADA. *n.f.* Baño, chapuzón. *Bath, swim, dip.*

BAÑADERA. *n.f.* (Acad.) Bañera. *Bath,*

bathtub.

BAÑADO. *n.m.* (Acad.) Terreno húmedo a trechos cenagoso y a veces inundado por las aguas pluviales o por las de un río o laguna cercana. *Area of marshland.*

BAÑO. *n.m.* Cuarto de baño. *Bathroom.*

BAQUETEAR. *v.* (Acad.) •Tratar a la BA-QUETA a alguien, tratar con poca consideración. *To mistreat, to abuse of someone.*

BAQUÍA. *n.f.* Conocimiento de una región. *Intimate knowledge of a region, local expertise.* || **2.** (Acad.) Habilidad y destreza para obras manuales. *Skill in using one's hands.* || **3.** •De BAQUIANO. Skilfully, expertly. *Like an old hand.*

BAQUIANO. *adj.* Que conoce una región. *Familiar with a region.* || **2.** *n.m.* Guía. *Guide, local expert.*

BARAJA. *n.f.* Juego de naipe. *Playing cards.* || **2.** •Jugar BARAJA. *To play cards.*

BARAJUSTAR. *v.* Irse, escaparse. *To leave, escape.*

BARANDILLA. *n.f.* Adral de carro. *Rail, sideboard (of a cart).*

BARATERO. *adj.* Que vende barato. *Who sells cheap (shopkeeper).* || **2.** •Tienda BARATERA. Tienda que vende artículos a bajo precio. *Cut-rate store.* || **3.** *n.m.* Tendero que ofrece artículos a bajo precio. *Cut-rate merchant.*

BARBA. *n.f.* (Acad.) Flecos de un pañolón, rebozo, colcha, etc. *Fringe.* •Un chal con BARBAS. *A fringed shawl.*

BARBACOA. *n.m.* (Acad.) Zarzo cuadrado u oblongo, sostenido con puntales, que sirve de camastro. *Platform bed, board bed supported on props, makeshift cot.* || **2.** (Acad.) Casita construida en alto sobre árboles o estacas. *Small hut on piles, lookout platform.* || **3.** Armazón que sirve de sostén a las plantas trepadoras. *Wooden or reed latice frame.* || **4.** Conjunto de madera verde sobre un hueco a manera de parrilla. *Barbacue frame for roasting meat.* || **5.** Carne asada de esta manera. *Meat roasted in this manner.* || **6.** (Acad.) Zarzo o tablado tosco en lo alto de las casas, donde se guardan granos, fru-tos, etc.). *Loft, attic to keep fruits, vegetables and other agricultural products.*

BARBEAR. *v.* Afeitar. *To shave.* || **2.** Derribar (res). *To throw, fell (cattle).*

BARBERA. *adj.* Tinto (vino). *Red (wine).* || **2.** (Acad.) Navaja de afeitar. *Razor.*

BARBIJO. *n.m.* (Acad.) Barbiquejo, cinta de sujetar que pasa por debajo de la barba. *Chin strap.*

BARCHILÓN, NA. *n.m&f.* (Acad.) Enfermero (enfermera) de un hospital. *Auxiliary nurse, hospital aide.*

BARDOMA. *n.f.* Cineo, fango, barro. *Dirt, filth, mud.*

BARRA. *n.f.* Grupo de hinchas, seguidores. *Fans.* || **2.** (Acad.) Público que asiste a las sesiones de un tribunal, asamblea o corporación. *Audience at a court session.* || **3.** Desembocadura de un río. *Mouth of a river.* || **4.** Acción o participación en una mina. *Share in a mine.* || **5.** •Hacerle BARRA a alguien. Alentar a una persona. *To cheer somebody on.*

BARRACA. *n.f.* (Acad.) Edificio en que se depositan cueros, lanas, maderas, cereales u otros efectos destinados al tráfico. *Large storage shed.* || **2.** Cuartel militar. *Barracks.*

BARRACÓN. *n.m.* Sitio que cada vendedor ocupa en las plazas del mercado. *Market stall.*

BARRANCO. *n.m.* Despeñadero. *Cliff.*

BARRAQUERO. *n.m.* Dueño o administrador de una **barraca**. *Owner or manager of a* **barraca***.*

BARRERO. *n.m.* Extensión de tierra salitrosa. *Salt marsh.*

BARRETA. *n.f.* Especie de piqueta que usan los albañiles. *Bricklayer's hammer.*

BARRETEAR. *v.* Trabajar con la BARRETA. *To drill, bore.*

BARRIADA. *n.f.* Barrio pobre, marginal. *Slum area, shantytown.*

BARRIAL. *n.m.* Pantano, barrizal. *Bog, quagmire.* || **2.** (Acad.) Perteneciente o relativo al barrio. *Pertaining to the neighborhood or local people.*

BARRIDA. *n.f.* Barrido, baridura. *Sweep, sweeping.* || **2.** Redada. *Police raid, sweep.*

BARRIL. *n.m.* Cometa hexagonal. *Hexagonal kite.*

BARRIO. *n.m.* •Barrio de tolerancia. Barrio chino. *Red-light district.*

BASEBALL. *n.m.* Béisbol. *Baseball.*

BASEBALLISTA. *n.m.* Jugador de béisbol. *Baseball player.*

BASKETBALL. *n.m.* Baloncesto. *Basketball.*

BASQUETBOL. *n.m.* (Acad.) Baloncesto. *Basketball.*

BASQUETBOLISTA. Jugador de baloncesto. *Basketball player.*

BASTA. *n.f.* Vuelta (de pantalones). *Trouser cuff.*

BASTO. *n.m.* (Acad.) Almohadilla inferior de la silla de montar. *Saddle pad.*

BASURAL. *n.m.* (Acad.) Basurero, sitio donde se echa la basura. *Garbage dump.*

BATACAZO. n.m. (Acad.) Triunfo inesperado de un caballo en una carrera. *Unexpected win by a racehorse.* || **2.** •Dar el batacazo. *To be the surprise winner in a horserace.*

BATACLÁN. *n.m.* Estriptise, striptease. *Burlesque show, striptease show.*

BATACLANA. *n.f.* Striptisera. *Striptease artist.*

BATAHOLA. *n.f.* Pandemonio, caos. *Pandemonium.*

BATATAR. *n.m.* Campo sembrado de batatas. *Sweet potato field.*

BATATAZO (variante de **batacazo**). || **2.** Cualquier triunfo o suceso afortunado y sorprendente. *Stroke of luck; fluke, lucky shot; unexpected win.*

BATEA. *n.f.* Vasija plana de madera destinada al lavado de ropa. *Shallow pan used for washing clothes.*

BATERÍA. *n.f.* •Dar batería. Dar guerra, causar molestias. *To make trouble for, give a lot of work to.* ~Los niños dan mucha batería a las madres. *Children make life difficult for their mothers.* || **2.** Trabajar con esfuerzo. *To work diligently, to keep at it.*

BATERISTA. *n.m&f.* Batería. *Drummer.*

BAÚL. *n.m.* Maletero del automóvil. *Trunk (of a car).*

BAYONETA. *n.f.* Nombre alterno de la yucca. *Alternate name for yucca.*

BAYONETEAR. *v.* Matar con bayoneta. *To bayonet.*

BE. *n.f.* •Be grande, larga. Be de burro, be de Barcelona. *The letter "b" (as opposed to the letter "v").* Note: Both of these letters have the same sound in Spanish).

BEBESTIBLE. *adj.* Potable. *Drinkable.*

BEBIDA. *n.f.* •Tener malas bebidas. Ponerse agresivo por causa de la bebida. *To get violent from overdrinking.*

BECADO. *n.m&f.* Becario. *Person who has obtained a scholarship.*

BEISBOLERO. *adj.* Que tiene relación con el béisbol. *Relative to baseball.* || **2.** *n.m.* Jugador de béisbol. *Baseball player.*

BEISBOLISTA. *n.m.* Jugador de béisbol. *Baseball player.*

BEJUCO. *n.m.* Liana. *Liana.*

BEJUQUEADA. *n.f.* Paliza, golpiza. *Beating, thrashing.*

BEJUQUEAR. *v.* (Acad.) Varear, apalear, azotar con un **bejuco**. *To beat, thrash with a reed.*

BELDUQUE. *n.m.* Cuchillo grande con hoja puntiaguda. *Large pointed knife.*

BELLACO. Difícil de gobernar (caballería). *Vicious, difficult to control.*

BEMBA. *n.f.* (Acad.) Boca de labios gruesos y abultados. *Thick lips.*

BEMBO. *adj.* De labios gruesos. *Thick-lipped.*

BEMBÓN. *adj.* (Acad.) Bezudo. *Thick-lipped.*

BEMBUDO (variante de **bembo**).

BENCINA. *n.f.* Gasolina. *Gasoline.*

BENCINERA. *n.f.* Estación de servicio. *Gas station.*

BENCINERO. *adj.* Motor BENCINERO. *Gas engine.* || **2.** Encargado en una estación de servicio. *Gasoline station attendant.*

BENEFICIAR. *v.* Preparar (res, cerdo). *To dress.* || **2.** Matar para vender (animal). *To slaughter and sell.* || **3.** Preparar en los BENEFICIOS productos agrícolas. *To process agricultural products.*

BENEFICIO. *n.m.* Matanza. *Slaughter, slaughtering.* || **2.** Preparación (de un animal). *Dressing.* || **3.** Matadero. *Slaughterhouse.* || **4.** (Acad.) Ingenio o hacienda donde se benefician productos agrícolas. *Coffee plantation, sugar refinery.*

BERMA. *n.f.* Arcén. *Hard shoulder.*

BERMUDA. *n.f.* Gramínea en prados y sabanas. *Meadow grass.*

BERRINCHUDO. *adj.* Enojadizo. *Touchy, irascible, bad-tempered.*

BETARAGA. *n.f.* Betarrata. *Beetroot, beet.*

BICHERÍO. *n.m.* Conjunto de bichos. *A swarm of insect, bugs.*

BICHO. *n.m.* Cualquier animal raro. *Odd-looking creature.* || **2.** •De puro BICHO. Por testarudez. *Out of sheer stubborness.* || **3.** •Matar el BICHO. *To have a drink.*

BIDEL. *n.m.* Bidet. *Bidet.*

BIFE. *n.m.* Bistec. *Steak.*

BILLETERA. *n.f.* Billetero, cartera. *Wallet.*

BILMA. *n.f.* Bizma. *Poultice.*

BILMAR. *v.* Bizmar. *To poultice.*

BINCHA. *n.f.* Cinta con que se ciñe la cabeza o se sujeta el pelo. *Headband.*

BIÓGRAFO. *n.m.* Cinematógrafo. *Movie theater.*

BIRIQUÍ. *n.m.* Berbiquí. *Carpenter's brace.*

BISTEQUE. *n.m.* Bistec. *Steak.*

BITOQUE. *n.m.* (Acad.) Cánula de la jeringa. *Injection tube of a syringe.*

BLANQUEADA. *n.f.* Blanqueo. *Bleaching, whitewashing.*

BOCABAJEAR. *v.* aplastar, reprimir. *To crush, put down.*

BOCADO. *n.m.* Correa atada a la boca del caballo y que hace las veces de freno. *Bit.*

BOCATERO. *adj.* Jactancioso, fanfarrón. *Bragging, boastful.*

BOCATOMA. *n.f.* Boca de agua. *Water intake, inlet pipe.*

BOCHINCHE. *n.m.* Riña, pelea. *Fight, brawl.* || **2.** Alboroto, desorden. *Racket, ruckus.*

BOCHINCHEAR. *v.* •Armar BOCHINCHES. *To cause an uproar or commotion.*

BOCHINCHERO. *adj.* Alborotador. *Rowdy.* || **2.** *n.m.* Alborotador. *Troublemaker, brawler.*

BOCHINCHOSO (variante de **bochinchero**).

BOCINA. *n.f.* Trompetilla. *Ear-trumpet.* || **2.** Tapacubos. *Hubcap.*

BODEGA. *n.f.* Tienda de comestibles. *Grocery store.*

BODEGAJE. *n.m.* Derecho de almacenamiento en una bodega. *Storage charges.*

BOFE. *n.m.* •Echar el BOFE (los BOFES). Jadear, quedar sin aliento. *To pant, be out of breath.*

BOGA. *n.m.* Remero. *Rower, oarsman.*

BOHÍO. *n.m.* Cabaña. *Hut, shack.*

BOICOTERO. *n.m.* Boicoteo. *Boycott.*

BOIQUIRA. *n.f.* Culebra de cascabel. *Rattlesnake.*

BOJOTE. *n.m.* (Acad.) Lío, bulto, envoltorio, paquete. *Bundle, parcel, package.*

BOL. *n.m.* Aguamanil, lavafrutas. *Finger bowl.*

BOLA. *n.f.* Pelota. *Ball, football.* || **2.** (Acad.) La bola empleada como arma ofensiva y para cazar o sujetar animales, boleadoras. *Lasso with balls.* || **3.** •Dar BOLA (a alguien). (Acad.) Prestar atención a alguien. *To pay attention to, take notice of.*

BOLADA. *n.f.* Suerte. *Piece of luck, lucky break.* || **2.** Ganga. *Bargain, lucky piece of business.* || **3.** Mentira. *Fib, lie.*

BOLADO. *n.m.* Asunto, negocio. *Affair, business.* || **2.** •Hazme un BOLADO. Hazme un favor. *Do me a favor.*

BOLEAR. *v.* Rechazar en una votación, bochar. *To reject a candidate in an election.* || **2.** Despedir a un empleado. *To fire, dismiss.* || **3.** Reprobar en un examen. *To fail an exam.* || **4.** Encabritarse el caballo, volcarse de espaldas. *To rear and fall, roll over.*

BOLETA. *n.f.* Billete. *Ticket.* || **2.** •Boleta de calificaciones. Boletín de calificaciones, boletín de notas. *Report card.* || **3.** Boleta electoral, papeleta. *Ballot paper.* || **4.** Borrador. *Draft (document).* || **5.** Certificado. *Certificate.* •Certificado de sanidad. *Health certificate.*

BOLETAJE. *n.m.* Conjunto de boletos o boletas. *Tickets.*

BOLETERÍA. *n.f.* (Acad.) Taquilla, casillero o despacho de billetes. *Box office, ticket office.* || **2.** Agencia de venta de localidades. *Ticket agency.* || **3.** Recaudación. *Gate, takings.*

BOLETERO. *n.m.* (Acad.) Persona que vende **boletos.** *Ticket clerk.*

BOLETO. *n.m.* Billete. *Ticket.* || **2.** Billete de lotería. *Lottery ticket.*

BOLICHE. *n.m.* Boliviano. *Native of Bolivia.* || **2.** (Acad.) Establecimiento comercial o industrial de poca importancia, especialmente el que se dedica al despacho y consumo de bebidas y comestibles. *Small, cheap restaurant.*

BOLILLO (mus.). *n.m.* Palillos de tambor. *Drumstick.*

BOLSA. *n.f.* (Acad.) Bolsillo de las prendas de vestir. *Pocket.* || **2.** •Como una bolsa de papas. *Like a sack of potatoes.* ~Se cayó como una bolsa de papas. *He went down like a sack of potatoes.*

BOLSEAR. *v.* (Acad.) Quitarle a alguien furtivamente lo que tenga de valor. *To pick someone's pocket.*

BOLSIQUEAR. *v.* (Acad.) **Bolsear,** quitar a alguien una cosa del bolsillo. *To pick someone's pockets.*

BOLSÓN. *n.m.* Cartapacio en que llevan los estudiantes los libros. *School bag.*

BOMBA. *n.f.* Rumor. *False rumor.* || **2.** (Acad.) Embriaguez. *Drinking spree.* || **3.** •Estar en bomba. *To be drunk.* || **4.** •Pegarse una bomba. *To get drunk.*

BOMBACHA. *n.f.* (Acad.) Calzón o pantalón bombacho. *Baggy trousers.*

BOMBACHO. *adj.* Ancho, suelto (ropa). *Baggy.*

BOMBEAR. *v.* Hacer funcionar un bomba (de agua). *To pump.*

BOMBEO. *n.m.* Acción de bombear. *Pumping.*

BOMBERO. *n.m.* Empleado que dispensa gasolina. *Gasoline station attendant (person who 'pumps' gasoline).*

BOMBILLA. *n.f.* (Acad.) Caña delgada que se usa para sorber el mate. *Metal tube for drinking mate.*

BOMBILLO. *n.m.* (Acad.) Bombilla eléctrica. *Electric light bulb.*

BONCHE (angl.). *n.m.* Montón. *Bunch, load.*

BONETERÍA. *n.f.* Tienda de ropa interior. *Notions store.*

BONGO. *n.m.* Barco pequeño. *Small boat.*

BONIATA. *adj.* Planta no venenosa. *Edible, non-poisonous (plant).*

BONITURA. *n.f.* Hermosura. *Beauty, attractiveness.*

BOQUETA. *adj.* (Acad.) Que tiene el labio hendido. *Harelipped.*

BORBOJA. *n.f.* Burbuja. *Bubble.*

BORDEJADA (mar.). *n.f.* Bordada, camino que entre dos viradas hace una embarcación cuando navega de bolina. *Board, course made on one track.*

BORDEJEAR. *v.* Bordear. *To skirt, go around.*

BORDÍN. *n.m.* Casa de huéspedes. *Boarding house.*

BORDINQUERO. *n.m.* Encargado de una casa de huéspedes. *Boarding house keeper.*

BORDONETE. *n.m.* Lechino, clavo de hilas que se pone en las llagas. *Small roll of lint for keeping a wound open.*

BORLARSE. *v.* Doctorarse, tomar la borla de doctor. *To become a doctor, take a higher degree.*

BORONA. *n.f.* Migaja. *Breadcrumb.*

BORRACHERÍA. *n.f.* Taberna. *Tavern, bar.*

BORRACHO. *adj.* Demasiado maduro. *Over-ripe.*

BORRADOR. *n.m.* Goma de borrar. *Eraser.*

BOTADA. *n.m.* Niño abandonado. *Abandoned child.* || **2.** *n.f.* Acción de tirar, arrojar. *Throw, throwing.* || **3.** Despedida (trabajo). *Dismissal.*

BOTADERO. *n.m.* Vertedero. *Rubbish dump.* || **2.** Vado. *Ford.*

BOTADO. *adj.* Muy barato o casí regalado. *Cheap, given away, dirt cheap (coll.).* || **2.** Despedido. *Fired, kicked out.*

BOTADOR. *adj.* (Acad.) Derrochador, manirroto. *Spendthrift, wasteful.*

BOTADURA. *n.f.* Despilfarro. *Waste of money.*

BOTAMANGA. *n.f.* Bocamanga. *Cuff.*

BOTANEARSE. •BOTANEARSE a alguno. Hablar en contra de alguien. *To speak ill of someone.*

BOTANEO. *n.m.* Chisme, calumnia. *Gossip, slander.*

BOTÁNICA. *n.f.* Sitio donde se venden hierbas medicinales. *Store where medicinal herbs are sold.*

BOTAR. *v.* Tirar. *Throw away.* || **2.** Despedir de un trabajo. *To fire, dismiss.* ~LO BOTARON de su trabajo. *They sacked him from his job.* || **3.** Perder. *To loose.* || **4.** Malgastar, derrochar. *To waste, squander.* || **5.** Arrojar, lanzar. *To hurl, fling, throw.* || **6.** Echar de un lugar. *To throw out.* || **7.** -se. Apresurarse. *To rush.* || **8.** •Se prohibe BOTAR basura. *No dumping.*

BOTARATE. *n.m.* (Acad.) Persona derrochadora, manirrota. *Spendthrift.*

BOTERO. *n.m.* Trapero. *Ragman.*

BOTIJA. *n.f.* •Poner a uno como BOTIJA verde. *To call someone every name under the sun.* || **2.** Tesoro enterrado. *Buried treasure.*

BOTIJUELA. *n.f.* Botijo. *Earthenware.*

BOTONAR. *v.* Abotonar. *To button up.* || **2.** Poner botones a una prenda. *To sew on buttons.*

BOTOTO. *n.m.* (Acad.) Calabaza para llevar agua. *Gourd or calabash for carrying water.*

BÓVEDA. *n.f.* •BÓVEDA de seguridad. Cámara acorazada. *Bank vault.*

BOX. *n.m.* Boxeo. *Boxing.*

BOZAL. *n.m.* Dícese del negro recien traido de Africa (hist.). *Said of the negro recently brought from Africa (hist.).* || **2.** Que habla mal el castellano. *Speaking broken Spanish.* || **3.** (Acad.) Bozo, ramal o cordel que, anudado al cuello de la caballería, forma un cabezón. *Halter, headstall.*

BRAGATERO. *n.m.* Que se casa por dinero. *Who marries for money.*

BRAMADERO. *n.m.* Poste al que se atan los animales. *Hitching post.*

BRASERO. *n.m.* Chimenea. *Hearth, fireplace.*

BRAVO. *adj.* Picante. *Hot, strong.* || **2.** Enojado. *Angry.*

BRAZADA. *n.f.* Braza (medida). *Fathom.*

BREQUE. *n.m.* Freno. *Brake.* || **2.** Coche grande de cuatro ruedas. *Break (vehicle).* || **3.** Wagón de equipaje (ferro.). *Baggage car.*

BREQUEAR. *v.* Frenar. *To break.*

BREQUERO. *n.m.* Guardafrenos. *Brakeman.*

BRETELES. *n.m.* Tirantes. *Suspenders.*

BREVA. *n.f.* (Acad.) Tabaco en rama, elaborado a propósito para masticar. *Chewing tobacco.*

BREVEMENTE. *adv.* En breve. *Shortly, very soon.*

BREVETE. *n.m.* Carné (carnet) de conducir. *Driving license.*

BRILLOSO. *adj.* Brillante. *Shiny.*

BRIN. *n.m.* Tela gruesa de lino para pintar al óleo. *Canvas used for oil painting.*

BRINCO. *n.m.* •BRINCO de cojito. Salto con un solo pie. *Hop.* || **2.** •De (en) un BRINCO. *In a jiffy.*

BRISERA. *n.f.* (Acad.) Especie de guardabrisa. *Glass shade, lamp chimney (for lamp or lantern).*

BROCEARSE. *v.* (Acad.) Esterilizarse una mina. *To become exhausted (mine).* || **2.** Echarse a perder un negocio. *To fall through, fail, fold.*

BROCEO. *n.m.* (Acad.) Acción y efecto de **brocearse**. *Exhaustion, becoming exhausted (mine).*

BROCHE. *n.m.* Cufflink. *Gemelo.* || **2.** Sujetapapeles. *Paper clip.*

BRONCA. *n.f.* (Acad.) Enojo, enfado, rabia. *Anger, fury.* || **2.** •Tener BRONCA a alguien. (Acad.) Tener entre ojos. *To be mad at someone.*

BRONCE. *n.m.* Campana. *Bell.*

BROTARSE. *v.* salirle granos a uno. *To come out in spots.*

BRUJO. *n.m.* Curandero. *Medicine man.*

BRUTAL. *interj.* ¡Fabuloso! *Great!*

BRUTO. *adj.* •A lo BRUTO. Tosca o groseramente. *Roughly, crudely.*

BUCHACA. *n.f.* (Acad.) Bolsa de la tronera de la mesa de billar. *Billiard-table pocket.*

BUCHE. *n.m.* Bocio. *Goiter, thyroid.* || **2.** Paperas. *Mumps.*

BUDÍN. *n.m.* Pastel. *Cake.*

BUENA. *adj.* •Estar en la BUENA. Estar de suerte. *To be on a roll.*

BUENO. *adv.* •¡Qué bueno!. ¡Qué bien!. *Great!.*

BUEY. *n.m.* Cornudo. *Cuckold.*

BUEYADA. *n.f.* Manada de bueyes. *Drove of oxen.*

BUFET. *n.m.* Autoservicio. *Buffet, self-service.*

BUITREAR. *v.* Matar. *To kill.*

BUITRÓN. *n.m.* Horno en que se funde la plata de las minas. *Silver-smelting blast furnace.*

BULLA. *n.f.* Pelea. *Quarrel, brawl.*

BULLADO. *adj.* Que se presta a comentarios. *Sensational, much talked about.*

BULLARANGA. *n.f.* Bullanga. *Noise, row.* || **2.** Disturbio. *Riot.*

BULLERO. *adj.* Bullicioso. *Noisy, boisterous.*

BULTO. *n.m.* Bolso. *Briefcase.*

BUMPER (angl.). *n.m.* Parachoques. *Bumper.*

BUROCRÁTICO. *adj.* Relativo al gobierno. *Government (attrib.), state (attrib.).* ~Un empleo BUROCRÁTICO. *A government or civil job.*

BURUDANGA. *n.f.* Trastajo. *Piece of junk.*

BUS. *n.m.* Autobús. *Bus.*

BUSCAPLEITOS. *n.m.* Pendenciero, entrometido. *Brawler, troublemaker.*

BUSCAR. *v.* Llamar a alguien o preguntar por él. *To ask for, call for.*

BUSETA. *n.f.* Autobús pequeño. *Small bus, microbus.*

BUTACA. *n.m.* •Correrle la BUTACA a alguien. Ganarle por mano a alguien. *To edge somebody out.*

BUTAQUE. *n.m.* Butaca pequeña. *Small armchair.*

BUZONERO. *n.m.* Empleado de correo que recoge las cartas de los buzones. *Postal employee who collects from letterboxes.*

C

CABADO. *adj.* Se dice de la fiera que por haber probado carne humana es más temible. *Man-eating.*

CABALGAR. *v.* ••Cabalgar a pelo. Cabalgar sin montura. *To ride bareback.*

CABALLADA. *n.f.* Animalada, borricada. *Stupidity, foolishness.*

CABALLAZO. *n.m.* (Acad.) Encontrón que da un jinete a otro o a alguno de a pie, echándole encima el caballo. *Jolt or trampling with a horse.*

CABALLO. *n.m.* ••Caballo AGUILILLA. Caballo muy veloz en el paso. *Very fast horse.* || **2.** ••Caballo de totora. (Acad.) Haz de totora, de tamaño suficiente para que, puesta sobre él a horcajadas una persona, puede mantenerse a flote. *Small reed boat.*

CABECEADA (dep.). *n.f.* Cabeceo, cabezada. *Nod, shake of the head.* || **2.** Cabezada. *Action of heading a soccerball, header.* || ••Dar CABECEADAS. *To nod off.*

CABELLOS. *n.m.* (Acad.) Huevos hilados. *Sweetened strands of egg yolk.* || **2.** (Acad.) Fideos finos. *Angel hair pasta.*

CABEZA. *n.f.* ••Andar en CABEZA. Andar sin sombrero, con la cabeza descubierta. *To be hatless, be bareheaded.*

CABEZADA. *n.f.* (Acad.) Cabecera de un río. *Source, headwaters.*

CABILDANTE. *n.m.* (Acad.) Regidor o conseja. *Town councilman.*

CABLA. *n.f.* Ardid, maña. *Trick.* || **2.** Cábala. *Superstition.*

CABLISTA. *adj.* Persona que usa de **cablas**. *Sly, cunning.*

CABRO. *n.m.* Macho cabrío. *He-goat, billy goat.*

CABRÓN. *n.m.* Persona vil, despicable, infame; canalla. *Swine.* || **2.** (Acad.) Rufián que trafica con mujeres públicas. *Pimp.*

CÁBULA. *n.f.* Ardid, maña. *Trick.*

CABULERO. *adj.* Que usa de **cábulas**. *Sly, cunning.*

CABURÉ. *n.m.* Buho pequeño. *Pigmy owl.*

CABUYA. *n.f.* Fibra o cuerda de cabuya. *Hemp rope.* || **2.** (Acad.) Cuerda, y especialmente la de pita. *Cord, string.* || **3.** ••Dar CABUYA. (Acad.) Amarrar con cuerdas o cadenas. *To tie, fasten, bind.* || **4.** •Ponerse en la CABUYA. (Acad.) Coger el hilo, poner al tanto de algún asunto. *To get to the point of, to become fully informed about.* || **5.** •Verse a uno las CABUYAS. Conocérsele la intención, versele el juego. *To see what somebody is up to, to see through somebody's scheme.*

CACAHUAL. *n.m.* Terreno plantado de cacaos. *Cacao plantation.*

CACAHUERO. *n.m.* (Acad.) Proprietario de huertas de cacao, y por extensión, individuo que se ocupa especialmente en esta almendra, ya como cultivador, zarandero, cargador de sacos de ella o negociante exportador. *Cacao planter, dealer or merchant; cacao plantation hand, loader or screener of cacao or cacao beans.*

CACALOTE. *n.m.* (Acad.) Rosetas de maíz. *Popcorn.*

CACAO. *n.m.* •No valer un CACAO. Ser una cosa de poco valor, insignificante. *To be worthless, insignificant.* || **2.** •Pedir CACAO. Pedir misericordia. *To beg for mercy.*

CACAOTAL. *n.m.* Terreno poblado de cacaos. *Cacao plantation.*

CACHA. *n.f.* Cuerno. *Horn (bull).* || **2.** Engaño. *Deception, trick.* || **3.** Cachete. *Cheek.*

CACHADA *n.f.* (Acad.) Cornada de un animal. *Goring.*

CACHAFAZ. *n.m.* (Acad.) Pícaro, desvergonzado. *Rascal, scoundrel, rogue.*

CACHAR. *v.* (Acad.) Cornear, dar cornadas. *To gore, but with the horns.* ‖2. (Acad.) En algunos juegos, coger al vuelo una pelota que un jugador lanza a otro. *To catch (ball, etc.).* ‖ 3. Agarrar (persona). *To grab, catch a hold of.* ~La CACHÉ del brazo. *I caught, grabbed her by the arm.* ‖ 4. (Acad.) Sorprender a alguien, descubrirle. *To catch in the act.* ‖ 5. (Acad.) Burlarse de una persona, hacerla objeto de una broma, tomarle el pelo. *To kid, pull one's leg, make fun of, poke fun at.*

CACHARPAS. *n.f.* (Acad.) Trebejos, trastos de poco valor. *Useless objects, odds and ends.*

CACHAZO. *n.m.* Golpe. *Thrust, butt.* ‖ 2. Cornada. *Goring.*

CACHEAR. *v.* Acornar, cornear. *To gore.*

CACHERÍA. *n.f.* Negocio pequeño. *Small retail shop or business.*

CACHETADA. *n.f.* Bofetada. *A hard slap on the face.* ‖ 2. ••Caer como una CACHETADA. Caerle mal a uno, caerle como un balde de agua. *To come as a shock.*

CACHETAZO (variante de **cachetada**).

CACHETEAR. *v.* (Acad.) Golpear a uno en la cara con la mano abierta. *To slap.*

CACHETÓN. *adj.* (Acad.) Cachetudo. *Chubby-cheeked.* ‖ 2. Sin vergüenza, descarado. *Impudent, barefaced.*

CACHIMBA. *n.f.* Pipa de fumar. *Pipe.* ‖ 2. Cartucho vacío de arma de fuego. *Empty cartridge.*

CACHIMBO (variante de **cachimba**).

CACHIRULO. *n.m.* Trampa. *Cheating.* ~Le hicieron CACHIRULO. *They cheated him.*

CACHITO. *n.m.* ••Espera un CACHITO. Espera un poco. *Just a minute, hang on a minute.* ‖ 2. ••Un CACHITO de café. Un poquito de café. *A drop of coffee.*

CACHO. n.m. (Acad.) Cubilete. *Dice box*

(for shooting dice). ‖ 2. Cuerno. *Horn.*

CACHUDO. *adj.* (Acad.) Dícese del animal que tiene los cuernos grandes. *Long-horned.*

CACHUPÍN. *n.m.* (Acad.) Español establecido en América. *Spanish settler in America.*

CACICA. *n.f.* Mujer que ejerce el cacicazgo. *Woman chief.* ‖ 2. Mujer del cacique. *Wife of a local boss.*

CACIMBA. *n.m.* Pozo de agua, manantial. *Well, spring.*

CACIQUE. *n.m.* El que domina los asuntos políticos o administrativos. *Local boss, local ruler, chief.*

CADETE. *n.m.* (Acad.) Aprendiz o meritorio de un establecimiento comercial. *Apprentice, office boy.*

CAEDIZO. *n.m.* Colgadizo. *Lean-to.*

CAER. *v.* CAER parado. Tener suerte. *To be lucky.*

CAFÉ. *n.m.* (Acad.) Reprimenda. *Reprimand, telling-off.* ‖ 2. ••CAFÉ negro. Espresso. *Espresso coffee.*

CAFETEAR, *v,* (Acad.) Reprender. *To reprimand.*

CAFETELERO. *adj.* Lo relativo a la sembra de café. *Coffee growing.* ~Indústria CAFETALERA. *Coffee-growing industry.*

CAFETERÍA. *n.f.* Café. *Coffee shop.* ‖ 2. Café o restaurante en que uno mismo se sirve. *Cafeteria, self-service restaurant.*

CAIMÁN. *n.m.* ‖ 1. Persona astuta y disimulada, ventajista en los negocios, ambiciosa y voraz. *Fox, cunning person, schemer.* ‖ 2. Reptil parecido al cocodrilo. *Alligator.*

CAIMANEAR. *v.* Cazar caimanes. *To hunt alligators.*

CAJEAR. *v.* Zurrar, azotar. *To beat, thrash.*

CAJETA. *n.f.* (Acad.) Dulce de leche de cabra, sumamente espeso. *Caramel topping, filling.* ‖ 2. Dulce con forma del molde en que se cuajó. *A confection set to jell in a wooden box.* ‖ 3. Caja en que se guarda estos dulces. *Small round sweet box.* ‖ 4. •De CAJETA. Excelente, de primera calidad. *Excellent, first class.*

CAJÓN. *n.m.* (Acad.) Ataúd, caja en que se pone un cadáver para enterrarlo. *Coffin, casket.*

CALABACERO. *n.m.* (Acad.) Jícaro. *Calabash.*

CALADOR. *n.m.* (Acad. Barrena acanalada para sacar muestras de los granos sin abrir los bultos que las contienen, a fin de conocer su clase o calidad. *Sampler (for extracting samples from bales).*

CALAMBUR. *n.m.* Juego de palabras. *Pun.*

CALAR. v. Sacar muestras con el CALADOR. *To take a sample of.*

CALCULADOR. *adj.* Interesado, egoísta. *Selfish, mercenary.*

CALENTAR. v. Provocar. *To get someone mad, to bug someone.* || **2. -se.** Enfadarse. *To get annoyed, to get mad.*

CALESITA. *n.f.* (Acad.) Tiovivo. *Merry-go-round.*

CALETA. *n.f.* (Acad.) Barco que va tocando, fuera de los puertos mayores, en las calas o caletas. *Boat which stops at all ports.* || **2.** Puerto pequeño. *Small port.*

CALICHE. *n.f.* (Acad.) Yacimiento de caliche; terreno en que hay tal caliche. *Nitrate field.*

CALICHERA (variante de **caliche**).

CALIDEZ. *n.f.* Calor humano. *Warmth.* ~Es una persona de gran CALIDEZ. *She's a very warm person.*

CALIENTE. *adj.* Enfadado. *Mad, annoyed.*

CALIFICADO. *adj.* Preparado, capacitado. *Skilled, qualified.*

CALIFICARSE. v. Inscribirse en los registros electorales. *To register as a voter.*

CALIFORNIA. *n.f.* Carrera de caballos. *Horse race.*

CALILLA. *n.f.* (Acad.) Molestia, pejiguera. *Pest, nuisance, annoyance.*

CALLANA. *n.f.* (Acad.) Vasija tosca que usan los indios americanos para tostar maíz o trigo. *Indian earthenware pan for toasting corn.*

CALLAR. v. Acallar, calmar. *To quiet down.*

CALLE. *n.m.* •Aplanar CALLES. Holgazanear, haraganear. *Lo loaf around, hang around (the streets).*

CALMO. *adj.* Sereno, tranquilo (río, mar); sosegado (persona). *Calm, tranquil (river, sea); serene, calm (person).* || **2.** Árido (tierra). *Barren.*

CALZA. *n.f.* (Acad.) Empaste de un diente o muela. *Tooth filling.*

CALZÓN. *n.m.* Pantalón. *Trousers, pants.* || **2.** Pantaletas. *Panties.*

CALZONUDO. *adj.* Dominado por la mujer. *Henpecked.* || **2.** Débil de carácter. *Wimpish.*

CAMA. *n.f.* ••Estar de CAMA. Estar hecho polvo, estar reventado. *To be dead tired.* || **2.** ••CAMA camarote. Litera. *Bunk bed.* || **3.** •CAMA matrimonial. Cama de matrimonio. *Double bed.*

CAMAGUA. *n.f.* (Acad.) dícese del maíz que empieza a madurar o del que se seca sin haber madurado. *Ripening or unripened corn.*

CAMARETA. *n.f.* (Acad.) Mortero usado en las fiestas populares y religiosas para disparar bombas de estruendo. *Small cannon fired during public festivities.*

CAMARÍN. *n.m.* Coche cama. *Sleeping compartment, car.*

CAMARÓN. *n.m.* Gamba. *Shrimp.*

CAMAROTERO. *n.m.* (Acad.) Camarero que sirve en los barcos. *Steward, stateroom attendant.*

CAMBADO. *adj.* (Acad.) Dícese del estevado o patizambo. *Bowlegged, knock-kneed.*

CAMBIAR. v. ••Mándese a CAMBIAR. *Kindly leave immediately.*

CAMBIO. *n.m.* •Hacer un CAMBIO. Cambiar de marcha. *To change gears.* || **2.** Marcha. *Gear.* ~Un coche de 5 CAMBIOS. Un coche de 5 marchas. *A car with a five-speed gearbox.*

CAMILUCHO. *adj.* (Acad.) Dícese del indio jornalero del campo. *Indian day-laborer.*

CAMINAR. *v.* Andar, funcionar (reloj, motor). *To work.* ‖ **2.** Ir bien, ir adelante (asunto). *To progress.* ~Parece que el asunto va CAMINANDO. *Things seem to be progressing.*

CAMINERO. *n.m.* Constructor de camino. *Road builder.*

CAMIONETA. *n.f.* Break. *Station-wagon.*

CAMISETA. *n.f.* Camisón. *Nightdress.*

CAMISÓN. *n.m.* (Acad.) Vestido, traje de mujer. *Woman's dress.*

CAMOTAL. *n.m.* (Acad.) Terreno plantado de **camotes**. *Sweet potato field.*

CAMOTE. *n.m.* Enamoramiento. *Affection, infatuation.* ‖ **2.** Batata. *Sweet potato.* ‖ **3.** (Acad.) Amante, querida. *Mistress, lover.*

CAMPANAZO. *n.m.* Campanada. *Stroke, chime.*

CAMPAÑA. *n.f.* (Acad.) Campo, terreno fuera del poblado. *Countryside.*

CAMPEAR. *v.* (Acad.) Salir en busca de alguna persona, o animal o cosa. *To search the countryside for a person or an animal.* ‖ **2.** Acampar. *To camp, go camping.*

CAMPERO. *n.m.* Agricultor, ganadero. *Farm worker.* ‖ **2.** (Acad.) Aplícase a la persona muy práctica en el campo, así como en las operaciones y usos peculiares de los cortijos o estancias. *Expert in farming matters.* ‖ **3.** (Acad.) Dícese del animal muy adiestrado en el paso de los ríos, montes, zanjas, etc. *Nimble-footed, sure-footed (a wading or climbing animal).*

CAMPISTA. *n.m.* (Acad.) Arrendador o partidario de minas. *Mine leasholder.*

CAMPO. *n.m.* Espacio, lugar. *Space, room.* ~No hay CAMPO. *There's no room.*

CAMUFLAR. *v.* Disimular, disfrazar (materal de guerra, contrabando). *To camouflage.* ‖ **2.** Ocultar, encubrir. *To disguise, cover up.*

CANA. *n.f.* (Acad.) Cárcel. *Jail, jug (coll.).*

CANALETA. *n.f.* (Acad.) Canalón, conducto que recibe y vierte el agua de los tejados. *Gutter alongside the eaves of a roof.*

CANALIZACIÓN. *n.f.* Alcantarilla, alcantarillado. *Sewage, drains, sewage system.*

CANARIO. *adj.* Amarillo. *Yellow.*

CANASTA. *n.f.* Cesta. *Basket.* ‖ **2.** ••CANASTA familiar. *Family shopping basket (to calculate the retail price index).*

CANCAGUA. *n.f.* (Acad.) Arenilla consistente, usada para ladrillos, hornos, braseros y como cemento en las construcciones. *Fine sand used in making bricks, ovens, and as a cement in contruction.*

CANCANEAR. *v.* Tartamudear. *To stammer.* ‖ **2.** Expresarse con dificultad. *To express oneself with difficulties.* ‖ **3.** Leer sin dar sentido a lo que se lee. *To read haltingly, falter in reading.*

CANCANEO. *n.m.* Acción y efecto de **cancanear**. *Stuttering, stammering.*

CANCEL. *n.m.* (Acad.) Cancela, puerta o verja que separa del zaguán el vestíbulo o el patio. *Outer door, outer gate.* ‖ **2.** Biombo, mampara. *Folding screen.*

CANCELAR. *v.* Saldar, liquidar. *Pay, settle (debts).*

CANCHA. *n.f.* (Acad.) Campo de fútbol. *Soccer field.* ‖ **2.** (Acad.) Habilidad que se adquiere con la experiencia. *Self-assurance, confidence.* ~Tiene mucha CANCHA con los niños. *She has a real way with kids.* ‖ **3.** (Acad.) Hipódromo. *Racetrack.* ‖ **4.** (Acad.) Corral o cercado espacioso para depositar ciertos objetos. *Fenced yard (for lumber, junk, etc.).* ~CANCHA de madera. *Lumber yard.* ‖ **5.** (Acad.) Lugar en que el cauce de un río es más ancho y desembarzado. *Long wide reach of a river.* ‖ **6.** (Acad.) Maíz o habas tostadas. *Toasted beans or corn.* ‖ **7.** Terreno, espacio o sitio llano y desembarazado. *Open space, track of level ground.* ‖ **8.** •¡CANCHA! Interjección que se emplea para pedir paso. *Make way!*

CANCHEAR. *v.* (Acad.) Buscar entretenimiento para no trabajar seriamente. *To shirk or shun work, to goof off (coll.).*

CANCHERO. *n.m.* (Acad.) Se aplica al trabajador encargado de una cancha. *Groundsman (in a playing field)* ‖ **2.** (Acad.) Ducho y experto en determinada actividad. *Adroit,* *skilled, experienced; self-assured, confident.*

CANCILLER. *n.m.* Ministro de Asuntos Exteriores. *Foreign Minister.*

CANDALLERO. *n.m.* Cojinete que soporta los ejes de los tornos (min.). *Axle seat shaft bearing.*

CANDELA. *n.f.* Fuego. *Fire.* || **2.** Lumbre *(cigarillos). Light.* || **3.** ••Dar CANDELA. Molestar, fastidiar. *To annoy, pester.*

CANDELEJÓN. *adj.* (Acad.) Cándido, inocentón o de cortos alcances. *Dunce, fool.*

CANDELILLA. *n.f.* Luciérnaga. *Glowworm.*

CANGA. *n.m.* (Acad.) Mineral de hierro con arcilla. *Clayey iron ore.*

CANGALLA. *n.f.* (Acad.) Persona cobarde, pusilánime, despreciable. *Coward.* || **2.** (Acad.) Desperdicios de los minerales. *Slag, taillings.*

CANGILÓN. *n.f.* Huella que dejan en el suelo las ruedas de los carruajes. *Rut, cart or wagon rut.* || **2.** Bache en el camino. *Pothole, hole in the ground.*

CANGREJO. *n.m.* Misterio. *Mistery, enigma.*

CANGRO. *n.m.* Cáncer. *Cancer.*

CANILLA. *n.f.* Tibia, espinilla. *Shinbone.* || **2.** Pierna flaca. *Thin leg.*

CANILLERA. *n.f.* (Acad.) Espinillera, almohadilla que proteje la parte anterior de la pierna. *Shin guard, shin pad.* || **2.** (Acad.) Temblor de pierna originado por el miedo o por otra cosa. *Trembling of the knees due to fear.*

CANILLITA. *n.m.* (Acad.) Vendedor callejero de periódicos. *Newsboy, newspaper vendor.*

CANILLÓN (variante de **canilludo**).

CANILLUDO. *adj.* (Acad.) Zanquilargo, personas de canillas o piernas largas. *Long-legged.*

CANOA. *n.f.* (Acad.) Canal de madera u otra materia para conducir el agua. *Water conduit or duct.* || **2.** (Acad.) Especie de artesa o cajón de forma oblonga que sirve para dar de comer a los animales (comedero). *Feeding trough.*

CANSADOR. *adj.* Que causa molestia o aburrimiento. *Wearisome, tiring, exhausting.*

CANSERA. *n.f.* Tiempo perdido. *Time lost, wasted effort.*

CANSÓN. *n.m.* Persona que cansa o aburre. *Tiring or boring person.*

CANTALETA. *n.f.* (Acad.) Estribillo, repetición enfadadosa. *Constant nagging or scolding.* || **2.** ••La misma CANTALETA. La misma cantinela. *The same old tune.*

CANTALETEAR. *v.* (Acad.) Repetir las cosas hasta causar el fastidio. *To harp on, repeat continually.* || **2.** Embromar. *To make fun of.*

CANTAMISA. *n.f.* (Acad.) Acto de cantar su primera misa un sacerdote. *Occasion on which a priest celebrates his first mass.*

CANTERO (Acad.). *n.m.* Cuadro de tierra sembrada o cultivada. *Piece of land that can be worked or cultivated.*

CANTIDAD. *n.f.* •Una gran cantidad. *Lots of, loads of (coll.).* ~Había CANTIDAD de gente. *There was a whole bunch of people.* || **2.** •¡Cualquier CANTIDAD! Un montón, una barbaridad.

CANTIL. *n.m.* (Acad.) Borde de un despeñadero. *Brink of a precipice.*

CANTINA. *n.f.* (Acad.) Taberna, bar. *Bar, saloon, tavern.*

CANTINFLISMO. *n.m.* Parloteo, palabrería, cháchara. *Babble, empty chatter.*

CANTÓN. *n.m.* Vecindario, territorio, barrio, lo de uno; por extensión, casa. *Place (house).* ~Vamos a mi CANTÓN. *Let's go to my place.* || **2.** Tela de algodón que imita al casimir (Acad.). *Fine crepe used in dressmaking.*

CANUTERO. *n.m.* (Acad.) Mango de la pluma de escribir. *Penhandle.*

CANUTO (Variante de **canutero**).

CAÑA. *n.f.* Caña de azucar. *Sugar cane.* || **2.** Aguardiente de caña. *Uncured brandy or rum.* || **3.** Paja. *(Drinking) straw.*

CAÑABRAVA. *n.f.* Junco. *Reed, bamboo.*

CAÑADA . *n.f.* (Acad.) Terreno bajo y húmedo entre dos lomas. *Bed of stream.* || **2.** Cauce pobre y reducido de agua que contiene la **cañada**. *Stream.*

CÁÑAMO. *n.m.* Hilo cualquiera hecho de fibra. *Hemp, hempfiber.*

CAÑAZO. *n.m.* Aguardiente de caña.*Sugar cane brandy, raw cane liquor.*

CAÑERO. *adj.* Relativo a la caña de azúcar. *Sugar cane (used as attribute before a noun).* ~Machete CAÑERO. *Sugar-cane knife.* || *n.m.* **2.** Cultivador o vendedor de **caña**. *Sugar cane planter or vendor.*

CAÑINQUE. *adj.* (Acad.) Enclenque. *Feeble, weak, sickly, emaciated.*

CAÑONERA. *n.f.* Pistolera. *Holster for a pistol.*

CAÑONERO. *n.m.* Huelguista. *Striker.*

CAPACHO. *n.m.* Sombrero viejo y desgastado. *Old, frayed hat.*

CAPACITAR. *v.* Autorizar. *To empower, authorize.*

CAPAZ. *adj.* •Es CAPAZ. Puede que, a lo mejor. *It's possible that, there's a chance that.* ~Llévate el paraguas, es CAPAZ que llueva. *Take your umbrella , it may rain.* || **2.** •¡Es CAPAZ!. *I wouldn't put it past him!*

CAPELO. *n.m.* Campana de cristal que sirve para cubrir comestibles en cafés y restaurantes. *Bell glass, glass cover.* || **2.** (Acad.) Capirote de doctor. *Academic cap, doctor's gown.*

CAPI. *n.m.* (Acad.) Maíz. *Corn.*

CAPIA. *n.f.* (Acad.) Maíz blanco y muy dulce que se emplea en la preparación de golosinas. *Variety of sweet corn.*

CAPIROTADA. *n.f.* (Acad.) Plato criollo que se hace con carne, maíz tostado y queso, manteca y especias. *Native dish of meat, corn, cheese and spices.*

CAPORAL (agr.). *n.m.* Capataz de una finca rural. *Foreman, headman.*

CAPOTERA. n.f. (Acad.) Percha para la ropa. *Clothes hanger or clothes rack.*

CARACHENTO. *adj.* (Acad.) Carachoso. *Mangy, scabby.*

CARACOL. *n.m.* Concha. *Shell.*

CARACOLEANTE. *adj.* Serpenteante (camino). *Twisting, snaking.*

CARÁCTER (angl.). *n.m.* Personaje. *Character (liter.).*

CARACÚ. *n.m.* Tuétano de los huesos de los animales. *Bone marrow.*

CARANGA. *n.f.* Piojo. *Louse.*

CARAPÁLIDA. *n.f.* Rostro pálido. *Paleface.*

CARAPINTADA. *adj./n.m.* Golpista. *Participant in a coup, rebel.*

CARÁTULA. *n.f.* Portada o primera página de un libro. *Title page, cover of a magazine.*

CARAVANAS. *n.m.* (Acad.) Pendientes, arracadas. *Earrings.*

CARBONADA. *n.f.* (Acad.) Guisado compuesto de carne en trozos, choclos, zapallo, patatas, arroz y, en ocasiones durazno.*Meat stewed with rice, pumpkin, potatoes and corn.*

CARCA. *n.f.* (Acad.) Olla en que se cuece la chicha. *Pot in which chicha, a native beer, is cooked or fermented.*

CARCAJ (Acad.). *n.m.* Funda de cuero en que se lleva el rifle al arzón de la silla. *Leather rifle case (on a saddle).*

CARCAMÁN. *n.m.* Extranjero inmigrante de poca educación y pretensions.*Low-class foreigner.* || **2.** Persona vieja y generalmente achacosa, carcamal. *Decrepit old person.*

CAREAR. *v.* Enfrentarse dos gallos de riña. *Confront, size up (cockfighting).*

CAREO. *n.m.* Acción de carear dos gallos de riña. *Confrontation, sizing up (cockfighting).*

CARGADOR. n.m. (Acad.) Mozo de cordel. *Porter.*

CARGAR. *v.* Llevar consigo habitualmente una cosa. *To carry, use, have, wear.* ~CARGAR anteojos. *To wear glasses.* ~CARGAR revólver. *To pack a gun.*~¿CARGAS dinero? *Do* *you have any money with you?*

CARGOSEAR. *v.* (Acad.) Importunar, molestar. *To annoy, pester, bother, importune.*

CARGOSO. *adj.* (Acad.) Cargante, que molesta, incomoda o cansa. *Bothersome, annoying, tiresome.*

CARGUERO. *n.m.* Bestia de carga. *Best of burden.* || **2.** Mozo de cordel. *Porter.*

CARIBE. *adj.* Antropófago. *Cannibalistic.* || **2.** *n.m.* Persona cruel e inhumana. *Savage, cruel and inhuman person.*

CARICATO. *n.m.* Caricatura. *Caricature.*

CARILARGO. *adj.* Que tiene larga la cara (por disgusto o preocupación). *Disgusted, annoyed.*

CARIMBO. *n.m.* (Acad.) Hierro para marcar esclavos. *Branding iron.*

CARINCHO. *n.m.* Guisado hecho con papas, carne y ají. *Stew made with meat, potatoes and green peppers.*

CARIÑO. *n.m.* (Acad.) Regalo, obsequio. *Gift, token of affection.* || **2.** Saludos. *Regards, love.* ~Dale CARIÑOS a tu esposa. *Give my regards to you wife.* || **3.** •CARIÑOS. *Love (in the closing of a letter).* || **4.** Caricia. *Hug, kiss.* || **5.** •Hacer CARIÑO. *To hug, cuddle, kiss.*

CARNAZA. *n.m.* Chivo expiatorio. *Fall guy, scapegoat.* || **2.** •Echar a uno de CARNAZA. *To put the blame on, make a scapegoat of someone.*

CARNE. *n.m.* •CARNE molida. Carne picada. *Ground beef.* || **2.** •CARNE de res. Carne de vaca. *Beef.* || **3.** Parte más dura del tronco de los árboles. *Heart, hardest part (tree).*

CARNEADA. *n.f.* Matanza de animales para su consumo. *Butchering, slaughtering of animals.*

CARNEAR. *v.* (Acad.) Matar y descuartizar las reses, para aprovechar su carne. *To slaughter, butcher animals.* || **2.** (Acad.) Herir, y matar con arma blanca en un combate o en un alcance. *To knife to death.*

CARNERAJE. *n.m.* (Acad.) Carnerada. *Flock of sheep.*

CARNERO. *n.m.* (Acad.) Persona que no tiene voluntad ni iniciativa propias. *Timid or easily led person, sheep, lamb.* || **2.** Nombre que vulgarmente se da a la llama, la alpaca y la vicuña. *Llama, alpaca, vicuña.*

CARÓN. *adj.* Carilleno, carigordo. *Broadfaced.* ~Es muy CARONA. *She has a very big face.*

CARPA. *n.f.* (Acad.) Tienda de campaña, toldo. *Tent.* || **2.** Puesto, tenderete. *Market stall.*

CARPIDORA. *n.f.* (Acad.) Instrumento para **carpir**. *Weeding hoe, rake.*

CARPIR. *v.* (Acad.) Limpiar o escardar la tierra, quitando la hierba inútil o perjudicial. *To weed, rake, hoe.*

CARRAMPLÓN. *n.m.* (Acad.) Fusil. *Type of musket.*

CARRASPOSO. *adj.* Aspero al tacto. *Rough, harsh.*

CARRERA. *n.f.* ••Hacer CARRERA (baloncesto). Dar (hacer) pasos. *To travel (basketball).*

CARRETEL. *n.m.* (Acad.) Carrete de hilo para coser. *Spool, reel.*

CARRETERAR (aviac.). *v.* Rodar por la pista de aterrizaje. *To taxi (plane).*

CARRETÓN. *n.m.* Carro grande y tosco. *Large cart.*

CARRIEL. *n.m.* (Acad.) Garniel, maletín de cuero. *Valise, traveling-bag.*

CARRO. *n.m.* (Acad.) Coche, automóvil. *Car.* || **2.** Vehículo en general: automóvil, tranvía, vagón de ferrocarril, caruajes, etc. *Any vehicle, (especially, car, auto).* ||**3.** Taxi. *Cab, taxi.* || **4.** •CARRO sport. Coche deportivo. *Sports car.*

CARROZO. *n.m.* Hueso de la fruta. *Stone, pit, core.*

CARRUAJERO. *n.m.* (Acad.) El que fabrica carruajes. *Coach builder.*

CARTA. *n.f.* •CARTA postal. Tarjeta postal. *Postcard.*

CARTERA. *n.f.* (Acad.) Bolso de las mujeres. *Handbag, purse.*

CARTON (angl.). *n.m.* Dibujos animados.

Cartoon.

CASA. *n.f.* •CASA de altos. (Acad.) Casa que además de la planta baja tiene otro u otros pisos. *House with more than one floor.*

CASCABEL. *n.m.* Víbora. *Rattlesnake.*

CASCABELA (variante de **cascabel**).

CÁSCARA. *n.f.* Corteza. *Bark.*

CASCO. *n.m.* Edificio vacío. *Empty building.* || **2.** Gajo de naranja, granada, etc. *Slice of fruit.*

CASCORVO. *adj.* (Acad.) Patizambo, zancajoso. *Bow-legged.*

CASERÍA. *n.f.* Clientela. *Customers, clientele.*

CASERO. *n.m.* (Acad.) Parroquiano, cliente. *Customer.*

CASETERA. *n.f.* Platina a cassete. *Cassette deck.*

CASILLA. *n.f.* ••Casilla POSTAL. (Acad.) Apartado de correos. *Post-office box.*

CASIMERO. *adj.* Bizco. *Cross-eyed.*

CASINETE. *n.m.* (Acad.) Cierta tela de calidad inferior al casimir. *Imitation cashmere fabric.*

CASO. *n.m.* •No haber CASO. Ser inútil. *To be useless, to be of no avail.* ~Se lo dije veinte veces, pero no hay CASO, no lo entiende. *I told him a hundred times, but to no avail; he just won't understand.*

CASQUILLO (Acad.). *n.m.* Herradura. *Horse-shoe.*

CASTILLA. *n.f.* Bayetón, tela de lana (Acad.) *Wool coating.*

CASUALIDAD. *n.f.* •De CASUALIDAD. Por casualidad. *By chance.*

CASUALMENTE. *adv.* Precisamente, justamente. *Precisely, exactly.*

CATA (variante de **cateo**).

CATANA. *n.f.* Pequeña embarcación. *Small boat.*

CATARRIENTO. *adj.* Catarroso. *Subject to cold.*

CATATAR. *v.* (Acad.) Hechizar, fascinar. *To bewitch, enchant.*

CATEADOR. *n.m.* (Acad.) El que hace catas para hallar minerales. *Prospector.*

CATEAR *v.* (Acad.) Explorar terrenos en busca de alguna veta de metal. *To make test borings in, explore (mining).* || **2.** (Acad.) Allanar la casa de alguno. *To break into, search (one's house).*

CÁTEDRA. *n.f.* •Dar CÁTEDRA. Dictar cátedra. *To lecture.*

CATEO. *n.m.* (Acad.) Acción y efecto de catear. *Prospecting.*

CATINGA. *n.f.* (Acad.) Olor fuerte y desagradable propio de algunos animales y plantas. *Body odor.*

CATINGUDO. *adj.* Que tiene **catinga** o mal olor. *Stinking.*

CATIRE. *adj.* Rubio. *Blond, fair.*

CATIRO (variante de **catiro**).

CATITA. *n.f.* (Acad.) Cotorrita muy inquieta *Parrot.*

CAUCHERO. *n.m.* (Acad.). Colector de caucho *Rubber worker.* || **2.** *adj.* Relativo al caucho. *Pertaining to rubber.* ~Negocio CAUCHERO. *A company dealing in rubber.*

CAUCHO (auto). *n.m.* Neumático. *Tire.*

CAUDILLAJE. *n.m.* (Acad.) Caciquismo, tiranía. *Domination by political bosses.* || **2.** (Acad.) Conjunto o sucesión de caudillos. *Group of succession of political bosses.*

CAUDILLO. *n.m.* (Acad.) Persona que ejerce influencia decisiva en los asuntos públicos de un pueblo. *Tyrant, political boss.*

CAUSANTE. *n.f.* Causa. *Cause.*

CAUTELAR. *v.* Defender. *To protect, defend.*

CAYUCA. *n.f.* Embarcación india de una pieza. *Indian canoe.*

CAZUELA. *n.f.* Guisado compuesto de gallina, maíz tierno, ají y otras legumbres. *Chicken stew.*

CEBA. *n.f.* Cebo de arma de fuego. *Cannon charge, priming.*

CEBADO. *adj.* (Acad.) Dícese de la fiera que por haber probado carne humana, es más temible. *Man-eating (said of a wild beast* *which has tasted human flesh and is therefore more dangerous.*

CEBICHE. *n.m.* (Acad.) Plato de pescado o marisco crudo cortado en trozos pequeños y preparado en un adobo de jugo de limón o naranja agria, cebolla picada, sal y ají. *Dish of raw fish marinated in lemon juice.*

CÉDULA. *n.f.* •CÉDULA de identidad. Tarjeta de identidad. *Identification card.*

CEJA. *n.f.* Camino estrecho, vereda. *Narrow road path.*

CÉLEBRE. *adj.* Agraciado, hermoso, aplicado especialmente a las mujeres. *Pretty (woman).*

CELOSO. *adj.* Sensible (mecanismo). *Highly sensitive.* || **2.** Dícese del arma de fuego que se dispara demasiado fácilmente. *Delicate, liable to go off (firearm).*

CEMENTO. *n.m.* Pegamento. *Glue.*

CENTAVO. *n.m.* Centésima parte de un peso (moneda americana). *Cent (coin).*

CEPILLAR. *v.* (Acad.) Adular. *To flatter, butter up.*

CEPILLAZO. *n.m.* Dicho o acto adulatorio o servil. *Adulation, flattery.*

CEPILLO. *n.m.* Adulador. *Flatterer.*

CERCO. *n.m.* Cerca, valla. *Fence.* || **2.** Seto. *Hedge.*

CEREZA. *n.f.* (Acad.) Cáscara del grano de café. *Coffee bean.*

CEROTE. *n.m.* •Estar hecho un CEROTE. Estar muy sucio. *To look unkempt, to look like a mess.*

CERQUILLO. *n.m.* Fleco, flequillo o pelo recortado sobre la frente. *Bangs (of hair).*

CERRERO. *adj.* (Acad.) Dícese de la persona inculta, brusca. *Uncouth, rough.*

CESANTE. *adj.* Desempleado. *Unemployed, jobless, laid off.* || **2.** *n.m.* Persona sin trabajo. *Unemployed person.*

CESE. *n.m.* •CESE del fuego. Alto el fuego. *Cease-fire.*

CESTO. *n.m.* Canasta (baloncesto). *Basket.*

CHABACANEAR *v.* Comportarse una persona de forma chabacana. *To do or say coarse things.*

CHABOLAS. *n.f.* •Barrio de CHABOLAS. *Shanty-town.*

CHÁCARA. *n.f.* (Acad.) **Chacra**, granja. *Small farm.* || **2.** Llaga, úlcera. *Sore, ulcer.* || **3.** Bolsa, garniel. *Large leather bag.*

CHACARERÍA. *n.f.* Conjunto de **chácaras** o **chacras**. *Group of small farms.* || **2.** Cultivo de una chacra, horticultura. *Farm work, horticulture.*

CHACARERO. *n.m.* (Acad.) Persona que trabaja en una **chácara**. *Farmer (who works a chácara).* || **2.** (Acad.) Dueño de una chacara o granja. *Owner of a chacra (or small farm)* || **3.** Aparcero. *Sharecropper.* || **4.** Mayoral. *Farm overseer.* || **5.** Peón. *Farm laborer.* || **6.** *adj.* (Acad.) Perteneciento o relativo a la **chacra**. *Pertaining to a chácara (or small farm).*

CHACHALACA. *n.f.* (Acad.) Persona locuaz. *Chatterbox.*

CHACRA. *n.f.* Finca rural, granja. *Small farm.* || **2.** Alquería. *Farmhouse.* || **3.** Productos que proviene de la chacra. *Farm produce.*

CHAFALOTE. *n.m.* Chafarote. Ordinario, de modales poco finos. *Common, rude, bad-mannered.*

CHAFAROTE. *n.m.* Espada ancho o cuchillo grandes. *Machete.*

CHALA. *n.f.* (Acad.) Hoja de la mazorca de maíz. *Tender leave of corn.*

CHALÁN. *n.m.* (Acad.) Picador, domador de caballos. *Horse-breaker.*

CHALANEAR. *v.* (Acad.) Adiestrar caballos. *To break or train horses.*

CHALÍN. *n.m.* (Acad) Chal angosto. *Narrow shawl.*

CHALÓN. *n.m.* Mantón o pañuelo doble que usan las mujeres. *Shawl, wrap.*

CHALONA. *n.f.* Carne de oveja curada. *Dried salted mutton.*

CHAMARRA. *n.f.* Saco corto. *Short jacket.*

CHAMBÓN. *adj*. Torpe, tosco. *Clumsy.*

CHAMBONADA. *n.f.* Tosquedad. *Clumsiness.* || **2.** Chapucería, obra mal hecha. *Botch, botched job.*

CHAMBONEAR. *v.* (Acad.) Hacer chambonadas. *To botch, bungle a job, make foolish mistakes.* || **2.** Ganar al juego de pura suerte. *To have a stroke of luck, win by chance.*

CHAMPA. *n.f.* Tepe, cepellón, raigambre. *Sod, turf.*

CHAMPEAR. *v.* (Acad.) Tapar o cerrar con cesped o tepes una presa o portillo. *To fill with sod.*

CHAMPUDO. *adj*. Desgreñado, de pelo revuelto. *Dishevelled.*

CHAMUCHINA. *n.f.* Populacho, gentuza. *Rabble, riffraff.* || **2.** Reunión de chiquillos. *Group of children.* || **3.** Quemadura, **chamusquina**. *Scortching.*

CHANCA. *n.f.* (Acad.) Trituración. *Grinding, crushing.* || **2.** (Acad.) Tunda, paliza. *Beating.*

CHANCACA. *n.f.* Azúcar macabado, panocha prieta. *Crude brown sugar in block.*

CHANCADORA. *n.f.* (Acad.) Trituradora. *Grinder, crusher.*

CHANCAR. *v.* (Acad.) Triturar, machacar, moler, especialmente minerales. *To crush, grind.*

CHANCE (angl.). *n.m.* Oportunidad, posibilidad. *Chance, opportunity, prospects.*

CHANCHA. *n.f.* Hembra del chancho. *Sow, female pig.* || **2.** •Hacer la CHANCHA. Faltar a clase, hacer novillos. *To miss class, to play hooky.*

CHANCHADA. *n.f.* (Acad.) Cochinada, acción grosera o desleal. *Dirty trick.* ~Su socio le ha hecho una CHANCHADA. *His partner played a dirty trick on him.* || **2.** Porquería, suciedad, cochinada. *Mess.* ~¡Qué CHANCHADA está haciendo este niño! *What a mess this child is doing!*

CHANCHERÍA. *n.f.* (Acad.) Tienda donde se vende carne de **chancho** y embuchados. *Pork butcher's shop.*

CHANCHERO. *n.m.* (Acad.) Persona que cuida **chanchos** o cerdos, los cría para venderlos o negocia comprándolos y vendiéndolos. *Pig farmer, pork butcher.*

CHANCHITO. *n.m.* Hucha. *Piggybank.*

CHANCHO. *n.m.* Cerdo. *Pig.* ~No comas como un CHANCHO. *Don't eat like a pig.* || **2.** Persona sucia. *Slob.* || **3.** (Ajedrez) Pieza que se queda encerrada sin posibilidad de movimiento. *Blocked piece (chess).* || **4.** •Hacerse el CHANCHO rengo. Hacerse el desentendido. *To play dumb.* || **5.** •Quedar como CHANCHO. Quedar mal. *To let someone down.* || **6.** •Ser dos personas como CHANCHOS. Ser amigos inseparables. *To be close friends.* || **7.** *adj*. (Acad.) Puerco, sucio, desaseado. *Dirty, filthy.*

CHANCLETA. *n.f.* (Acad.) Niña, en especial la recién nacida. *Newborn girl (derog.).*

CHANFLE. *n.m.* (Dep.) Efecto (en la bola, pelota). *Spin.* Darle CHANFLE a la pelota. *To put a spin on the ball.*

CHANGA. *n.f.* (Acad.) Chanza, burla, broma, chuscada. *Joke, jest.*

CHANGO. *n.m.* (Acad.) Niño, muchacho. *Child.*

CHANTAR. *v.* (Acad.) Vestir o poner. *To put on.* || **2.** Plantar, decir a uno claridades. *Not to mince words, to say something straight to someone's face.*

CHAPA. *n.f.* Cerradura. *Lock.*

CHAPARRO. *adj*. Achaparrado. *Short, squat.* ~Casas CHAPARRAS y pobretonas. *Squat, shabby houses.* || **2.** *n.m.* Petiso. *Short, squat.* ~¡Vamos, CHAPARRO, que se hace tarde! *Let's go shorty, we'll be late!*

CHAPEAR. *v.* Desyerbar. *To weed.* || **2.** Limpiar la tierra. *To clear the ground.*

CHAPETÓN. *adj*. Poco diestro, novato. *Inexperienced, unskillful.* || **2.** Torpe, tosco. *Clumsy, awkward.* || **3.** Persona recién llegada de Europa. *Newly arrived from Europe.* || **4.** Chaparrón. aguacero. *Downpour, shower.*

CHAPULÍN. *n.m.* (Acad.) Langosta, cigarrón. *Locust, large grasshoper.*

CHAPUZON. *n.m.* Aguacero, chaparrón. *Downpour, shower.*

CHARAMUSCA. *n.f.* Leña menuda para hacer fuego. *Firewood, kindling.*

CHARANGA. *n.f.* Baile familiar. *Informal dance.*

CHARANGO. *n.m.* (Acad.) Especie de bandurria, de cinco cuerdas, cuya caja se construye, generalmente, con un caparazón de armadillo o quirquincho. *Five-stringed guitar.*

CHAROL. *n.m.* (Acad.) Bandeja, pieza para servir, presentar o depositar cosas. *Tray.*

CHAROLA (Variante de **charola**).

CHARQUEAR. *v.* Herir a puñaladas. *To slash, cut to pieces.* || **2.** Infamar. *To vilify, malign.* || **3.** (Acad.) Hacer **charqui**. *To dry, jerk (meat).*

CHARQUI. *n.m.* (Acad.) Tasajo, carne salada. *Dried beef, jerked meat.*

CHARQUICÁN. *n.m.* (Acad.) Guiso hecho con **charqui**, ají, patatas, judías y otros ingredientes. *Stew made with charqui and other vegetables.*

CHARUTO. *n.m.* Puro envuelto en una hoja de maíz. *Cigar wrapped in corn husk.*

CHASCA. *n.f.* (Acad.) Cabello enmarañado. *Matted or tangled hair.*

CHASQUE (variante de **chasqui**).

CHASQUI. *n.m.* (Acad.) Mensajero, emisario. *Messenger, courrier.*

CHATO. *adj.* •Quedarse CHATO. Quedarse frustrado en sus empeños. *To fail at an undertaking.*

CHATRE. *adj.* Vestido elegantemente. *Elegantly dressed.*

CHAUCHA. *n.f.* Papa temprana. *Early or small potato.*

CHEQUEAR (angl.). *v.* Facturar el equipaje. *To check in one's luggage, check in.* ||**2.** (Acad.) Examinar, verificar, controlar. *To check, inspect, examine.*

CHEQUEO. *n.m.* Examen, revisión, inspection. *Check, check-up, examination.*

CHEQUERA. *n.f.* (Acad.) Talonario de cheques. *Checkbook.*

CHÉVERE. *adj.* (Acad.) Primoroso, gracioso, bonito, elegante, agradable. *Great, fantastic, groovy (coll.).* ~¡Qué CHÉVERE! *This is fantastic!*

CHÉVERES. *n.m.* Trastos, cachivaches, trebejos. *Odds and ends, bits and pieces, trinkets.*

CHIBOLO. *n.m.* (Acad.) Cualquier cuerpo pequeño y esférico. *Small round body, mass.* || **2.** (Acad.) Chichón. *Bump, bruise.*

CHICANA. *n.f.* Sofistería, argucia, artería. *Cunning, subterfuge.*

CHICANEAR. *v.* Enredar, recurir a ardides. *To be cunning, tricky.*

CHICANERÍA. *n.f.* Sofistería, artería. *Chicanery.*

CHICANERO. *adj.* Que usa de **chicanas** o malos procedimientos. *Cunning, tricky, crafty.*

CHICANO. *adj.* (Acad.) Dícese del ciudadano de los Estados Unidos de América, perteneciente a la minoría de origen mexicano allí existente. *Person of Mexican extraction born in the United States.* || **2.** Propio del **chicano**. *Pertaining to Mexican Americans born in the United States.*

CHICHE. *adj.* (Acad.) Pequeño, delicado, bonito. *Exquisite.* ~Esta joya es un CHICHE. Esta joya es una preciosura. *This is a delightful jewel.* || **2.** Pequeño, gracioso (juguete, baratija). *Small, cute.* ~¡Este juguete es un CHICHE! *What a cute, little toy!* || **3.** *n.m.* Persona digna de confianza. *Trustworthy person.* || **4.** Persona inteligente. *Intelligent person.* || **5.** Local decorado con gusto o casa pequeña, cómoda y elegantemente puesta. *Comfortable, well decorated, small shop or house.* ~Este cuarto es un CHICHE. *This is really a nice and elegant room.* || **6.** *n.m.* Pecho de la mujer. *Woman's breast.* || **7.** (Acad.) Juguete, entretenimiento de niños. *Toy.*

CHICHERÍA. *n.f.* (Acad.) Casa o tienda donde se vende **chicha**. *Place where chicha* *is made or sold.*

CHICHERO. *n.m.* (Acad.) Persona que fabrica o vende **chicha**. *Chicha vendor or maker.*

CHICHIGUA. *n.f.* (Acad.) Nodriza. *Nursemaid.*

CHICO. *adj.* Joven. *Young.* ‖ **2.** Partido (billar, naipes). *Game, round.*

CHICOTAZO. *n.m.* (Acad.) Golpe dado con el **chicote**, látigo. *Whipping, lashing.*

CHICOTE. *n.m.* (Acad.) Látigo. *Whip.*

CHICOTEAR. *v.* (Acad.) Dar chicotazos. *To flog, whip, lash.* ‖ **2.** Pegar, dar una paliza. *To beat up.*

CHIFLAR. *v.* Silbar. *To whistle.*

CHIFLÓN. *n.m.* (Acad) Viento colado o corriente muy sútil del aire. *Draught of air.*

CHILENA. *n.f.* (fútbol).) Tijereta, tiro de tijera. *Scissor's kick.*

CHILLAR. *v.* Protestar. refunfuñar, lamentarse. *To shout, protest.* ‖ **2. -se.** Picarse, ofenderse. *To become annoyed, to take offense.* ‖ **3.** Llorar. *To sob.*

CHIMBO. *adj* (Acad.) Dícese de una especie de dulce hecho con huevos, almendras y almibar. *Desert made with sugar, almonds and egg yolks.*

CHINA. *n.f.* Hembra, mujer. *Woman.* ‖ **2.** Amante, concubina. *Mistress.* ‖ **3.** Término cariñoso aplicado a la mujer. *Term of endearment.* ~Mi CHINITA. *My darling., my sweet one.* ‖ **4.** Esposa, novia. *Wife, girlfriend.* ~Mi CHINITA. *My wife, my girlfriend.* ‖ **5.** Sirvienta. *Maid.*

CHINGANA. *n.f.* (Acad.) Taberna en que se suele haber baile y canto. *Low class barroom with a dance floor.* ‖ **2.** Fiesta o reunión en que se bebe y baila. *Noisy party with drinking and singing.*

CHINGANEAR. *v.* Parrandear. *To go on a binge or spree.*

CHINGARSE. *v.* (Acad.) No acertar, fracasar, frustrarse, fallar. *To fail, miscarry.* ~La fiesta se CHINGÓ. *The party was a flop.* ~El cohete se CHINGÓ. *The rocket failed to go off.*

CHINO. *n.m.* Mestizo. *Half-breed.* ‖ **2.** *adj.* (Acad.) Dícese de la persona aindiada. *Of Indian descent.* ‖ **3.** (Acad.) Criado, sirviente. *Servant.*

CHIQUERO. *n.m.* Corral para cerdos, gallinas u otros animales, pocilga. *Pigpen, pigsty.* ‖ **2.** Lugar muy sucio o en desorden. *Messy or dirty place.*

CHIQUILÍN. *adj.* Infantil, pueril. *Childish.* ~¡No seas CHIQUILÍN!. *Don't act like a kid, don't be a baby!* ‖ **2.** *n.m.* Persona inmadura. *Cry-baby, big kid.*

CHIQUITITO. *adj.* Pequeño. *Small.* ~La casa es CHIQUITITA pero cómoda. *The house is small but confortable.* ‖ **2.** Muy pequeño. *Very small, tiny.* ‖ **3.** *n.m.* Niño pequeño. *Small child.*

CHIRIPA. *n.f.* ••De CHIRIPA. Por casualidad. *By pure luck.*

CHIRIPAZO. *n.m.* Acierto casual o excepcional,. *Stroke of luck.*

CHIRLEAR. *v.* Chirlar, dar cuchilladas. *To wound, knife.*

CHIRRIÓN. *n.m.* Látigo. *Heavy leather whip.*

CHISCHÍS. *n.m.* Llovizna. *Drizzle or rain.*

CHIVA. *n.f.* Perilla. *Goatee.*

CHIVAR. *v.* (Acad.) Fastidiar, molestar, engañar. *To annoy, upset.* ‖ **2.** (Acad.) Enojarse, irritarse. *To get annoyed.*

CHIVATEAR. v. Retozar los muchachos con estruendo. *To indulge in horse-play, to have a noisy free-for-all.*

CHIVUDO. *adj.* (Acad.) Que lleva barba larga. *Long-bearded.*

CHOCANTE. *adj.* (Acad.) Antipático, fastidioso, presuntuoso. *Unpleasant, shocking, offensive; vulgarly witty.*

CHOCANTERÍA. *n.f.* (Acad.) Impertinencia, cosa desagradable y molesta. *Rude remark, impertinence, coarse joke.*

CHOCAR. *v.* (aut.) Chocar con. *To crash, have an accident.* ~Me CHOCÓ el auto. *He crashed my car, he had an accident with my car.*

CHOCLO. *n.m.* (Acad.) Mazorca tierna de maíz. *Corncob, ear of corn.* ‖ **2.** (Acad.) Humita. *Flavored corn paste wrapped in corn leaves.*

CHOCOLATE. *n.m.* Sangre. *Blood.*

CHOLO. *n.m.* (Acad.) Meztizo de sangre europea e indígena. *Half-breed.* ‖ **2.** Peruviano. *Peruvian.* ‖ **3.** *adj.* (Acad) Dícese del indio que adopta los usos occidentales. *Half-civilized Indian.*

CHOMPA. *n.f.* (Acad.) Jersey de punto, ligero, poco ceñido, con mangas y abotonadura al cuello. *Sweater.*

CHONTAL. *adj.* (Acad.) Aplícase a la persona rústica e inculta. *Uncivilized (person).*

CHORREADO. *adj.* (Acad.) Sucio, manchado. *Dirty, stained.*

CHOTEAR. *v.* Mofarse de alguien. *To make fun of.*

CHÚCARO. *adj.* (Acad.) Arisco, bravío. Dícese principalmente del ganado vacuno y del caballar y mular aún no desbravado. *Wild, untamed (animal).* ‖ **2.** Huraño, arisco (persona). *Unsociable.*

CHUCEAR. *v.* Herir, pinchar con arma punzante. *To prick, goad.*

CHUCHO. *n.m.* (Acad.) Escalofrío. *Shivers, shakes.* ‖ **2.** (Acad.) Fiebre producida por el paludismo, fiebre intermitente. *Malaria fever.* ‖ **3.** (Acad.) Pez pequeño como el arenque y de carne muy estimada. *Small herring-like fish.*

CHUCHOCA. *n.f.* (Acad.) Especie de frangollo o maíz cocido y seco, que se usa como condimento. *Corn toasted, pounded and cooked into meal.*

CHUECO. *adj.* Torcido. *Crooked.* ‖ **2.** Patizambo. *Bow-legged.* ‖ **3.** *adv.* De forma torcida. *Crookedly.* ~Camina CHUECO. *He walks crookedly.* ‖ **4.** •Pelea CHUECO. *He fights dirty.* ‖ **5.** (fig.) •Ganó el partido CHUECO. *He won the match dishonestly.*

CHULLA. *adj.* Dícese del objeto que usándose en número par, se queda solo. *Odd, single item of a pair (glove, shoe, etc.).*

CHUMBE. *n.m.* (Acad.) Ceñidor o faja. *Girdle, sash (to hold skirt).*

CHUÑO. *n.m.* (Acad.) Fécula de papa. *Potato starch.*

CHUPA. *n.f.* Borrachera. *Drunkenness.*

CHUPADO. *adj.* •Estar CHUPADO. Estar borracho. *To be drunk, plastered (coll.).*

CHUPADOR. *n.m.* Persona dada a las bebidas. *Heavy drinker.* ‖ **2.** Fumador. *Smoker.*

CHUPAFLOR. *n.m.* (Acad.) Colibrí. *Humming bird.*

CHUPAR. *v.* Beber. *To drink.* ~Le gusta CHUPAR. *He likes to drink.* ‖ **2.** Fumar. *To smoke.* ‖ **3.** -se. Aguantar, sufrir (cosas desagrades). *Put up with, endure.* ~¡Tuve que CHUPARME una película tan aburrida! *I had to put up with such a boring movie!* ‖ **4.** •CHÚPATE esa! *So there! Put that in your pipe and smoke it (coll.).*

CHUPE. *n.m.* (Acad.) Guisado hecho de papas en caldo, al que se añade carne o pescado, mariscos, huevos, ají, tomate y otros ingredientes. *Stew of fresh fish or clams, bread, eggs, cheese, tomato, etc.* ‖ **2.** Sopa. *Soup.*

CHUPETE. Chupadura. *Lick, suck.*

CHUPO. *n.m.* Divieso. *Boil.*

CHUPÓN. *n.m.* (Acad.) Chupetón. *Pacifier.* ‖ **2.** Biberón. *Feeding-bottle.* ‖ **3.** (Acad.) Chupada. *Lick.*

CHURUMBELA. *n.f.* Bombilla para tomar el maté. *Tube through which mate tea is drunk.*

CHURRASCO. *n.m.* Bistec. *Steak.*

CHURRETEAR. *v.* Manchar. *To spot, stain, dirty.*

CHUSPA. *n.f.* Bolsa. *Bag, pouch.*

CIDRACAYOTE. *n.m.* Variedad de calabaza que se emplea en la confección de dulces. *Gourd, calabash.*

CIENTISTA. *n.m.* Científico. *Scientist.*

CIERRERELÁMPAGO. *n.m.* (Acad.) Cremallera de prendas de vestir, bolsos, etc. *Zipper.*

CIGARRERÍA. *n.f.* (Acad.) Tienda donde se vende cigarrillos. *Tabacco shop.*

CIMARRÓN. *adj.* (Hist). Propio del esclavo que huía buscando la libertad. (Before a noun) *Runaway, fugitive.* || **2.** Salvaje (animal), silvestre (planta). *Wild (plant), wild, untamed (animal).* || **3.** Rudo, rústico. *Rough, uncouth.* || **4.** Dícese del marino indolente. *Lazy (sailor).* || **5.** *(fig)* Rebelde, desenfrenado. *Wild, unruly.* || **6.** *n.m.* Animal salvaje. *Wild animal.* || **7.** (Hist) Esclavo que huía buscando la libertad. *Runaway, fugitive slave.* || **8.** ••Negro CIMARRÓN (variante de **cimarrón**).

CIMARRONADA. *n.f.* (Acad.) Manada de animales **cimarrones**. *Herd of wild animals.*

CIMBRAR. *v.* Dejar de improviso una dirección y tomar otra en una carrera. *To change direction suddenly.*

CIMBRÓN. *n.m.* Temblor o sacudida nerviosa violenta. *Shudder.* || **2.** Sacudida (de un terremoto). *Tremor, shake, jolt.* || **3.** (Acad.) Tirón fuerte y súbito del lazo u otra cuerda. *Violent jerk or pull.* || **4.** Estremecimiento o vibración fuerte de una cosa flexible (de lazo, etc.). *Crack.*

CIMBRONAZO (variante de **cimbrón**).

CINCHADA. *n.f.* Cinchadura. *Girthing, cinching.* || **2.** Juego de tira y afloja con una cuerda. *Tug of war.*

CINCHADO. *adj.* (Acad.) Dícese del animal cuyo pelaje presenta una o más fajas de distinto color en la barriga. *Animal with multicolor stripes on its belly.*

CINCHONA. *n.f.* Corteza del árbol de la quina. *Quinine bark.*

CINCO. *adj.* Moneda de cinco centavos. *Five-cent piece.* || **2.** Guitarra de cinco cuerdas. *5-stringed guitar.* || **3.** ••No entendió ni CINCO. *He didn't understand a thing.*

CINETECA. *n.f.* Archivo cinematográfico. *Film archive.*

CINTA. *n.f.* Lata. *Tin, can.*

CINTILLO. *n.m.* Cinta angosta para el cabello. *Hairband.*

CITADINO. *n.m.* Gente que vive en la ciudad. *City-dweller.*

CIUDAD. *n.f.* •Ciudad BALNEARIA. Centro turístico costero. *Coastal resort.*

CÍVICO. *n.m.* Policía. *Policeman.*

CLARO. *adj.* Por supuesto, claro que sí. *Of course, please do.* || **2.** ••COPIAR en claro. Copiar algo (de algo). *To copy something out.*

CLIENTELISMO. *n.m.* Sistema de repartirse los empleos entre los del partido victorioso. *Spoil system.*

CLÓSET. *n.m.* (Acad.) Ropero empotrado en la pared. *Built-in closet.* || **2.** Aparado, alacena. *Cupboard.* || **3.** Botiquín, armario del cuarte de baño. *Bathroom cabinet.*

COBIJA. *n.f.* (Acad.) Manta para abrigarse. *Blanket.* || **2.** (Acad.) Ropa de cama y especialmente la de abrigo. *Bedclothes.*

COBRE. *n.m.* Centavo. *Penny.* || **2.** ••Estar sin un COBRE. *To be penniless.* || **3.** •ENSEÑAR el cobre. Revelarse como hombre necio o sin importancia. *To show one's true colors.*

COCACHO. *n.m.* (Acad.) Coscorrón, golpe con los nudillos en la cabeza. *Rap on the head with the knuckles.*

COCADA. *n.f.* (Acad.) Especie de turrón. *Kind of nougat.*

COCAL. *n.m.* (Acad) Cocotal. *Coconut grove.*

COCAVÍ. *n.m.* (Acad.) Provisión de coca y, en general, de víveres que llevan los que viajan a caballo. *Provisions carried on a trip.*

COCINADA. *n.f.* Período de cocción. *(period of) cooking, cooking time.*

COCOA. *n.m.* Cacao. *Cocoa.*

COCOTAL. *n.m.* Plantío de cocoteros. *Coconut plantation.*

COCUYO. *n.m.* Luciérnaga. *Firefly, glowworm.*

CODEAR. *v.* (Acad.) Pedir con insistencia. *To sponge (something out of someone).*

COGOTUDO. *n.m.* (Acad.) Plebeyo enriquecido. *Self-made man, parvenu.*

COIMA. *n.f.* (Acad.) Cohecho, gratificación, con que se soborna. *Bribe.*

COIMEAR. *v.* (Acad.) Recibir o dar coima. *To give or receive a bribe.*

COIMERO. *n.m.* (Acad.) Persona que da

coimas o que las recibe. *Bribe taker.*

COJUDEZ. *n.f.* (Acad.) Cualidad de **cojudo**. *Stupidity.*

COJUDO. *adj.* (Acad.) Tonto, bobo. *Stupid.*

COLA. *n.f.* Nalgas. *Bottom, behind.* || **2.** •Hacer COLA. Hacer autostop. *To hitchhike, to thumb a ride.*

COLADERA. *n.f.* Cloaca. *Drain.*

COLECTIVO. *n.m.* Autobús. *Bus.*

COLITA. *n.f.* •Hacer COLITA. Hacer autostop. *To hitchhike, to thumb a ride.*

COLLERA. *n.f.* Gemelos de camisa. *Cufflinks.*

COLOCAR. *v.* Volver a poner en su lugar. *To put back, to put away.*

COLONIAJE. *n.* (Acad.) Nombre que algunas repúblicas dan al período histórico en que formaron parte de la nación española. Período colonial. *Colonial period.*

COLOR. *n.m.* •Zapatos de COLOR. Zapatos marrones. *Brown shoes.* ••Huevos de COLOR. Huevo moreno. *Brown eggs.*

COLORADO. *adj.* Verde, subido de tono (chiste). *Off-colored, risqué.*

COLUMPIO. *n.m.* Mecedora. *Rocking chair.*

COMBI. *n.m.* Microbús. *Minibus.*

COMBO. *n.m.* (Acad.) Mazo, almádana. *Sledgehammer.*

COMEDIA. *n.f.* Telenovela. *Soap opera.*

COMEDIDAMENTE. *adv.* En una forma servicial y complaciente. *In an helpful and obliging way.*

COMEDIDO. *adj.* Atento, servicial, complaciente. *Obliging, well-meaning.* || **2.** *n.m.* Persona atenta y servicial. *A well-meaning person, an obliging soul.*

COMEDIMIENTO. *n.m.* Acción de **comedirse**, de ofrecerse para algo. *Helpfulness.*

COMEDIRSE. *v.* Ofrecerse o disponerse para alguna cosa. *To volunteer, offer to help.*

COMEDOR. *n.m.* Coche comedor, vagón restaurante. *Dinning car.*

COMELÓN. *adj.* Comilón. *Hearty.* || **2.** *n.m.* Hearty eater, glutton.

COMELONA. *n.f.* Comida variada y muy abundante. *Feast, lavish meal.*

COMERCIAL (Angl.). *n.m.* Anuncio, emisión publicitario. *Commercial.*

COMIDA. *n.f.* Cena. *Evening meal, dinner.*

COMO. *adv.* ••¿A CÓMO estamos hoy? ¿A qué fecha estamos? *What is today's date?* || **2.** ••¡CÓMO no!. Por supuesto, claro que sí. *Of course, certainly, with pleasure.* . || **3.** ••Vino a COMO las dos. Vino a eso de las dos. *He came at around two o'clock.* || **4.** En el caso de que. *In the event that.*~ COMO vengas tarde no comerás. *If you come late you won't eat.* || **5.** ••COMO quien dice. Por así decirlo. *So to speak.*

COMPADRAZCO. *n.m.* Amistad. *Close friendship.*

COMPADRE. *n.m.* Amigo. *Friend, pal.*

COMPADREO. *n.m.* Camaradería. *Companionship, close contact.*

COMPETENCIA. *n.f.* (Acad.) Competición deportiva. *Competition.*

COMPLETAR. *v.* Rellenar (formulario). *To fill out*

COMPLEXIÓN. *n.f.* Tez. *Complexion.*

COMPLICACIÓN. *n.f.* Implicación. *Involvement.*

COMPONER. *v.* Arreglar (zapato, reloj, radio). *To repair, fix.* || **2.** (Acad.) Restituir a su lugar los huesos dislocados. *To set (bone).* || **3. -se.** Mejorarse, sanarse. *To get better.*

COMPULSORIO. *adj.* Obligatorio. *Compulsory.*

COMÚN. *adj.* ••COMÚN y silvestre. Común y corriente. *Ordinary, simple.* ~Una blusa COMÚN y silvestre. *An ordinary blouse.*

COMUNA. *n.f.* Ayuntamiento, municipio. *Municipality, town council.*

CON. *prep.* ••Me peino CON Gerardo. Me peina Gerardo. *Gerardo does my hair.*

CONCENTRACIÓN. *n.f.* (com.) Fusión, unión. *Merger.*

CONCHA. *n.f.* ••Tener CONCHA. Ser descarado. *To have a lot of nerve.*

CONCHABADO. *n.m.* Sirviente. *Servant.*

CONCHABAR. *v.* (Acad.) Asalariar, contratar a alguno para un servicio de orden inferior, generalmente doméstico. *To hire, employ.* || **2. -se**. Entrar a servir a sueldo. *To get a job as a servant.*

CONCHABO. *n.m.* (Acad.) Contrato de servicio doméstico. *Hiring.*

CONCHO. *n.m.* Residuo, sedimento, borra. *Dregs, sediment, residue.* || **2.** Resto de comida. *Left-overs.*

CONCHUDO. *adj.* (Acad.) Sinvergüenza, caradura. *To have a lot of nerve.* ~¡Qué tipo tan CONCHUDO. *He's go a lot of nerve!* || **2.** *n.m.* Bobo, tonto. *Simple, stupid, naive.*

CONCRECIÓN. *n.f.* Realización (sueños, proyectos). *Realization.*

CONCRETO. *n.m.* Hormigón, cemento armado. *Concrete.*

CONCUÑO. *n.m.* (Acad.) *Concuñado. Spouse of one's own spouse's brother or sister.*

CONDUCTOR. *n.m.* (mús.) Director. *Conductor.*

CONECTAR. *v.* Poner en contacto. *To put someone in touch with someone.*

CONEJO. *n.m.* •Andar de CONEJO. Actuar, obrar clandestinamente. *To be operating under cover.*

CONEXIONES. *n.f.* Amistades, relaciones con las que se puede contar. *Connections.*

CONFERENCISTA. *n.m.* (Acad.) Conferenciante. *Lecturer.*

CONFIABLE. *adj.* Fidedigno, fiable (información). *Reliable.*

CONFIANZUDO. *adj.* Que se toma excesivas confianzas. *Forward.*

CONFLICTIVO. *adj.* Atormentado. *Troubled.* ~Es una persona muy CONFLICTIVA. *She's a very troubled person.*

CONFORMARSE. *v.* Resignarse. *To resign oneself.*

CONFORMIDAD. *n.f.* Resignación. *Resignation.*

CONGENITAL (angl.). *adj.* Congénito. *Congenital.*

CONGO. *n.m.* Negro. *Negro.* || **2.** Hoja del tabaco obtenida de la segunda cosecha. *Second crop of tobacco leaf.*

CONGRESAL. *n.m.* Congresista. *Congressman, delegate.*

CONMUTADOR. *n.m.* (Acad.) Centralita telefónica. *Switchboard.* || **2.** Central. *Telephone exchange.*

CONNOTADO. *adj.* Destacado. *Distinguished, emminent.*

CONNUBIO. *n.m.* Complicidad. *Complicity.* || **2.** •En CONNUBIO con. *In league with, in cahoots with (coll.).*

CONOCOCIENCIA. *n.f.* Novia. *Girlfriend, sweetheart.*

CONORTE. *n.m.* Comodidad. *Comfort.*

CONQUÉ. *n.m.* Dinero. *Money.*

CONSCRIPCIÓN. *n.f.* Reclutamiento. *Conscription, recluting, military draft.*

CONSCRIPTO. *n.m.* Recluta. *Conscript.*

CONSECUENCIA. *n.f.* Honradez. *Integrity.*

CONSEJERO. *n.m.* Consejal. *Councilman.*

CONSERVATISMO. *n.m.* Conservadurismo. *Conservatism.*

CONSIDERACIÓN. *n.f.* ••De mi MAYOR consideración (carta). *To whom it may concern, dear sir, madam.*

CONSISTENTE. *adj.* Consecuente, congruente. *Consistent.*

CONSISTIR. *v.* •CONSISTIR de. Consistir en. *To consist of.*

CONSTANCIA. *n.f.* Comprobante (documento). *Documentary proof, written evidence.* ~Para que quede CONSTANCIA de la fecha. *In order to give proof of the date.*

CONSTIPADO. *adj.* Estreñido. *Constipated.*

CONTACTO. *n.m.* Interrumptor. *Switch, contact breaker.*

CONTADO. *n.m.* •De CONTADO. Al contado. *For cash, cash down.* || **2.** ••Al CONTADO rabioso. Al contado. *Cash.*

CONTADOR. *n.m.* Ábaco. *Abacus.* || **2.** Contable. *Accountant, bookkeeper.* || **3.** Certified public accountant.*Contable diplomado.* || **4.** Cajero. *Cashier.* || **5.** (jur.) Síndico administrador, jurídico, de quiebras. *Receiver.* || **6.** CONTADOR de navío. Contador (de navío), comisionario. *Purser.*

CONTADURÍA. *n.f.* Contabilidad. *Accounting.*

CONTENTA. *n.f.* Declaración escrita en que declara que una obligación ha sido pagada. *Acknowledgment of payment, release.*

CONTENTAR. *v.* Reconciliar. *To reconcile.* ~RECONCILIAR a dos personas. *To reconcile two people.* || **2. -se.** Reconciliarse. *To be (become) reconciled.*

CONTEO. *n.m.* (Acad.) Recuento. *Count, survey.*

CONTESTA. *n.f.* Respuesta. *Answer.*

CONTRA. *n.f.* Dificultad. *Snag.* || **2.** Contraveneno. *Antidote.* || **3.** •En CONTRA mía/suya/nuestra (en mi/su/nuestro) contra. *Against me/him/us.* ~No sé porqué todos parecen estar en CONTRA mío (mi CONTRA). *I don't really know why everyone seems to be against me.*

CONTRALOR. *n.m.* (Acad.) Funcionario encargado de examinar la contabilidad y la legalidad de los gastos oficiales. *Comptroller, treasury inspector.*

CONTRALORÍA. *n.f.* Oficina del **contralor.** *Comptroller's office, treasury inspector's office.*

CONTRAMATAR. *v.* Estropear a alguien golpeándolo contra algo. *To bang someone against something.* || **2. -se.** Chocar. *To crash, collide into something.*

CONTRAPUNTEAR. *v.* (Acad.) Cantar versos improvisados dos o más cantantes populares. *To compete in a verse duel.* || **2.** (Acad.) Estar en contrapunteo o disputa dos o más personas. *To quarrel, wrangle.* || **3.** (Acad.) Rivalizar. *To compete.*

CONTRAPUNTEO. *n.m.* (Acad.) Confrontación de pareceres. *Argument.*

CONTRAPUNTO. *n.m.* Desafío de dos o más poetas populares. *Poetic competition with improvised verses.*

CONVERSA. *n.f.* Charla. *Talk, chat.* || **2.** Lisonjas. *Smooth talk.*

CONVERSACIÓN. *n.f.* Charla. *Chat, chatting.* ~Me las encontré de gran CONVERSACIÓN. *I found them gabbing away.*

CONVERSADA. *n.f.* Charla. *Chat, talk.*

CONVERSADOR. *adj.* Charlatán. *Talkative.* || **2.** *n.m.* Charlatán. *Chatterbox.* || **3.** Zalamero. *Smooth talker.*

CONVERSAR. *v.* Charlar. *To chat, gab (coll.).*

CONVERTIBLE. *adj.* (Acad..) Descapotable. *Convertible.*

CONVERTIR. *v.* (dep.) Marcar un tanto. *To score.*

CONVICTO. *n.m.* Preso. *Convict.*

CONVIDAR. *v.* Ofrecer. *To offer.* ~Le CONVIDO con un café. *She offered him a cup of coffee.*

COPERA. *n.f.* Anfitriona. *Hostess.*

COPETÍN. *n.m.* (Acad.) Aperitivo, trago de licor. *Aperitif.*

COPETÓN. *adj.* Copetudo, engreído.*Stuck up, haughty.*

CORACHA. *n.f.* Saco de cuero. *Leather bag.*

CORAJE. *n.m.* Valor. *Bravery, courage.*

CORDÓN. *n.m.* (Acad.) Bordillo. *Curb.*

CORNER. *n.m.* Esquina (boxeo). *Corner.*

CORONTA. *n.f.* (Acad.) Zuro o carozo. *Corncob.*

CORRELÓN. *adj.* Corredor. *Fast, good at running.*

CORRENTADA. *n.f.* Lugar del río donde la corriente es más impetuosa. *Place in a river where the current is strongest.*

CORRENTOSO. (Acad.) Torrentoso (río). *Fast-flowing, rapid.*

CORRETEAR. *v.* Perseguir. *To chase, pursue.* || **2.** Hostigar. *To harass.*

CORTADA. *n.f.* Cortadura, tajo.*Cut, slash.*

CORTE. *n.m.* Reducción, rebaja (impuestos). *Cut.* || **2.** Tribunal. *Court.* || **3.** •Corte Suprema. Tribunal supremo. *Supreme Court.*

COSA. *n.f.* •Cosa que. Para que. *So that.* ~Despierta temprano, cosa que no llegues tarde. *Get up early so you won't be late.*

COSIACA. *n.f.* Cosa insignificante. *Small thing, triffle.*

COSTEÑO. *adj.* Dícese de la persona que vive o proviene de la costa. *Coastal dweller.* || **3.** Costanero. *Pertaining to the coast.*

COSTILLA. *n.f.* Costilla (de vaca). *T-bone steak.* || **2.** •Reir a costillas de uno. Reir a expensas de uno. *To laugh at someone's expense.*

COSTURAR. *v.* Coser. *To sew.*

COSTUREAR (Variante de **costurar**).

COTEJO. *n.m.* Partido. *Game, match.*

COTIZAR. *v.* (Acad.) Imponer una cuota. *To fix (subscription, contribution to pay).*

COTO. *n.m.* (Acad.) Bocio, papera. *Goiter.*

COTONA. *n.f.* (Acad.) Camisa fuerte de algodón, u otra materia, según los países. *Coarse cotton undershirt.*

COTUDO. *adj.* (Acad.) Que tiene **coto** o bocio. *Suffering from goiter.*

COTUFAS. n.f. Palomitas de maíz. *Popcorn.*

COYOTERO. *adj.* (Acad.) Dícese del perro amaestrado para perseguir a los coyotes. *Coyote-hunting dog.* || **2.** (Acad.) Trampa de coyotes. *Coyote trap.*

CRACK. *n.m.* El que se destaca en la práctica de un deporte. *Ace, star.*

CREÍDO. *adj.* Vanidoso, envanecido. *Conceited, vain.* || **2.** Crédulo, confiado. *Credulous, trusting.*

CREMA. •Crema agria (ácida). *Sour cream.* || **2.** •Crema batida. Nata montada. *Whipped cream.* || **3.** •Crema líquida. Nata líquida. *Single cream.* || **4.** ••Crema doble. Nata para montar. *Double cream.*

CRESPO. *adj.* Rizado. *Curly.* || **2.** *n.m.* Curl. Rizo.

CRIANDERA. *n.f.* Nodriza. *Wet nurse.*

CRIOLLO. *adj.* Se dice del nacido en Hispanoamérica. *Born in Latin America.* || **2.** (Hist.) Hijos de los primeros colonizadores de Latinoamérica. *Children of early Spanish and Portuguese settlers.* || **3.** (Acad.) Propio de algún país de Hispanoamérica. *Pertaining to the country (in Latin America).* ~Costumbres criollas. *Native customs.* ~Cocina criolla. *Typical cuisine of the country.* || **4.** •A la criolla. (Acad.) Sin mucha etiqueta, sin muchos cumplimientos. *Any old way.* || **5.** ••Hablar en criollo. Hablar en cristiano. *To speak plain Spanish.* Note. «In Latin America the noun and the adjective *criollo* often denote what is indigenous and national as opposed to what is foreign. Thus, *un manjar criollo* is a typical dish; *un caballo criollo* is a native horse of a breed peculiar to the country in question; In Argentina un buen criollo means a good Argentinian, an Argentinian of good stock». (*Gran Diccionario Larousse*).

CRONISTA. *n.m.* Periodista. *Reporter, journalist.*

CRUDO. *n.m.* Tela burda, especie de arpillera. *Coarse cloth, sackcloth.*

CRUZAR. *v.* Dar segunda reja a las tierras de labor cruzando los surcos perpendicular a los primeros. *To plough a second time.*

CUADRA. *n.f.* Manzana (distancia entre dos esquinas). *City block.*

CUADRADO. a*dj.* Cerrado de mente. *Inflexible, rigid.*

CUADRAR. *v.* Sentar (ropa). *To suit, become (clothes).* ~Este abrigo le sienta muy bien. *This coats suits you very well.*

CUAL. Que. *Which.* ~¿A cuál escuela estudias? ¿A qué escuela estudias?. *Which school do you study at?*

CUARTA. *n.f.* Látigo corto. *Short horsewhip.*

CUARTERÍA. *n.f.* Conjunto de cuartos de una casa. *Dilapidated rooming house.*

CUARTERÓN. *n.m.* Hijo de blanco y mulata. *Person of mixed race, quadroon.*

CUARTO. *n.m.* •Es un cuarto para las dos.

Son las dos menos cuarto. *It's two o'clock.* ||
2 ••Esa moda ya tuvo su CUARTO de hora. *That fashion has had it day.*

CUBILETE. *n.m.* Chistera. *Top hat.* || **2.** Sombrero hongo. *Bowler hat.* || **3.** Ardid, intriga (especialmente en política. *Intrigue.*

CUCAR. *v.* Molestar, provocar, azuzar. *To urge on, incite, provoke.*

CUCHARA. *n.f.* •Despacharse con la CUCHA-RA grande (o cucharón). Guardar para sí la parte más grande. *To keep the lion's share.* || **2.** Albañil experto. *Skilled bricklayer.*

CUCHILEAR. *v.* Azuzar. *To incite, egg on.*

CUCHILLA. *n.f.* Cordillera, cadena de montañas. *Mountain range.* || **2.** Cortaplumas. *Pocket knife.*

CUCHILLAZO. *n.m.* Cuchillada. *Slash.*

CUCHILLERO. *n.m.* Se dice del pendenciero cuya arma predilecta para la pelea es el cuchillo. *Knife-carrying brawler.*

CUCURUCHO. *n.m.* (Acad.) Parte más alta de algo. *Attic (house), top (tree).* || **2.** (Acad.) colina, elevación natural del terreno. *Hill.*

CUCHUGO. *n.m.* (Acad.) Cada una de las dos cajas de cuero que suelen llevarse en el arzón de la silla de montar. *Saddlebag.*

CUENTA. *n.f.* •Haz CUENTA de que no voy. *Just imagine that I'm not going.*

CUERAZO. *n.m.* (Acad.) Latigazo. *Lash.* || **2.** (Acad.) Caída, costalada. *Fall, blow.*

CUERDA. *n.f.* •Estar en su CUERDA. Estar en su elemento. *To be in one's element.* || **2.** •Estar con CUERDA. Estar decidido y jovial. *To be ready and willing.*

CUEREADA. *n.f.* Preparación de cueros, curtido. *Tanning.*

CUERIZA. *n.f.* Paliza (en especial con látigo). *Beating, thrashing (especially with a wip).* || **2.** Zurra. *Spanking.*

CUERUDO. *adj.* Se dice de las caballerías lerdas. *Slow, sluggish (horse).* || **2.** Se aplica a la persona fastidiosa. *Annoying.*

CUETE. *n.m.* Petardo. *Rocket.* || **2.** •Como CUETE. Como cohete. *Like a shot.* ~Pasó como CUETE. *He shot past.*

CUI (variante de **cuy**).

CUICO. *n.m.* Extranjero. *Foreigner.*

CUIDADO. *n.m.* •¡Pierda Ud. CUIDADO¡ ¡No hay de que¡ *Don't mention it!*

CULATA. *n.f.* Cada uno de los lados de una casa. *Sides of a house.*

CULECO. *n.m.* adj. Se dice de la persona muy casera. *Home-loving.*

CULILLO. *n.m.* (Acad.) Miedo, especialmente con los verbos dar, entrar y tener. *Fear.* ~Me da CULILLO ir al cementerio. *Going to the cementary gives me the creeps.*

CUMPA. *n.m.* compadre, amigo. *Pal, buddy.*

CUMPLEAÑERO. *n.m.* se dice de la persona que celebra su cumpleaños. *Person celebrating a birthday.*

CUMPLIDO. *adj.* Puntual. *Punctual.*

CUÑA. *n.f.* Persona de influencia. *Influential person, big shot (coll.).*

CUOTA. *n.f.* Plazo. *Payment, installment.* || **2.** •CUOTA inicial. Entrega inicial, entrada. *Down payment.* || **3.** •Carretera de CUOTA. Carretera de peaje. *Toll road/freeway.*

CUPO. *n.m.* || **1.** Cabida, capacidad. *Space, room, capacity.* || **2.** •No haber CUPO. No quedar asientos (teatro, cine). *Full house, 'sold out' (theater).*

CURACA. *n.m.* (Acad.) Cacique, potentado o gobernador. *Cacique, chief.*

CURAGUA. *n.f.* (Acad.) Maíz de grano muy duro y hojas dentadas. *A type of coarse, hard-grained corn or maize.*

CURCHUNCO. *adj.* Corcovado. *Hunchbacked.*

CURITA. *n.f.* Tirita. *Band-Aid.*

CURRUTACO. *adj.* Bajito, rechoncho. *Short, squat.*

CURSANTE. *n.m.* Estudiante. *Student.*

CURSERA. *n.f.* (Acad.) Diarrea, o cagalera. *Diarrhea.*

CURTIEMBRE. *n.f.* (Acad.) Tenería, curtiduría. *Tannery, tanning.*

CURTIRSE. *v.* Ensuciarse. *To get dirty, dirty one's clothes.*

CUSCO. *n.m.* (Acad.) Cuzco (perro pequeño, gozque). *Small yapping dog.*

CUSI CUSÍ. *adj.* Así, así. *So-so.*

CUY. *n.m.* Conejillo de Indias. *Guinea pig.*

D

DACTILAR. *adj.* •Cartera DACTILAR. Carné de conducir. *Driver's licence.*

DAMA. *n.f.* •DAMAS y caballeros. Señoras y señores. *Ladies and gentlemen.*

DAMASCO. *n.m.* Albaricoque. *Apricot (fruit), apricot (tree).*

DANCING. *n.m.* Baile. *Dance.* || **2.** Lugar donde se baila. *Dance hall.*

DANTA. *n.f.* Tapir. *Tapir.* || **2.** Anta. *Elk, moose.*

DAÑO. *n.m.* Maleficio, mal de ojo. *Spell, curse.*

DARSE. *v.* •DARSE por bien servido. Darse por satisfecho. *To be pleased, satisfied with the results.*

DE. *prep.* •DE no. Si no. *If not.*

DEBAJO. *adv.* Abajo. *Underneath.*

DECESADO. *n.m.* Muerto. ~LOS DECESADOS. Los muertos. *The dead, the deceased.*

DECESO. *n.m.* La muerte. *Death.*

DECIR. *v.* •Y no se DIGA. Y no digamos. *Not to mention.* ~Le gustan las matemáticas y no se DIGA la física. *He loves mathematics, not to mention physics.*

DECLARADO. *adj.* Pretendido, supuesto. Ostensible. ~Un enemigo DECLARADO. *A professed enemy.*

DECOLAJE. *n.m.* Despegue. *Take-off.*

DECOLAR. *v.* Despegar. *To take off.*

DEDO. *n.m.* •Ir al DEDO, tirar DEDO. Hacer autostop, hacer dedo. *To hitchhike.*

DEJAR. *v.* •DEJAR saber. Informar, comunicar. *Inform, let it be known.*

DELANTE. *adj.* •DELANTE mío, nuestro, etc. Delante de mí, de nosotros, etc. *In front of me, of us, etc.*

DEMANDAR. *v.* Requerir. *Require.* ~Es una arte que DEMANDA mucho talento. *It's an art that requires much talent.*

DEMASIADO. *adj.* Excesivamente, muy. ~Ricardo es DEMASIADO bueno. *Richard is a very good person.*

DEMECHADO. *adj.* Despeinado. *Wild, ruffled, tousled (hair).*

DEMERITAR. *v.* (Acad.) Empañar, quitar mérito. *To discredit.*

DEMORA. *n.f.* Tardanza, retraso. *Delay.*

DEMORAR. *v.* Tardar. *To take (time).* ~Demoró tres días en terminar el trabajo. *It took him three days to complete the work.* || **2.** Retrasar. *To delay.* ~Tuvo que DEMORAR el viaje. *He had to delay the trip.* || **3.** •¡No DEMORES! *Don't take long!*

DEMORÓN. *adj.* Lento, tardo (persona). *Slow.* || **2.** *n.m.* Persona lenta, tortuga (coll.). *Slowpoke.*

DENGUE. *n.m.* (Acad.) Contoneo. *Affected gait, hip-swaying, waggle.*

DENGUEAR. *v.* (Acad.) Contonearse. *(woman) To sway one's hips, walk with a waggle, show off as one walks, walk affectedly.*

DENOMINACIÓN. *n.f.* (fin.) Valor. *Denomination.* ~Billete de baja DENOMINACIÓN. *Small-denomination bill.*

DENTISTERÍA. *n.f.* (Acad.) Consultorio del dentista, clínica dental. *Dentist's office, dental clinic.* || **2.** (Acad.) Odontología. *Dentistry, odontology.*

DENTRO. *adv.* Adentro. *Inside.*

DENUNCIO. *n.m.* (Acad.) Denuncia.

Report.

DEPARTAMENTO. *n.m.* (Acad.) Provincia, división de un territorio sujeta a una autoridad administrativa. *Department, administrative district, province.* || **2.** Apartamento. *Apartment.*

DEPOSITAR. *v.* Pagar la fianza. *To post bail.*

DERECHA. *n.f.* •Político de DERECHAS. *Right-wing politician.*

DERECHO. *adj.* Afortunado. *Lucky.* || **2.** Dichoso. *Happy, content.*

DERRIBA. *n.f.* (Acad.) Desmonte, acción y efecto de desmontar. *Clearing or felling of trees.*

DERRUMBARSE. *v.* Fracasar. *To fail.*

DESABRIDO. *adj.* Soso, insípido (persona). *Boring, dull.*

DESACOMODAR. *v.* Desordenar. *To untidy, mess up.* || **2.** -se. Hacerse un lío. *To get mixed up.*

DESAGUISADO. *n.m.* Barrullo, confusión, desorden. *Mess, disorder.*

DESALOJAR. *v.* Desahuciar. *To evict.*

DESALOJO. *n.m.* Desahucion. *Eviction.*

DESANGRE. *n.m.* Desangramiento. *Bleeding, loss of blood.*

DESANIMACIÓN. *n.f.* Desánimo, falta de animación. *Tediousness, listlessness.*

DESANIMADO. *adj.* Se dice de fiestas o reuniones faltos de animación. *Dull (parties, etc.).*

DESAPERCIBIDO. *adj.* Inadvertido. *Unnoticed.*

DESARRAJAR. *v.* Descerrajar. *To break open, force the lock of.*

DESATERRAR. *v.* (Acad.) Escombrar, desembarazar de escombros o tierras un lugar para allanarlo. *To clear of rubble or earth.*

DESATIERRE. *n.m.* Escombrera. *Rubbish or rubble dump.*

DESATORNILLADOR. *n.m.* Destornillador. *Screwdriver.*

DESAYUNARSE. *v.* Desayunar. *To have* breakfast. || **2.** Enterarse. *To find out.*

DESBARRANCADERO. *n.m.* Despeñadero. *Precipice.*

DESBARRANCAR. *v.* Despeñar. *To fling over a precipice.* || **2.** Arruinar. *To ruin.* || **3.** -se. Despeñarse. *To fall over a precipice.*

DESBOTONAR. *v.* (Acad.) Quitar los botones y la guía a las plantas, especialmente a las del tabaco, para impedir su crecimiento y para que ganen en tamaño las hojas. *To remove buds from tobacco plants.*

DESCACHALANDRADO. *adj.* Desaliñado. *Sloppy, untidy, slovenly.*

DESCACHAR. *v.* Descornar. *To dehorn.*

DESCACHAZAR. *v.* (Acad.) Quitar la cachaza al guarapo. *To remove scum from sugar cane juice.*

DESCAMINAR. *v.* Empobrecer, arruinar (a alguien). *To Ruin.*

DESCARRILLAR. *v.* Descarrilarse. *To derail, jump the track (coll.).* || **2.** Irse por las ramas. *Get off the track, wander from the point.*

DESCHAPAR. *v.* (Acad.) Descerrejar una cerradura. *To break (lock).*

DESCHAVETADO. *adj.* (Acad.) Chiflado, que ha perdido la chaveta. *Crazy, mad, off one's rocker.*

DESCHAVETARSE. *v.* Perder la cabeza. *To loose one's head.* || **2.** Atolondrarse. *To be bewildered; to be stunned, amazed.* || **3.** Perder el juicio. *To go crazy, go mad, go off one's rocker.*

DESCOMEDIDAMENTE. *adv.* Groseramente. *Disrespectfully.*

DESCOMEDIDO. *adj.* Desatento. *Toughtless, impolite, discourteous.*

DESCOMPLETAR. *v.* Dejar incompleto lo que antes estaba completo. *To make incomplete, impair the completeness of.*

DESCOMPONERSE. *v.* Estropearse, averiarse. *To break down, get out of order.*

DESCOMPOSTURA. *n.f.* Malestar. *Sickness.*

DESCOMPUESTO. *adj.* Estropeado, averiado (máquina). *Out of order, broken, inoperable.* || **2.** (Acad.) Borracho. *Half drunk.*

DESCONCHABAR. *v.* Dislocar. *To dislocate a joint.*

DESCONGESTIONAR. *v.* Disolver. *Disperse, break up (a crowd).*

DESCONTROLADO. *adj.* Se dice del que no tiene o ha perdido el control de si mismo. *Upset.*

DESCOTADO. *adj.* Escotado. *Low-cut, with a low neckline (dress).*

DESCREENCIA. *n.f.* Descreimiento. *Unbelief* .

DESCREMAR. *v.* Extraer la crema de la leche. *To skim milk.*

DESCUAJERINGADO. *adj.* Desvencijado, destartalado. *Rickety, beat-up, dilapidated.*

DESCUAJERINGAR. *v.* Desvencijar. *To break into pieces.* || **2.** Desordenar. *To mess up, make untidy.* || **3. -se.** Dehacerse. *To fall to pieces.*

DESCUERAR. *v.* (Acad.) Desollar, despellejar. *To skin, remove the skin from.* || **2.** Hablar mal de una persona. *To difame, tear a person to pieces.*

DESCUERNAR. *v.* Descornar. *To dehorn.*

DESCUIDO. *n.m.* •En un DESCUIDO. Cuando menos se piensa. *When least expected.*

DESECHO. *n.f.* Sendero, vereda. *Side path.* || **2.** Atajo. *Shortcut.*

DESEMBARAZAR. *v.* Dar a luz la mujer. *To give birth to.*

DESEMBARAZO. *n.m.* Parto. *Birth, delivery.*

DESEMBOZADAMENTE. *Adj.* Sin embozo, sin ocultar intenciones. *Openly.* || **2.** Desvergonzadamente. *Shamelessly.*

DESEMPACAR. *v.* Desembalar, desempaquetar. *To unpack.*

DESEMPASTADO. *adj.* Sin encuadernar (libro). *Unbound book.*

DESEMPASTAR. *v.* Quitar las cubiertas o pastas a un libro. *To take the cover off books.*

DESEMPEÑARSE. *v.* (Acad.) Actuar, trabajar, dedicarse a una actividad satisfactoriamente. *To make out, acquit oneself, manage.*

DESENCAMINADO. *adj.* Descaminado. *To be on the wrong track.*

DESENCANTADO. *adj.* Decepcionado. *Disillusioned, disenchanted, disappointed.*

DESENCONTRARSE . *v.* No hallarse las personas que se buscan. *To miss each other, to fail to meet up.* || **2.** No concordar las opiniones. *To converge (opinions).* || **3.** Tener opiniones opuestas dos personas. *To be of different opinion.*

DESENDEUDARSE. *v.* Librarse uno de sus deudas. *To pay one's debts.*

DESENLATAR. *v.* Sacar algo de una lata. *To remove from a can.*

DESENROSCAR. *v.* Desatornillar. *To unscrew, unwind, untwist.*

DESENTECHAR. *v.* (Acad.) Destechar. *To tear the ceiling off.*

DESENTEJAR. *v.* (Acad.) Destejar. *To remove the tiles from, to leave unprotected.*

DESENYUGAR. *v.* Desyugar, quitar el yugo. *To remove the yoke, to unyoke.*

DESENYUNTAR (variante de **desenyugar**).

DESESPERO. *n.m.* Desesperación. *Despair, desesperation, impatience, hopelessness.*

DESEXILIO. *n.m.* Vuelta al país después del exilio. *Return from exile.*

DESGALILLARSE. *v.* Gritar con fuerza. *To yell or scream at the top of one's voice.*

DESGAÑOTAR. *v.* Matar cortando el gaznate. *To kill by cutting the windpipe (birds).*

DESGARRADOR. *adj.* Conmovedor, muy emocionante. *Heartrending.*

DESGARRAR. *v.* (Acad.) Arrancar la flema. *To cough up.*

DESGARRO. *n.m.* (Acad.) Flema. *Phlegm.*

DESGRACIADO. *n.m.* Persona infame, despreciable. *Despicable person.*

DESGUAÑANGAR. *v.* (Acad.) Desvencijar, descuajaringar. *To damage, break; to* *take apart, loosen.*

DESHECHA. *n.m.* (Acad.) Desecho, atajo. *Short cut.* || **2.** Desvío. *Detour.*

DESHECHO. *adj.* (Acad.) Desaliñado. *Slovenly.* || **2.** (Variante de **deshecho**).

DESHIJAR. *v.* (Acad.) Quitar los chupones a las plantas. *To remove suckers from a plant.*

DESINTELIGENCIA. *n.f.* Disensión, oposición en los pareceres. *Disagreement, difference of opinion.*

DESLAVE. *n.m.* Derrubio. *Landslide, avalanche.*

DESMALEZAR. *v.* Deshierbar. *To weed.*

DESMANCHAR. *v.* Limpiar de manchas. *To remove the stains from (a garnment).* ||**2.** -se. (Acad.) Abandonar el grupo o compañía de que se forma parte, alejarse de amistades. *To withdraw.* || **3.** (Acad.) Desbandarse, huir, salir corriendo. *To bolt out, escape.* || **4.** (Acad.) Salirse de la manada una animal. *To stray from a herd.* || **5.** (Acad.) Descarriarse, desorientarse. *To get lost, go astray.*

DESMENTIDO. *n.m.* (Acad.) Mentís, comunicado en que se desmiente algo públicamente. *Public denial.*

DESMERITAR. *v.* Desacreditar. *To discredit.*

DESMONETIZAR. *v.* (Acad.) Depreciar, desacreditar. *To discredit.*

DESMONTE. *n.m.* (Acad.) Mineral pobre acumulado en la boca de una mina. *Discarded ore or rock.*

DESMOTAR. *v.* Quitar al algodón su semilla. *To cotton gin.*

DESMOTE. *n.m.* Acción de desmotar. *Ginning.*

DESOCUPACIÓN. *n.f.* (Acad.) Paro forzoso, desempleo. *Unemployment.*

DESOCUPADO. *adj.* (Acad.) Desempleado, sin trabajo. *Unemployed.*

DESOCUPARSE. *v.* (Acad.) Parir, dar a luz. *To give birth.*

DESOREJADO. *adj.* (Acad.) Desasado (sin asas). *Without handles.* || **2.** (Acad.) Tonto. *Stupid.* || **3.** (Acad.) Que tiene mal oído para

la música. *Tone-deaf, having no ear for music.*

DESPABILARSE. *v.* (Acad.) Escabullirse, marcharse. *To vanish.*

DESPACHADOR. *n.m.* Excavador. *Excavator.*

DESPACIO. *adv.* •Hablar DESPACIO. Hablar en voz baja. *To speak softly.* || **2.** *n.m.* Lentitud. *Slowness.* || **3.** Retraso. *Delay.*

DESPACIOSAMENTE. *adj.* Despacio. *Slowly.*

DESPACIOSO. *adj.* Lento. *Slow.*

DESPANCAR. *v.* (Acad.) Separar la panca de la mazorca de maíz. *To husk corn.*

DESPARRAMAR. *v.* (Acad.) Divulgar una noticia. *To spread around.*

DESPARRAMO. *n.m.* (Acad.) Acción de desparramar. *Scattering, sprinkling, spreading.* || **2.** Fuga desordenada. *Disorderly flight.* || **3.** Divulgación de una noticia. *Spreading (of news).*

DESPELOTADO. *adj.* Poco metódico. *Disorganized.*

DESPELOTE. *n.m.* Caos, lío. *Shamble, mess.*

DESPELUCAR. *v.* (Acad.) Despeluzar, descomponer. *To dishevel, tousle, rumple.*

DESPENAR. *v.* Rematar, ayudar a morir al moribundo. *To kill, finish off.*

DESPERCUDIDO. *adj.* Avivado, despabilado. *Alert, smart, awake.* || **2.** (Acad.) De piel clara. *Fair-skinned.*

DESPERCUDIR. *v.* Avivar, despabilar a alguien. *To liven up, make smart, wise up.* || **2.** Limpiar o lavar lo que está percudido. *To cleanse or wash what is soiled or stained.* || **3.** -se. Avivarse, despabilarse. *To become smart or alert.* || **4.** Blanquearse, clarearse la piel. *To turn, go white (skin).*

DESPERNANCARSE. *v.* (Acad.) Esparrancarse, despatarrarse. *To straddle ungracefully, to spread one's legs wide.*

DESPESTAÑARSE. *v.* Trabajar excesivamente con la vista de noche. *To burn the midnight oil.*

DESPEZUÑARSE. *v.* (Acad.) Desvivirse, poner mucho empeño en una cosa. *To be very eager to do something, to long for.* || **2.** (Acad.) Caminar muy de prisa, precipitarse. *To walk very quickly.*

DESPICHAR. *v.* (Acad.) Aplastar, despachurrar. *To crush, flatten.*

DESPILARAMIENTO. *n.m.* (Acad.) Acción y efecto de **despilarar**. *The act of removing props from a mine.*

DESPILARAR. *v.* (Acad.) Derribar los pilares de una mina. *To remove props from a mine.*

DESPINTAR. *v.* (Acad.) No apartar de la vista. *Not to let someone out of one's sight.* || **2.** Correrse (maquillaje). *To run, get smudged.*

DESPLANTE. *n.m.* Disparate. *Crazy idea.* || **2.** •Hacer un DESPLANTE. Dejar plantado. *To stand someone up.*

DESPOSTAR. *v.* (Acad.) Destazar, descuartizar una res o un ave. *To cut up (a slaughtered animal).*

DESPOSTE. *n.m.* (Acad.) Acción y efecto de **despostar**. *Cutting up (of slaughtered animals).*

DESPRESAR. *v.* (Acad.) Descuartizar, hacer presas un animal. *To carve (a fowl).*

DESRIELAR. *v.* Decarrilar. *To derail.* || **2.** -se. Descarrilarse. *To run off the rails, jump the track.*

DESTAJAR. *v.* Descuartizar una res. *To cut up, carve into pieces.*

DESTAPADOR. *n.m.* (Acad.) Abridor de botellas. *Bottle opener.*

DESTAPAR. *v.* Desatascar (caño, inodoro). *To unblock.* || **2.** (Acad.) Dar a conocer el nombre del tapado. *To reveal, uncover.*

DESTARTALAR. *v.* Descomponer, desbaratar. *To ruin, spoil, destroy.*

DESTEMPLARSE. *v.* (Acad.) Sentir dentera. *To have one's teeth on edge.* || **2.** Sentirse indipuesto, afiebrado. *To feel sick, feverish.*

DESTENDER. *v.* Deshacer. *To strip.* ~Dejo la cama DESTENDIDA. *He left his bed unmade.*

DESTERNERAR. *v.* (Acad.) Desbecerrar. *To wean (young calves).*

DESTILADERA. *n.f.* (Acad.) Filtro para clarificar un líquido. *Water filter.*

DESTORNILLARSE. *v.* •DESTORNILLARSE de risa. Desternillarse de risa. *To split one's sides laughing.*

DESTORNUDAR. *v.* Estornudar. *To sneeze.*

DESTORNUDO. *n.m.* Estornudo. *Sneeze.*

DESTRONCAR. *v.* (Acad) Descuajar, arrancar plantas o quebrarlas por el pie. *To uproot.*

DESUBICACIÓN. *n.f.* Desplazamiento. *Displacement.* || **2.** Desorientación. *Confusion, desorientation.*

DESUBICADO. *adj.* Desplazado. *Out of position.* Las vértebras están DESUBICADAS. *The vertabrae are out of position.* || **2.** Desorientado. *Confused, disoriented.* || **3.** No tener la mínima idea de algo. *Not to have a clue.*

DESUBICAR. *v.* Desorientar, confundir. *Disorient, confuse.* || **2.** -se. Desplazarse. *To move out of position.* || **3.** Confundirse, desorientarse. *To get confused, disoriented.*

DESURTIDO. *adj.* (Acad.) Dícese de la tienda que no está surtida. *Lacking in variety.*

DESYERBA. *n.f.* Desyerbo. *Weeding.*

DETALLE. *n.m.* •Al DETALLE. Al por menor. *Retail.*

DETRÁS. *Prep.* •DETRÁS mío, nuestro, etc. Detrás de mí, de nosotros, etc. *Behind me, us, etc.*

DEVELAMIENTO. *n.m.* Revelación. *Revelation, disclosure.* || **2.** Descubrimiento (estatua). *Unveiling.*

DEVOLVERSE. *v.* Regresar. *To go back, return.*

DÍA. *n.m.* •DÍA de por medio. *Every other day.*

DIABLO. *n.m.* •Donde el DIABLO perdió el poncho. (Acad.) En un lugar distante o extraviado. *In the back of beyond, in some* *forsaken spot.*

DIARIERO. *n.m.* (Acad.) Vendedor de diarios. *Newspaper boy.*

DIARIO. *adv.* Diariamente. *Daily.*

DIARISMO. *n.m.* Periodismo. *Journalism.*

DIARISTA. *n.m.* Dueño de un periódico. *Owner of a newspaper.* || **2.** Periodista. *Reporter, journalist.*

DIARRUCHO. *n.m.* Diario sin importancia, diarito de mala muerte. *A so-called newspaper.*

DICERES. *n.m.* Rumores. *Rumors.*

DICHA. *n.f.* Suerte. *Luck, good fortune.* ~¡Qué DICHA, han venido a verme! *How lucky, you have come to see me!*

DICTAR. *v.* (Acad.) Dicho de clases, conferencias, etc., darlas, pronunciarlas, impartirlas. *To give (class, course), deliver (lecture).*

DIENTE. *n.m.* •De los DIENTES para afuera. *He never means what he says.* || **2.** •Pelar el DIENTE. **a)** Coquetear. *To smile flirtatiously.* **b)** Reírse con frecuencia. *To be constantly smiling.*

DIENTUDO. *adj.* Dentudo. *Toothy, bucktoothed.*

DIFERENDO. *n.m.* (Acad.) Diferencia, desacuerdo, disprepancia entre instituciones o estados. *Dispute.*

DIFUNTEAR. *v.* (Acad.) Matar. *To kill someone.*

DILATAR. *v.* Tardar. *To delay, be slow.* || **2.** llegar tarde (tren, etc.). *To be late.*

DINERO. *n.m.* •Estar podrido en DINERO. *To be stinking rich.*

DINTEL. *n.m.* Umbral. *Threshold.*

DIOS. *n.m.* •Menos pregunta DIOS y perdona. Con que se elude dar explicaciones. *Ask no questions.*

DIPLOMARSE. *v.* Terminar una carrera universitaria. *To graduate.*

DIRECTORIO. *n.m.* Guía telefónica. *Telephone directory.*

DIRIGENCIA. *n.f.* Liderazgo. *Leadership.*

DISCAR. *v.* Marcar. *To dial.*

DISCERNIR. *v.* Otorgar (premio). *To award.* || **2.** Abjudicar. *To confer.*

DISCOTECA. *n.f.* Disquería, casa de música. *Record shop.*

DISCRIMEN. (Acad.) Discriminación. *Discrimination.*

DISPARADA. *n.f.* (Acad.) Acción de echar a correr de repente o de partir con precipitación; fuga. *Stampede, wild rush.* || **2.** •A la DISPARADA. (Acad.) A todo correr. *At full speed.*

DISQUETA. *n.f.* Disquete, disco flexible. *Floppy disk.*

DISTINGUIDO. *adj.* •DISTINGUIDO Señor. Estimado Señor. *Dear Sir.*

DITA. *n.f.* (Acad.) Deuda, obligación de pagar, satisfacer o reintegrar a otro una cosa, por lo común dinero. *Debt.*

DITERO. *n.m.* (Acad.) Persona que presta a DITA. *Lender.*

DIVERTIDO. *adj.* (Acad.) Achispado, ligeramente bebido. *To be tight.*

DIZQUE. *n.m.* (Acad.) Al parecer, presuntamente. *Apparently.*

DOBLAR. *v.* Torcer. *Turn.* Cuando llegue a la esquina, DOBLE a la derecha. *When you get to the corner, turn right.*

DOLAMA. *n.f.* Dolencia, achaque. *Chronic illness.*

DON. *n.m.* •Que le vendo DON?. ¿En qué le pueda ayudar amigo? *How can I help you pal?*

DONDE. *conj.* Si. *If.* ~DONDE vuelvas a hacer eso te mato. *If you do that again, I'll kill you.* || **2.** ¡Cómo!, ¡De ninguna manera! ~DONDE va a oírlo, si es sordo. *How is he supposed to hear, he's deaf.*

DOÑA. *n.f.* •No me toque la fruta, DOÑA. *Please do not handle the fruit, dear.* ||**2.** •La DOÑA. *The lady of the house, the boss, the woman in charge.*

DORMIDA. *n.f.* Sueño, siesta. *Sleep, nap.* •Echarse una DORMIDA. *To take a nap.* || **2.** (Acad.) Lugar donde se pernocta. *Night's* *lodging, place to sleep overnight.*

DRAGONA. *n.f.* Fiador de la espada. *Guard.*

DRAGONEAR. *v.* (Acad.) Hacer alarde, presumir de algo. *To boast, brag.* ‖ **2.** •Dragonear de. Hacerse pasar por. *To pass oneself off as, to pretend to be.* ~Dragonea de médico. *He passes himself off as a doctor.*

DROGA. *n.f.* (Acad.) Deuda, a veces la que no se piensa pagar. *Debts, bad debts.*

DROGUERO. *n.m.* (Acad.) Moroso, mal pagador. *Swindler, cheat.*

DUEÑO. *n.m.* •Dueño de casa, proprietario. *Householder.*

DULCE. *adj.* •Dulce espera. Embarazo. *Pregnancy.*

DURAZNAL. *n.m.* Lugar poblado de **durazneros**. *Peach tree plantation.*

DURAZNERO. *n.m.* Melocotonero. *Peach tree.*

DUREX. *n.m.* Cinta Scotch. *Scotch tape.*

DURMIENTE. *n.m.* Traviesa. *Sleeper, tie.*

DURO. *adv.* (trabajar, estudiar). Mucho. *Hard.* ‖ **2.** •Duro y parejo. (Acad.) Con fuerza y constancia. *Long and hard.* ~Trabajaron duro y parejo. *They worked long and hard.*

E

ECHADA. *n.f.* (Acad.) Fanfarronada, bola, mentira. *Boast.*

EDAD. *n.f.* •La EDAD del chivateo. La edad del pavo, pubertad. *The awkward age.* || **2.** •Se quita la EDAD. Se saca la edad. *He pretends to be younger than he actually is.*

EFEMÉRIDES. *n.f.* Conmemoración de la declaración de la independencia. *Events to commemorate the declaration of independence.*

EGRESADO. *n.m.* (Acad.) Persona que sale de un establecimiento docente después de haber terminado sus estudios. *Graduate.*

EGRESAR. *v.* Terminar la carrera. *To graduate.* || **2.** Retirar, sacar (dinero). *To withdraw.* || **3.** Salir, partir, marcharse. *To go away, leave.* || **4.** Salir de una parte. *To go away from, emerge from, leave.*

EGRESO. *n.m.* Graduación. *Graduation.* || **2.** Salida, partida. *Departure, leaving, going away.* || **3.** Gastos, desembolso. *Expenditure, expense, debit.* || **4.** •Ingresos y EGRESOS. *Income and expenditure.*

EJEMPLARIZAR. *v.* Dar buen ejemplo, ejemplificar. *To set an example.*

ELECCIONARIO. *adj.* Electoral. *Electoral.*

ELEGANTOSO. *adj.* Elegante. *Elegant.*

ELEMENTO. *n.m.* Persona de pocos alcances. *Dimwit.*

ELENCO. *n.m.* Reparto (cine, teatro). *Cast*

ELEVADOR. (Acad.) Ascensor. *Elevator.*

EMBALAR. *v.* Ir a gran velocidad, aumentar la velocidad. *To step on the gas, put on speed.*

EMBARRADA. *n.f.* Desbarro, error grande. *Blunder, stupidity, foolish act.*

EMBARRAR. *v.* (Acad.) Calumniar, desacreditar a alguien. *To smear, damage someone's standing.* || **2.** (Acad.) Cometer un delito. *To blunder, commit a foolish act.* || **3.** (Acad.) Causar daño, fastidiar. *To annoy, irritate.*

EMBARRIALARSE (variante de **embarrarse**).

EMBELEQUERÍA. *n.f.* (Acad.) Embeleco, engañifa . *Deceit, fraud.*

EMBELEQUERO. *n.m.* Aspaventero. *Given to making a great fuss, highly emotional.*

EMBOCHINCHAR. *v.* (Acad.) Promover un bochinche, alborotar. *Agitate, stir up, arouse, create chaos.*

EMBOLSICAR. *v.* Meter en el bolsillo o en la bolsa. *To Put into one's pocket or purse.*

EMBORRASCAR. *v.* (Acad.) Hablando de minas, empobrecerse o perderse la veta. *To become exhausted (mine).*

EMBRETAR. *v.* Encerrar a lo animales en el **brete** o corral. *To pen, corral.*

EMBROMADO. *v.* (med.) Enfermo, fastidiado, malo. *In a bad way.* ~Ando EMBROMADO con este constante dolor de cabeza. *These constant headaches are driving me crazy.* || **2.** Se dice de quien está en situación económica difícil. *To be in financial trouble.* ~La situación económica nos tiene EMBROMADOS. *We're in a pretty bad way economically.* || **3.** Se dice de quien está atravesando por una situación difícil. *To be in a fix, having a tough time.* || **4.** Salir perjudicado. *To loose out, suffer the consequences.* ~Total, el que siempre resulta EMBROMADO soy yo. *In short, I'm* *alway the one who comes off worse.* || **5.** (problema) Espinoso. *Thorny.*

EMBROMAR. *v.* (Acad.) Molestar, fastidiar. *To pester, annoy, vex.* ~¡Déjame de EMBROMAR. *Stop pestering me, will you!* || **2.** Perjudicar, dañar (salud). *To harm, have an adverse affect on, be detrimental to.* ~Los antibióticos me EMBROMARON el estómago. *The antibiotics played havoc with my stomach.* || **3.** Arruinar (planes). *Ruin, spoil.* ~La lluvia nos EMBROMÓ los planes. *The rain spoiled our plans.* || **4.** Estropear, dañar (aparato, máquina). *Damage, break.* || **5.** Perjudicar. *To have an adverse effect.* ~La guerra nos EMBROMÓ a todos. *The war affected us greatly.* || **6.** Poner en un aprieto. *Put in a predicament, an awkward situation, a tight spot.* ~¡Ahora sí que estamos EMBROMADOS! *We really had it! (coll.).* || **7.** (Acad.) Detener, hacer perder el tiempo. *To hold up, detain.* || **8. -se.** Fastidiarse, jorobarse (coll.). *To get oneself into a mess, to put oneself in a predicament.* ~Me EMBROMÉ por no pagar la cuenta a tiempo. *I got myself into a mess by not paying the bill in time.* || **9.** •¡Que se EMBROME! *Serves him right!, that's his business!* ~¡Si no quiere venir que se EMBROME! *If he doesn't want to come, that's his business!* ~¡Que se EMBROME por estúpido. *It serves him right for being so stupid!* || **10.** Hacerse daño. *To hurt oneself.* ~Me EMBROMÉ la rodilla. *I hurt my knee.*

EMBULLAR. *v.* Meter bulla, alborotar. *To make a racket, to create a ruckus.*

EMBULLO. *n.m.* (Acad.) Bulla, broma, jarana *Noise, gaity, revelry.*

EMBURUJARSE. *v.* (Acad.) Arrebujarse, cubrise bien el cuerpo. *To wrap oneself up.*

EMBUTIDO. *n.m.* (Acad.) Entredós de bordado o de encaje. *Strip of lace.*

EMBUTIRSE. *v.* Darse un atracón. *To polish off, to stuff oneself with something.*

EMCAMPANAR. *v.* (Acad.) Elevar, encumbrar. *To raise, raise on high.*

EMPACAMIENTO. *n.m.* (Acad.) Acción y efecto de empacar o empacarse. *Packing.*

EMPACAR. *v.* (Acad.) Hacer el equipaje,

preparar las maletas. *To pack.* || **2. -se.** (Acad.) Plantarse una bestia. *To balk, shy (horse).* || **3.** Obstinarse, emperrarse. *To be obstinate, get stubborn.*

EMPAJAR. *v.* (Acad.) Techar de paja. *To thatch.*

EMPAMPARSE. *v.* (Acad.) Extraviarse en la pampa. *To get lost in the pampas.*

EMPAÑETAR. *v.* (Acad.) Embarrar, cubrir una pared con una mezcla de barro, paja y boñiga. *To plaster, parget.*

EMPAQUE. *n.m.* (Acad.) Descaro, desfachatez. *Nerve, brazenness, impudence.* || **2.** (Acad.) Acción y efecto de empacarse una animal. *Balking, shying (horse).*

EMPARRANDARSE. *v.* Parrandear. *To go on a binge.*

EMPASTADOR. *n.m.* (Acad.) Encuadernador de libros. *Bookbinder.*

EMPASTAR. *v.* (Acad.) Empradizar un terreno. *To turn into pasture land.*

EMPATAR. *v.* (Acad.) Empalmar, juntar una cosa con otra. *To join, connect, couple, tie firmly together.*

EMPAVONAR. *v.* Untar, pringar (Acad.). *To grease.*

EMPECINADO. *adj.* Obstinado, terco. *Stubborn, obstinate.* || **2.** Decidido, resuelto. *Determined.*

EMPECINAMIENTO. *n.m.* Terquedad. *Stubborness .*

EMPECINARSE. *v.* Obstinarse, encapricharse. *To get an idea into one's head, persist.*

EMPELLA. *n.f.* (Acad.) Pella, de menteca. *Pork fat.*

EMPELOTAR. *v.* (mec.) Desarmar, desmontar. *Strip down, dismantle.* || **2. -se.** (Acad.) Desnudarse, quedarse en pelota. *To undress.*

EMPEÑADURÍA. *n.f.* Casa de empeños. *Pawnshop.*

EMPEÑOSAMENTE. *adv.* Enpeñadamente. *With great determination.*

EMPEÑOSO. *adj.* (Acad.) Dícese del que

muestra tesón y constancia en perseguir un fin. *Persevering, dilligent.*

EMPIEZO. *n.m.* (Acad.) Comienzo. *Beginning, start.*

EMPIPADA. n.f. (Acad.) Atracón, hartazo. *Satiety, surfeit, bellyfull (coll.).*

EMPIPARSE. *v.* (Acad.) Apiparse, ahitarse. *To gorge oneself.*

EMPLASTO. *n.m.* (Med.) Parche. *Patch, dressing.* || **2.** Persona pesada o inoportuna. *Annoying person.*

EMPLEARSE. *v.* Conseguir trabajo. *To get a job.*

EMPLUMAR. *v.* (Acad.) Fugarse, huir, alzar el vuelo. *To run away.* || **2.** Emplumarlas (emplumárselas). Huir. *To run away.*

EMPONCHADO. *adj.* (Acad.) Dícese del que está cubierto con el poncho. *Wearing or covered with a poncho.* || **2.** Astuto, hipócrita. *Crafty, sharp.* || **3.** Sospechoso. *Suspicious.*

EMPONCHARSE. *v.* (Acad.) Ponerse el poncho. *To cover oneself with or wear a poncho.*

EMPOTRERAR. *v.* (Acad.) Herbajar, meter el ganado en el potrero para que paste. *To put cattle out to graze or pasture.* || **2.** Convertir un terreno abierto en un terreno cerrado. *To convert into fenced pasture, enclose.*

EMPOZAR. *v.* (Acad.) Quedar el agua detenido en el terreno formando pozas o charcos. *To form pools.*

EMPUJADA. *n.f.* (Acad.) Empujón. *Push, shove.*

EN. *prep.* En la mañana, tarde, noche. A la mañana, tarde, noche. *In the morning, evening, night.*

ENANCAR. *v.* (Acad.) Montar a las ancas. *To put somebody on the crupper (of one's horse).* || **2.** -se. Encabritarse el caballo. *To rear up.* || **3.** (Acad.) Meterse uno donde no le llaman. *To meddle, butt in, interfere.*

ENCABRESTRARSE. *v.* Obstinarse, emperrrarse. *To become obstinate, to dig one's heels in.*

ENCAJONAR. *v.* Atravesar el río un cauce agosto. *To flow through a narrow ravine.*

ENCALAMBRARSE. *v.* Acalambrarse. *To get cramp.* || **2.** (Acad.) Entumirse, aterirse. *To go numb.* || **3.** Aterirse. *To get stiff with cold.*

ENCAMOTADO. *adj.* Enamorado. *In love.*

ENCAMOTARSE. *v.* (Acad.) Enamorarse, amartelarse. *To fall madly in love with.*

ENCANAR. *v.* Encarcelar. *To jail, lock up.*

ENCANDELILLAR. *v.* (Acad.) Encandilar, deslumbrar. *To dazzle.* || **2.** (Acad.) Sobrehilar una tela. *To overcast, overstitch (fabric).*

ENCARGO. *n.m.* Embarazo. *Pregnancy.* || **2.** •Estar de encargo. Estar encinta. *To be pregnant.*

ENCARPETAR. *v.* (Acad.) Dar carpetazo, dejar detenido un expediente. *To file away, pigeonhole.* || **2.** No dar curso a un asunto. *To shelve, bury (plan, etc.).*

ENCARTUCHAR. *v.* (Acad.) Enrollar en forma de cartucho. *To make a cone of, roll up into a cone.*

ENCASQUILLADOR. *n.m.* (Acad.) Herrador. *Blacksmith.*

ENCASQUILLAR. *v.* (Acad.) Herrar caballerías o bueyes. *To shoe.*

ENCAUCHADO. *adj.* (Acad.) Dícese de la tela o prenda impermeabilizada con caucho. *Rubberized cloth, waterproof cape.*

ENCEGUECER. *v.* Perder la vista, volverse ciego. *To go blind.* || **2.** Ofuscarse el entendimiento debido a la vehemencia de una pasión o de una afecto. *To be blinded by passion, fury, etc.*

ENCEGUECIMIENTO. *n.m.* Ceguera. *Blindness.*

ENCERRADO. *adj.* Viciado (aire), mal ventilado (cuarto), donde falta el aire. *Stuffy.*

ENCHARCARSE. *v.* Enfangarse, embarrarse. *To get muddy.*

ENCHICHARSE. *v.* Embriagarse con **chicha**. *To get drunk.*

ENCHIQUERAR. *v.* Meter a los animales en el **chiquero**. *To pen, corral.*

ENCHISPARSE. *v.* Achisparse, emborracharse. *To get tight.*

ENCHUECAR. *v.* Torcer (metal). *To bend.* || **2.** Alaberarse (madera). *To warp.* || **3.** Retorcer (cara). *To twist.* || **4.** Inclinar (cuadro). *To tilt.*

ENCHUMBAR. *v.* Ensopar, empapar de agua. *To drench, soak.*

ENCIMA. *adv.* •Echarse ENCIMA. Suscitar el antagonismo de. *To antagonize.* ~Se echó ENCIMA a todos los de su oficina. *He antagonized everyone in the office.*

ENCIMAR. *v.* Poner una cosa sobre otra. *To stack up.* || **2.** Dar algo encima de lo debido, regalar. *To give as a bonus, to give extra.* ~Me ENCIMÓ dos más. *She gave me two extra ones.*

ENCLENQUE. *adj.* Muy flaco. *Terribly thin.*

ENCOMIENDA. *n.f.* (Acad.) Paquete postal. *Package, parcel.* || **2.** •ENCOMIENDA contra reembolso. *Parcel sent C.O.D.*

ENCOMIOSO. *adj.* Laudatorio. *Eulogistic, laudatory.*

ENCONCHARSE. *v.* Retraerse, meterse en su concha. T*o withdraw into one's shell.*

ENCORSELAR. *v.* (Acad.) Encorsetar. *To put a corset on.* || **2.** Estrechar, limitar (ideas, etc). *To restrict, confine.*

ENCUARTELAR. *v.* Acuartelar. *To put in barracks.*

ENCUERADO. *adj.* Desnudo. *Nude, naked.* || **2.** *n.m&f.* Persona desnuda. *Naked man or woman.* || **3.** •Revistas de ENCUERADAS. *Girlie magazines.*

ENCUERAR. *v.* (Acad.) Desnudar, dejar en cueros a una persona. *To undress, take someone's clothes off.* || **2.** -se. Desnudarse. *To undress, take one's clothes off.*

ENCURRUCARSE. *v.* Acurrucarse. *To squat, crouch.*

ENDENANTES. *adv.* (rur.) (Acad.) Hace poco tiempo. *A short time ago, a while ago.* || **2.** Hace tiempo. *Earlier, in the past, before.*

ENDEVERAS. *adv.* De veras. *Really, truly.*

ENDIABLADO. *adj.* Difícil, arriesgado. *Difficult, dangerous (road), complicated, tricky (affair).*

ENDIJA. *n.f.* Rendija, hendija. *Crack, crevice.*

ENFERMAR. *v.* Volver loco. *To drive someone mad.* || **2.** -se. Enfermar. *To fall ill, get sick.*

ENFERMOSO. *adj.* (Acad.) Enfermizo. *Sickly.*

ENFIESTADO. *adj.* De fiesta. *Partying, living it up.*

ENFIESTARSE. *v.* (Acad.) Estar de fiesta, divertirse. *To party, to live it up.*

ENGALLINAR. *v.* Intimidar, amedentrar. *To cow, intimidate.*

ENGARROTARSE. *v.* Entumecerse. *To go numb, get stiff.*

ENGARZARSE. *v.* (Acad.) Enzarzarse, enredarse unos con otros. *To get involved in something.*

ENGORDA. *n.f.* Engorde, ceba. *Fattening, fattening up.* || **2.** Ganado puesto a engordar. *Cattle fattened for slaughter.*

ENGRAMPADORA. *n.f.* Engrapadora. *Stapler.*

ENGRAMPAR. *v.* Engrapar. *To staple.*

ENGREÍDO. *adj.* Encariñado. *Affectionate.* || **2.** Mimado. *Spoiled.*

ENGREÍR. *v.* Mimar. *To spoil, pamper.* **2.** -se. ENGREÍRSE a (con). Encariñarse, apegarse a una persona o cosa. *To grow fond of.*

ENGUARAPARSE. *v.* (Acad.) Aguaraparse. *To acquire the taste of* **guarapo**.

ENHORQUETAR. *v.* (Acad.) Poner a hocajadas. *To place astride or astradle.* ||**2.** -se. Ponerse a horcajadas. *To sit astride.*

ENJUAGUE. *n.m.* Acondicionador. *Conditioner.* || **2.** •ENJUAGUE bucal. Enjuague (para la boca). *Mouthwash.*

ENJUGAMANOS. *n.m.* Toalla. *Towel.*

ENLATADO. *adj.* Programa de poca calidad. *Poor-quality program.*

ENLAZAR. *v.* Arrojar el lazo para aprisionar un animal. *To lasso, rope.*

ENLOZADO. *adj.* Se dice de los ustensilios de metal recubiertos de una capa de loza. *Enameled.* ‖ **2.** Esmaltado. *Glazed.*

ENLOZAR. *v.* (Acad.) Cubrir con un baño de loza o de esmalte vítreo. *To enamel, glaze.*

ENMONARSE. *v.* Emboracharse. *To get tight.*

ENMONTARSE. *v.* (Acad.) Cubrirse un campo de maleza. *To become overgrown.*

ENMUGRAR. *v.* Ensuciar. *To soil, dirty.*

ENOJADIZO. *adj.* Que se enoja con facilidad. *Irritable, touchy.*

ENOJADO. *adj.* Enfadado. *Angry, mad.*

ENOJAR. *v.* Enfadar. *To make someone angry.* ‖ **2.** -**se**. Enfadarse. *To get angry, get mad.*

ENOJO. *n.m.* Enfado. *Anger.*

ENOJÓN. *adj.* Enojadizo. *Short-tempered, touchy, irritable.*

ENOJOSO. *adj.* Aburrido. *Tedious, tiresome.* ‖ **2.** Incómodo, violento. *Awkward.*

ENQUÉ. *n.m.* Recipiente o saco en que se ha de traer o llevar algo. *Container in which something is to be carried.* ~ Lo traeré si encuentro ENQUÉ. *I'll bring it if I can find something (a bag) to put it in.*

ENRASTROJARSE. *v.* Cubrirse un campo de maleza. *To get covered with weeds.*

ENREDISTA. *n.m.* Enredador. *Troublemaker.*

ENREJAR. *v.* Poner el rejo o soga a un animal. *To put a halter on.*

ENRIELAR. *v.* Poner rieles. *To lay rails on.* ‖ **2.** Poner en el riel, encarrilar. *To put back on the rails.* ‖ **3.** Encauzar. *To guide, direct, put on the right track.*

ENROLARSE. *v.* Alistarse (ejército). *To enlist, sign up.*

ENROSTRAR. *v.* (Acad.) Dar en rostro, echar en cara, reprochar. *To reproach.*

ENSALMADO. *n.m.* Ensalmo. *Spell, incantation, black magic.*

ENSARTAR. *v.* Hacer caer en un engaño o trampa. *To trap, snare a person.* ‖ **2.** -**se**. Intervenir (en un asunto, negocio). *To get involved.*

ENSEGUIDA. *adv.* •ENSEGUIDA de. Inmediatamente despúes. *Right after, immediately after.* ~Salimos ENSEGUIDA de almorzar. *We left right after lunch.*

ENSERIARSE. *v.* (Acad.) Ponerse serio mostrando algún disgusto o desagrado. *To become serious.*

ENSIMISMARSE. *v.* Engreírse, envanecerse. *To get conceited or vain.*

ENSOPAR. *v.* (Acad.) Empapar, poner hecho una sopa. *To soak, drench.* ‖ **2.** Mojarse, empaparse. *To get soaked, drenched.* ‖ **3.** Mojar (galleta). *To dip, dunk.*

ENTABLAR. *v.* (Acad.) Igualar, empatar (ajedrez). *To draw.* ‖ **2.** Presentar una acción judicial. *To file a suit or legal action.*

ENTABLE. *n.m.* Empate (ajedrez). *Draw.* ‖ **2.** El orden en que está dispuesta una empresa, organización, etc. *Order, disposition, arrangement.*

ENTABLICAR. *v.* Poner tabiques. *To partition off, wall up, board up.*

ENTECHAR. *v.* Techar. *To roof.*

ENTEJAR. *v.* Tejar. *To tile.*

ENTEJE. *n.m.* Acción de tejar. *Tiling.*

ENTELERIDO. *adj.* (Acad.) Enteco, flaco, enclenque. *Weak, sickly, frail.* ‖ **2.** Acongojado, afligido, angustiado. *Distressed, upset.*

ENTENDER. *v.* •Darse a ENTENDER. Hacerse entender. *To make oneself understood.* ~No habla muy bien inglés, pero se da a ENTENDER. *He doesn't speak English that well, but he gets along.*

ENTERAR. *v.* (Acad.) Pagar, entregar dinero. *To pay, hand over.* ‖ **2.** Completar, integrar una cantidad. *To make up, complete, round off.* ‖ **3.** Mejorar, reponerse un enfermo. *To get better, get well.* ‖ **4.** -**se**. Recobrar lo perdido. *To recoup one's loss.*

ENTERCADO. *adj.* •ENTERCADO en hacer algo. Resuelto, decidido. *Determined to to something.*

ENTERO. *n.m.* (Acad.) Entrega de dinero,

especialmente en un oficina pública. *Payment.*

ENTERRAR. *v.* (Acad.) Clavar, meter un instrumento punzante. *To bury, trust into.*

ENTIERRO. *n.m.* Tesoro enterrado. *Buried treasure.*

ENTIZAR. *v.* Dar tiza al taco de billar. *To chalk.*

ENTONCES. *conj. & adv.* Pues. *Then.* ~ Nos veremos, ENTONCES, esta noche. *We'll see tonight, then.* || **2.** Por fin. *Finally.* ~ ¿Qué has resuelto ENTONCES? *What did you finally decide?* || **3.** Luego. *Then.* ~ ENTONCES, el vino a verme. *Then he came to see me.*

ENTONTAR. *v.* Entontecer. *To make foolish or stupid.*

ENTRABAR. *v.* (Acad.) Trabar, estorbar. *To get in the way of, interfere with.*

ENTRADA. *n.f.* •ENTRADA a. Entrada en. *Entry, entrance in.* ~La policía tuvo que forzar su ENTRADA al edificio. *The police had to force their way into the building.*

ENTRADOR. *adj.* Atrevido. *Daring, forward.* || **2.** Animoso, brioso. *Enterprising.* || **3.** Enamoradizo. *Flirtatious.*

ENTRAR. *v.* •ENTRAR a. **a)** Entrar en. *To go in, enter into.* ~ ENTRÓ al banco. Entró en el banco. *He went into the bank.* **b)** Incorporarse. *To enter.* ~ENTRÓ al convento de muy joven. *She entered convent at an early age.* **c)** Integrarse. *To join.* ~ ENTRÓ a la compañía de gerente. *He joined the company as a manager.* || **2.** •ENTRARLE a alguien. Dar jabón a; tratar de ligar con (una muchacha). *To try to make out with, flirt, pick up (girls, boys).*

ENTRE. *adv.* •ENTRE más... menos... *The more... the less...* ~ ENTRE más pide, menos le dan. *The more he asks for, the least they give him.*

ENTREFUERTE. *adj.* Se aplica a una clase de tabaco ni fuerte ni suave. *Medium strong tobacco.*

ENTREMÁS. *adj.* Cuanto más. *The more... the more...* ~ ENTREMÁS lo pienso, más convencido estoy. *The more I think of it, the more convinced I am.*

ENTREPISO. *n.m.* Entresuelo. *Mezzanine.*

ENTRESEMANA. *n.f.* Cualquiera de los días laborables de la semana. *Midweek, working days of the week.*

ENTRETENCIÓN. *n.f.* (Acad.) Entretenimiento, diversión. *Entertainment.*

ENTREVERO. *n.m.* Mezcla desordenada, revoltijo. *Jumble, mess.*

ENTROMPARSE. *v.* Enfadarse, poner trompa. *To fly off the handle.*

ENTRONCAR. *v.* (Acad.) Empalmar dos líneas de transporte. *Connect, meet, link up (railw.).*

ENTRONQUE. *n.m.* Entroncamiento. *Junction.*

ENVASAR. *v.* •ENVASAR un puñal en uno. *To plunge a dagger into someone.*

ENYERBAR. *v.* Hechizar. *To bewitch.* || **2.** -**se.** Cubrirse de maleza. *To become covered with grass.*

ENYUNTAR. *v.* Unir dos cosas de la misma especie. *To put together, join.*

EPA. *Interj.* (ante un accidente). *Whoops.*

EPISCOPAL. *adj.* (Acad.) Anillo EPISCOPAL. *Episcopal ring.*

EQUILIBRISTA. *n.m.* Político que se afilia al partido de más provecho. *Politician of shifting allegiance.*

EQUITADOR. *n.m.* (Acad.) Caballista, el que entiende de caballos. *Horseman.*

ERIZAR. *v.* Darle dentera a alguien. *To set one's teeth on edge.* || **2.** -**se.** Ponérsele a uno carne de gallina. *To get goose-bumps.*

EROGACIÓN. *n.f.* Desembolso, gastos. *Expenditure, outlay.*

EROGAR. *v.* Pagar, saldar (una deuda). *To pay, settle.*

ERRADO. *adj.* Equivocado. *Wrong, mistaken.*

ESAS. •En una de ÉSAS. El día menos pensado. *One of these days.*

ESCAPARATE. *n.m.* Ropero. *Wardrobe.*

ESCARAPELAR. *v.* Descascarar. *To scrape off, scall off, chip off.* || **2.** -**se.**

Descascararse. *To peel off, flake off.*

ESCOBERÍA. *n.f.* Fábrica de escobas. *Broom factory.*

ESCOBILLAR. *v.* (Acad.) En algunos bailes tradicionales, zapatear suavemente como si se estuviese barriendo el suelo. *To tap one's feet on the floor.*

ESCOBILLEO. *n.m.* (Acad.) Acción y efecto de **escobillar**, en algunos bailes tradicionales. *Tapping of one's feet on the floor in certain traditional dances.*

ESCONDIDA. *n.f.* (Acad.) Juego del escondite. *Hide-and-seek game.* ~Jugar a las ESCONDIDAS. *To play hide-and-seek.*

ESCONDIDO (variante de **escondida**).

ESCRIBANÍA. *n.f.* (Acad.) Notaría. *Notary's office, profession of notary.*

ESCRIBANO. *n.m.* Notario. *Notary, notary public.*

ESCRITORIO. *n.m.* Oficina, despacho. *Office.*

ESCUADRA. *n.f.* Equipo. *Team.*

ESCUCHA. *n.m.* Oyente. *Listener.*

ESCUCHAR. *v.* Oír. *To hear.* ~ Habla más fuerte que no te ESCUCHO. *Speak up, I can hardly hear you.*

ESCUELERO. *n.m.* Maestro de escuela (pey.). *Schoolmaster.*

ESCULCAR. *v.* Registrar para encontrar algo oculto. *To search.*

ESCULQUE. *n.m.* Registro, cateo. *Body search.*

ESCUPIDERA. *n.f.* (Acad.) Orinal, bacín. *Chamberpot.* || **2.** •Pedir la ESCUPIDERA. (Acad.) Acobardarse, tener miedo. *To get scared.* || **3.** (Acad.) Sentirse derrotado, considerarse vencido. *To give up.*

ESCURANA. *n.f.* Oscuridad. *Darkness.*

ESCURRIDO. *adj.* Confuso, avergonzado. *Embarrassed.* ~ Quedó muy ESCURRIDO. *He felt very embarrassed.*

ESPALDAR. *n.m.* Respaldo (de silla). *Back (of a chair).*

ESPANTO. *n.m.* Fantasma, aparecido. *Ghost.*

ESPARTILLO. *n.m.* Esparto. *Esparto (grass).*

ESPELUCAR. *v.* Despeluzar, despelucar. *To have one's hair chopped off.*

ESPERANZA. *n.f.* •¡Qué ESPERANZA! ¡Qué va! *You must be joking.*

ESPERMA. *n.f.* Vela. *Candle.*

ESPERNANCARSE. *v.* (Acad.) Abrirse de piernas. *To straddle, sit with the legs far apart.*

ESPIDÓMETRO. *n.m.* Velocímetro. *Speedometer.*

ESPINILLA. *n.f.* Grano. *Pimple.*

ESPINUDO. *adj.* Espinoso. *Thorny, prickly.*

ESPUELA. *n.f.* (Acad.) Garrón o espolón de las aves. *Spur.*

ESPUELEAR. *v.* Espolear. *To spur, spur on.*

ESQUELA. *n.f.* Carta. *Note, short letter.*

ESQUELETO. *n.m.* Bosquejo, borrador. *Rough draft, outline, preliminary plan.* || **2.** Formulario, impreso. *Blank, application form.*

ESQUINA. *n.f.* Tienda de comestibles situada generalmente en la esquina de una manzana. *Corner shop, village store.*

ESQUINADO. *n.m.* Se dice del mueble colocado contra un ángulo formado por dos paredes de una habitación. *Piece of furniture standing in a corner.*

ESQUINAR. *v.* Colocar un mueble en la esquina de una habitación. *To place a piece of furniture in the corner of a room.*

ESQUINERA. *n.f.* (Acad.) Rinconera, mueble. *Corner cupboard.*

ESQUIVADA. *n.f.* Acción de eludir un encuentro. *Evasion, dodge.*

ESTACA. *n.f.* Pertenencia mineral. *Mining property, mining claim.*

ESTACADA. *n.f.* Malecón. *Dike.* || **2.** Herida, punzada. *Jab, prick.*

ESTACAR. *v.* (Acad.) Sujetar, clavar con estacas, se usa especialmente cueros cuando se extienden en el suelo para que se sequen y mantengan estirados. *To stretch by fastening to stakes.*

ESTACIÓN. *n.f.* Emisora. *Radio station.*

ESTACIONAMIENTO. *n.m.* Aparcamiento. *Parking.* || **2.** Aparcamiento (lugar). *Parking lot.*

ESTACIONAR. *v.* Aparcar. *To park.* ~ Prohibido ESTACIONAR. *No parking.*

ESTACÓN. *n.m.* Pinchazo. *Prick, jab.*

ESTADÍA. *n.f.* Estancia, permanencia o demora en un lugar. *Stay.*

ESTAMPIDA. *n.f.* (Acad.) Huida impetuosa que emprende un persona, un animal o, especialmente un conjunto de ella.*Stampede.*

ESTAMPILLA. *n.f.* Sello (postal). *Stamp.*

ESTAMPILLADO. *n.m.* Sello (postal). *Stamp.* || **2.** •ESTAMPILLADO fiscal. *Fiscal or tax stamp.*

ESTAMPILLADORA. *n.f.* Franqueadora. *Postage meter.*

ESTAMPILLAR. *v.* Poner estampillas (sobre, paquete). *To stamp, put stamps on.* || **2.** Poner sello (documento). *To stamp.*

ESTANCIA. *n.f.* (Acad.) Hacienda de campo destinada al cultivo, y más especialmente a la ganadaría. *Farm, cattle ranch.*

ESTANCIERO. *n.m.* Dueño de una estancia. *Farmer, rancher.*

ESTANTE. *n.m.* (Acad.) Cada uno de los maderos que, hincados en el suelo, sirven de sostén al armazón de las casas en las ciudades tropicales. *Pillar supporting a house.* || **2.** Soporte. *Prop.*

ESTAQUEAR. *v.* Estacar cueros. *To stretch on stake (hide, skin).*

ESTATIZACIÓN. *n.f.* Nacionalización. *Nationalization.*

ESTATIZAR. *v.* Nacionalizar. *Nationalize.*

ESTEARINA. *n.f.* Vela. *Candle.*

ESTÉNCIL. *n.m.* Cliché. *Stencil.*

ESTERILLA. *n.f.* Mimbre, artículos de mimbre. *Wicker.*

ESTERO. *n.m.* Pantano, laguna. *Marsh.*

ESTILAR. *v.* Distilar, hacer caer gota a gota (Acad.). *To drip, to distill.*

ESTILOSO. *adj.* Elegante, con estilo. *Stylish.*

ESTITIQUEZ. *n.f.* (Acad.) Estipticidad, estreñimiento. *Constipation.*

ESTRELLÓN. *n.m.* (Acad.) Choque, encontrón. *Crash.*

ESTRICTEZ. *n.f.* (Acad.) Calidad de estricto, rigurosidad. *Strictness, severity.*

EXACERBANTE. *adj.* Irritante. *Irritating, provoking.*

EXFOLIADOR. *n.m.* (Acad.) Aplícase a un especie de cuaderno cuyas hojas solo están ligeramente pegadas para poder desprenderlas fácilmente. *Notepad.*

EXITOSAMENTE. *adv.* Con éxito. *Successfully.*

EXITOSO. *adj.* Que tiene éxito. *Successful.*

EXPEDITO. *adj.* Fácil. *Easy.*

EXPENDIO. *n.m.* (Acad.) En comercio, venta al por menor. *Retail sale.* || **2.** Tienda. *Store.*

EXPONENTE. *n.m.* Tipo representativo de lo mejor en su género.*Model, prime example.* ~El tabaco cubano es EXPONENTE de calidad. *Cuban tobacco is the best of its kind.*

EXTINGUIDOR. *adj.* •Manguera EXTINGUIDORA. *Fire hose.*

EXTINTO. *adj.* Difunto. *Late, deceased.* || **2.** La EXTINTA, el EXTINTO. *The deceased.*

EXTRAÑAR. *v.* Echar de menos. *To miss (friends, family).*

FACHO. *adj.* Facista. *Fascist.*

FACILONGO. *adj.* Fácil en extremo. *Extremely easy.* ~ Estuvo bien FACILONGO. *It was dead easy, it was a piece of cake.*

FACISTOL. *adj.* Vanidoso, fachendoso. *Vain, conceited person.*

FACTORÍA. *n.f.* Fábrica. *Plant, factory.*

FACTURADOR (variante de **facturista**).

FACTURERO (variante de **facturista**).

FACTURISTA. *n.m.* Encargado de facturar mecancías. *Person who bills or invoices.*

FAFARRACHO. *adj.* (Acad.) Dícese de la persona fachendosa, jactanciosa. *Boastful, vain.*

FAJAR. *v.* (Acad.) Pegar a uno, golpearlo. *To give, deliver (blows).* ~Los boxeadores se FAJARON duro. *The boxers really laid into each other.* || **2.** Atacar. *To attack.*

FAJO. *n.m.* Trago de aguardiente. *Swig of liquor.*

FALENCIA. *n.f.* (Acad.) Quiebra de un comercio. *Bankruptcy.*

FALLA. *n.f.* Fallo. *Shortcoming, defect.* ~ Debe haber una FALLA en el motor. *There must be something wrong with the motor.* || **2.** Lástima. *Pity, shame.* ~ Es una FALLA que no haya podido venir. *It's a pity she wasn't able to come.*

FALTAR. *v.* Ser grosero. *To be rude to, show disrespect for.* || **2.** •FALTAR al respeto. *To be disrespectul.* || **3.** •FALTAN 5 para las ocho. Son las 8 menos 5. *It's 5 to 8.*

FAMILIA. *n.f.* Pariente. *Relative.*

FANDADULERO. *adj.* Farolero. *Braggart, boaster.*

FANÉ. *adj.* Gastado, deslucido (ropa). *Worn, shabby.* || **2.** Marchito (plantas). *Whitered.* || **3.** Arrugado (billete, ropa). *Wrinkled.* || **4.** •Estar FANÉ. Estar estropeado (persona). *To be past one's prime.*

FAÑOSO. *adj.* (Acad.) Que habla con una pronunciación nasal oscura. *Nasal (manner of speaking, voice).*

FANTOCHEAR. *v.* Lucirse. *To show off.*

FARFULLA. *n.f.* Fanfarronería. *Bragging. boasting.*

FARREAR. *v.* (Acad.) Andar de farra o de parranda. *To paint the town red.* || **2.** -se. Despilfarrar, tirar. *To squander, blow.* ~ Se FAREÓ el sueldo en el casino. *He blew his money in the casino.*

FARRERO (variante de **farrista**).

FARRISTA. *n.m.* (Acad.) Juerguista, aficionado a la juerga o la farra. *Said of a person who likes to live it up, have a good time.*

FASTIDIARSE. *v.* Molestarse. *To get annoyed, get cross.* ~Se FASTIDIÓ por lo que dije. *He got annoyed at what I said.*

FAUCES. *n.m.* Colmillos. *Tusks.*

FAUL. *n.m.* (Dep.). Falta. *Foul.*

FAULEAR. *v.* (Dep.) Cometer una falta. *To foul.*

FAULERO. *n.m.* (Dep.) Jugador que juega sucio. *Dirty player, persistent fouler.*

FAVOR. *n.m.* •Si hace FAVOR. Por favor. *If you don't mind.* || **2.** •FAVOR de venir puntualmente. Hágame el favor de venir puntualmente. *Please try to be on time.*

FAVORECIDO. *adj.* Ganador (en un sorteo). *Winner.* Salió FAVORECIDO con el primer premio. *He was the lucky winner.*

FECHA. *n.f.* •FECHA de vencimiento. Fecha

de caducidad. *Expiration date.*

FECHADOR. *n.m.* Matasellos. *Date stamp.*

FENÓMENO. *n.m.* Fenomenal. *Great, fantastic.* ~ ¡Es un libro FENÓMENO!. *It's a great book!* || **2.** *Interj.* •¡FENÓMENO! *Great!* Mañana te invito a casa - ¡FENÓMENO! *I'm inviting you to my house tomorrow - Great!*

FEO. *adj.* Malo, desagradable. *Unpleasant, bad.* ~ ¡Qué FEO está el día! *What an awful day!.* ~Tiene un FEO sabor. *It has an unpleasant, disagreeable taste.* ~Huele FEO. *It smells bad, awful.* || **2.** •Ponerse FEO un asunto. Tomar mal cariz un asunto. ~La cosa se está poniendo FEA, ¡Vámonos! *Things are getting out of hand, let's go!* || **3.** Malísimo, horrible. *Terrible.* ~Me has dado cartas muy FEAS. *You have dealt me a terrible hand.* || **4.** *adv.* Malísimamente. *Terribly.* ~Canta FEO. *She sings terribly.*

FERIADO. *adj.* •Días FERIADOS. Días festivos. *Public holidays.* || **2.** *n.m.* Día festivo, fiesta. *Holiday.* ~ Mañana es FERIADO. *Tomorrow is a holiday.* ~ Cerramos domingos y FERIADOS. *We are closed on Sundays and holidays.*

FESTEJAR. *v.* Celebrar. *To celebrate.*

FESTEO. *n.m.* Fiesta. *Rowdy celebration or party.*

FIAMBRERÍA. *n.f.* (Acad.) Tienda donde se venden o preparan fiambres. *Delicatessen.*

FICHA. *n.f.* •Ser mala (buena) FICHA. Ser una buena pieza. *To be a rogue, a villain.*

FIERRO. *n.m.* (Acad.) Hierro, marca para el ganado. *Branding iron.* || **2.** Trozo de metal. *Piece of metal.* ~Le dió con un HIERRO en la cabeza. *He hit him over the head with a metal bar.* || **3.** Resortes. *Springs.*

FIESTITA. *n.f.* Diversión familiar. *Family get-together.*

FIFÍ. *n.m.* Petimetre, playboy. *Playboy, young man about town.*

FIJA. *n.f.* Caballo que se cree seguro ganador en una carrera. *Sure thing, sure winner.* || **2.** •¿Te FIJAS? ¿Viste? *See what I mean?*

FILMADORA. *n.f.* Máquina para filmar. *Film, cine camera.*

FILO. *n.m.* Hambre. *Hunger.* ~Tengo un FILO enorme. *I'm starved.*

FILOSO. *adj.* Afilado, que tiene filo. *Sharp, sharp-edged.*

FINANCISTA. *n.m.* Persona versada en finanzas, financiero. *Financier.*

FINCA. *n.f.* Casa de campo, quinta de recreo. *Country estate.*

FINCAR. *v.* Estribar, consistir. *To rest, lie.* ~El problema FINCA en su política oficial. *The problem rests in their official policy.*

FINTEAR. *v.* (Dep.) Fintar. *To feint, fake.*

FIRULETE. *n.m.* (Acad.) Volante. *Frill.* || **2.** Rúbrica. *Flourish (signature).* || **3.** Pasos rebuscados en el baile. *Elaborate twirl (in dancing).* || **4.** Adorno rebuscado. *Intricate decoration.* || **5.** (Acad.) Adorno supérfluo y de mal gusto. *Cheap adornment.*

FISCAL. *n.m.* Vecino a cargo de la iglesia en los pueblos pequeños sin cura residente. *Church warden.*

FLACÓN. *adj.* Muy flaco. *Skinny, very thin.*

FLACUCHENTO. *adj.* Flacucho. *Very thin.*

FLAQUENCIA. *n.f.* Flacura. *Thinness, skininess.*

FLATO. *n.m.* (Acad.) Melancolía, murria, tristeza. *Depresión, gloom.*

FLAUTA. *n.f.* •¡La gran FLAUTA! *Good grief!, you don't say!.* || **2.** •De la gran FLAUTA. Formidable, estupendo, fantástico, magnífico. *Terrific, tremendous.*

FLETAR. *v.* Transportar (pasajeros, mercancías). *To transport.* || **2.** Alquilar un vehículo para transportar personas o cargar. *To charter, hire.*

FLETE. *n.m.* (Acad.) Precio del alquiler de una nave o de otro medio de transporte. *Hire charge, rental charge.* || **2.** (Acad.) Carga que se transporta por mar o por tierra. *Transportation, carriage, transport.*

FLETERO. *adj.* (Acad.) Dícese de la embarcación, carro u otro vehículo que se alquila para transporte. *Cargo, charter or freight (used adjectively before names of transport vehicles).* || **2.** Dueños de vehículos que se alquilan. *Owner of vehicles for hire.*

FLOR. *n.f.* Excelente, fabuloso, magnífico. *Splendid, excellent.* ~Es una FLOR de ganga. *It's a heck of a bargain.* || **2.** En grado sumo. *To the ultimate degree.* ~Es un FLOR de estúpido. *He's a real idiot.*

FLORCITA. *n.f.* Florecita. *Little flower.* || **2.** •Andar de FLORCITA. Darse a diversiones y placeres. *To wander aimlessly, to loaf.*

FLOREAR. *v.* (Acad.) Florecer. *To flower, bloom, blossom.* || **2.** Adornar con flores, dibujos, bordados (vestido). *To add a flowery design to.* || **3. -se.** Lucirse en el desempeño de una actividad. *To show off, to perform brillantly.*

FLORERÍA. *n.f.* Floristería. *Florist, flower shop.*

FLUX. *n.m.* (Acad.) Terno, traje masculino completo. *Suit of clothes.*

FOCO. *n.m.* •Estar fuera de FOCO. *To be out of focus.* || **2.** Bombilla. *Light bulb.*

FOETAR. *v.* Dar latigazos. *To horsewhip.*

FOETAZO. *n.m.* Látigazo. *Lash.* || **2.** •Darle FOETAZO a alguien. *To horsewhip someone.*

FOETE. *n.m.* Látigo. *Whip.*

FOGAJE. *n.m.* Bochorno, calor sofocante. *Scorching heat, sultry weather.*

FOGÓN. *n.m.* (Acad.) Fuego de leña u otro combustible que se hace en el suelo. *Bonfire, campfire.*

FOGUEADO. *adj.* Perito, experto. *Expert, experienced.*

FOJA. *n.f.* Hoja. *Sheet.* || **2.** FOJA de servicios. *Service record.* || **3.** Volver a FOJA cero. *To be back to square one.*

FOLLÓN. *n.m.* (Acad.) Fullona, pendencia, gresca. *Row, quarrel, fight, squabble.*

FONDA. *n.f.* Restaurante de poca categoría. *Cheap restaurant.*

FONDEADO. *adj.* •Estar FONDEADO. Tener dinero. *To be wealthy.* || **2.** Quedar FONDEADO. Quedar sin dinero. *To be broke.*

FONDEARSE. *v.* Enriquecerse. *To get rich.* || **2.** Guardar dinero. *To save for the future.*

FONDERO. *n.m.* Encargado o dueño de una fonda. *Innkeeper, restaurant owner.*

FONDILLO(s). *n.m.* Trasero. *Seat, buttock, backside.*

FONDILLUDO. *adj.* De anchos fondillos o de asentaderas abultadas. *To have a large backside.*

FONDO. *n.m.* •¡FONDO blanco! ¡Salud y pesetas! *Bottoms up.*

FORCITO. *n.m.* Pequeño Ford. *Little Ford.*

FORMA. *n.f.* •En FORMA. **a)** Estupendo. *Terrific.* ~Una comida en FORMA. *A real good meal.* **b)** Fenomenal, estupendamente. ~Hoy nos divertimos en FORMA. *Today we really had a good time.*

FOUL. *n.m.* (Dep.) Infracción. *Foul.*

FRANCACHÓN. *adj.* Muy franco y llano en las maneras y el trato. *Too direct, too outspoken.*

FRANGOLLERO. *adj.* Que hace las cosas mal y de prisa. *Said of a person who does work in a slip-shod fashion.*

FRANGOLLÓN. *adj.* (Acad.) Que hace las cosas mal y de prisa. *Bungling.*

FRAZADA. *n.f.* Manta, cobija. *Blanket.*

FREEZER. *n.m.* Congelador. *Freezer.*

FREGADA. *n.f.* Restregadura. *Scrub, scrubbing.* ~ Este suelo necesita una buena FREGADERA. *This floor need a real good scrubbing.* || **2.** Suceso adverso, molesto o perjudicial. *Nuisance, drag, bother, hassle.*

FREGADERA. *n.f.* Molestia. *Inconvenience, nuisance.* ~Es una FREGADERA tener que ir hasta allí. *It's a real hassle having to go all that way.*

FREGADO. *adj.* (Acad.) Majadero, enfadoso, importuno, dicho de personas. *Annoying.* ~¡Que hombre más FREGADO!, hace 5 veces que me llama. *What a nuisance this man is!, he has already called me 5 times.* || **2.** Difícil. *Difficult, tricky, tough.* ~Fue un examen muy FREGADO. *It was a very difficult, tough test.* || **3.** Difícil (pesona). *Difficult.* ~ Con la edad se ha puesto muy FREGADO. *He has become very difficult in his old age.* || **4.** *n.m.* Persona difícil. *Difficult person.*

FREGAR. *v.* (Acad.) Fastidiar, molestar, jorobar. *Pester, annoy, bother.* || **2.** Acosar. *To worry, harrass.* || **3.** Malograr, arruinar. *To ruin, spoil, mess up (coll.).* ~El mal tiempo nos vino a FREGAR las vacaciones. *The bad weather ruined our vacations.* || **4.**Fastidiar, perjudicar, joder (vulg.). *To ruin, drag down, destroy.* ~El anterior gobierno no hizo más que FREGAR al país. *All the last government managed to do was to drag to country down.* || **5.** (Acad.) Desconcertar. *Stump.* ~Me FREGÓ con esta pregunta. *That question really stumped me.* || **6.** •FREGARLE la paciencia a alguien. No dejar ni a sol ni a sombra. *To get on someones nerve, to get on someone's back.* || **7.** •¡No FRIEGUES! *You're kidding! Really!* || **8.** •¡Déjate de FREGAR! *Stop bothering me! Leave me alone!* || **9. -se.** Fastidiarse. ~Si no quieres venir, te FRIEGAS. *If you don't want to come, that's your business (you're the one who is going to lose out).*

FREGÓN. *adj.* Molesto. *Trying, tiresome, annoying.* || **2.** Tonto. *Stupid.*

FRENADA. *n.f.* Frenazo. *Braking.*

FRENADO. (Acad.) Frenazo, acción y efecto de frenar súbita y violentamente. *Sudden braking, sudden halt, squeal of brakes.*

FRENILLO. *n.m.* Abrazadera (para los dientes). *Braces.*

FRESCO. *n.m.* (Acad.) Refresco, bebida fría y atemperante. *Soda.* || **2.** •Echar FRESCO. Decirle a uno las cuatro verdades. *To tell it like it is.*

FRESQUERÍA. *n.f.* Lugar donde se hacen y venden bebidas heladas o refrescos. *Ice cream parlor, soda fountain.*

FRIEGA. *n.f.* (Acad.) Molestia, fastidio. *Annoyance, nuisance.* || **2.** Zurra, paliza. *Thrashing.*

FRIGIDAIRE. *n.m.* Frigorífico, nevera. *Refrigerator.*

FRIJOL. *n.m.* Judía. *Bean.*

FRÍO. *n.m.* Fiebre intermitente. *Intermittent fever.* || **2.** Paludismo. *Malaria.*

FRIOLENTO. *adj.* Friolero, muy sensible al frío. *Very sensitive to cold.*

FRISA. *n.f.* (Acad.) Pelo de algunas telas, como el de la felpa. *Nap (on clothes)*

FRITANGA. *n.f.* Fritada. *Fried snacks.*

FRITAR. *v.* Freir. *To fry.*

FRUTILLA. *n.f.* (Acad.) Especie de fresón americano. *Strawberry.*

FRUTILLAR. *n.m.* Sitio donde se crían frutillas. *Strawberry field.*

FRUTILLERO. *n.m.* Vendedor ambulante de frutillas. *Strawberry seller.*

FUETAZO. *n.m.* Latigazo. *Lash.*

FUETE. *n.m.* Látigo. *Whip.*

FULMINANTE. *n.m.* Cápsula fulminante. *Percussion cap.*

FUNCIÓN. *n.f.* •Entrar en FUNCIÓNES. *To assume one's post.* || **2.** •FUNCIÓN continua. Sesión continua. *Continuous performance.*

FUNDIDO. *adj.* Se dice de quien está comercialmente arruinado. *Ruined, bankrupt.* || **2.** Agotado. *Worn out, exhausted.*

FUNDILLO. *n.m.* Fondillos (pantalones). *Seat (of pants)*

FUNDIRSE. *v.* (Acad.) Arruinarse, hundirse. *To go bankrupt.* El negocio se FUNDIÓ. *The business went bankrupt.*

FUROR. *n.m.* •Tener FUROR para algo. *To have a craving for, to have a passion for.*

FUSIL. *n.m.* Rifle. *Rifle.*

FUSTÁN. *n.m.* Enaguas. *Petticoat.*

FUSTANERO. *n.m.* El que fabrica fustanes. *Petticoat maker.*

FUTRE. *n.m.* Lechuguino, o simplemente persona vestida con atildamiento. *Dandy, fashionably-dressed man.*

G

GABELA. *n.f.* (Acad.) Provecho, ventaja. *Advantage, profit.*

GACETA. *n.f.* Periódico. *Newspaper.*

GACHO. *n.m.* Sombrero flexible. *Slouch hat.*

GACHUMBO. *n.m.* (Acad.) Cáscara leñosa y dura de varios frutos, de la que se hacen vasijas, tazas y otros ustensilios. *Hollowed-out fruit shell (used to make cups, etc.).*

GAFO. *n.m.* Despeado. *Footsore, dead-tired (from over walking).*

GALERA. *n.f.* (Acad.) Sombrero de copa redondeada, o alta y cilíndrica, y alas abarquilladas. *Top hat.*

GALERÓN. *n.m.* (Acad.) Romance vulgar que se canta en una especie de recitado. *Popular folk song.*

GALGUEAR. *v.* Sentir mucho apetito. *To be starving.* || **2.** Andar de un lado a otro buscando qué comer. *To wander about looking for food.*

GALLEGO. *n.m.* (pey.) Nombre genérico que se da a los españoles. *Spaniard, in particular immigrants (derog.).*

GALLERÍA. *n.f.* (Acad.) Gallera. *Cockpit.*

GALLERO. *adj.* (Acad.) Aficionado a las riñas de gallos. *Fond of cockfighting.* || **2.** *n.m.* Criador de gallos de riña. *Gamecock breeder.* || **3.** Persona que maneja los gallos de riña en la pelea. *Person in charge of cockfighting.*

GALLINA. *n.f.* •La GALLINA de arriba siempre ensucia la de abajo. En posición subalterna siempre se sufre. *The big fish eat the smaller ones.*

GALLINETA. *n.f.* (Acad.) Gallina de Guinea. *Guinea hen.*

GALLO. *n.m.* •GALLO de pelea. Gallo de riña. *Gamecock.* || **2.** •Haber GALLO encerrado. Haber gato encerrado. ~Aquí hay GATO encerrado. *There's something fishy about this.* || **3.** •Soltar un GALLO. Volverse chillona la voz de un adolescente. *To go squeaky (the voice of an adolescent).*

GALPÓN. *n.m.* (Acad.) Cobertizo grande con paredes o sin ellas. *Hut, shed.* || **2.** Almacén. *Store, storehouse.*

GALUCHA. *n.f.* Galope (Acad.). *Gallop, gait of a horse.*

GALUCHAR. *v.* (Acad.) Galopar. *To gallop.*

GAMBETA. *n.f.* (Acad.) En el fútbol, regate, movimiento del jugador para evitar que le arrebate el balón el contrario. *Dodge (in football).*

GAMBETEAR. *v.* Hacer **gambetas**. *To dodge (in football).*

GAMONAL. *n.m.* (Acad.) Cacique de pueblo. *Boss, chief, large landowner.*

GAMONALISMO. *n.m.* (Acad.) Caciquismo. *Exploitation of natives by large landowners.*

GANCHETE. *n.m.* •Ir de GANCHETE. Ir del brazo. *To go arm-in-arm.*

GANCHO. *n.m.* (Acad.) Horquilla para sujetar el pelo. *Hair pin.*

GANDIDO. *adj.* (Acad.) Comilón, hambrón. *Gluttonous.*

GANGOCHO. *n.m.* (Acad.) Guangoche, tela basta, especie de harpillera para embalajes, cubiertas, etc. *Burlap.*

GARAJE. *n.m.* Taller. *Garage, repair shop.*

GARAJISTA. *n.m.* Dueño o persona que cuida un garaje. *Garage owner or attendant.*

GARANDUMBA. *n.f.* (Acad.) Embarcación

grande a manera de balsa, para conducir carga siguiendo la corriente de los ríos. *Large river raft.*

GARAÑÓN. *n.m.* (Acad.) Caballo semental. *Stud horse, stallion.*

GARAPIÑA. *n.f.* (Acad.) Bebida muy refrigerante hecha de la corteza de la piña y agua con azúcar. *Drink made with fermented pineapple juice.*

GÁRGARA. *n.f.* Gargarismo, líquido para hacer gárgaras. *Liquid used for gargling.*

GARGAREAR. *v.* (Acad.) Hacer gárgaras. *To gargle.*

GARGÜERO. *n.m.* Garganta, gaznate, garguero. *Throat.*

GARRA. *n.f.* (Acad.) Pedazo de cuero endurecido y arrugado. *Dried, withered piece of leather.* || **2.** (Acad.) Desgarrones, harapos. *Rags, tatters.*

GARRAPATERO. *n.m.* Ave que se alimenta de las garrapatas del ganado. *Tick-eater (bird).*

GARRAPATICIDA. *n.f.* Sustancia química que mata las garrapatas. *Insecticide, tick-killing agent.*

GARRAPIÑADA. *n.f.* Almendras confitadas. *Caramel-coated peanuts or almonds.*

GARROCHA. *n.f.* (Dep.) Pértiga. *Vaulting pole.*

GARROCHISTA. *n.m.* Saltador con pértiga. *Pole-vaulter.*

GARÚA. *n.f.* (Acad.) Llovizna. *Drizzle, fine misty rain.*

GARUAR. *v.* (Acad.) Lloviznar. *To drizzle.*

GATAZO. *n.m.* •Dar el GATAZO. **a)** Engañar con aparencias. ~ No es de oro pero da el GATAZO. *It's not gold but it could pass for gold.* **b)** Parecer más joven de lo que en realidad es. *Not to show one's age.* ~Es cuarentona pero cuando se arregla da el GATAZO. *She's well into her forties but when she dresses up she looks pretty good (she fools you).*

GATEADO. *adj.* (Acad.) Se dice del caballo o yegua de color bayo oscuro y cebrado. *Light-colored horse with black streaks.*

GATEAR. *v.* Andar en aventurillas amorosas. *To be on the prowl.*

GAVERA. *n.f.* (Acad.) Gradilla o gálapo, molde para fabricar tejas o ladrillos. *Brick or tile-mold.*

GAVILÁN. *n.m.* (Acad.) Uñero, borde de la uña, especialmente la del dedo gordo del pie, que se clava en la carne. *Ingrown nail.*

GAVILLERO. *n.m.* Matón, salteador. *Gunman, trigger-man.*

GAZNATADA. *n.f.* (Acad.) Bofetada. *Smack, slap.*

GENTE. *adj.* (Acad.) Gente decente, bien portada. *Respectable people.* ~Es una familia muy GENTE. *They're a very decent family.* || **2.** (Acad.) Persona, individuo. *Person, individual.* ~ Había dos GENTES en el salón. *There were two persons in the hall.* ||**3.** •Ser (muy) GENTE. Ser como se debe, ser recto, irreprochable. *Kind, good.*

GERENCIAL. *adj.* Directivo, de dirección. *Managerial.*

GERENCIAR. *v.* (com.) Dirigir. *To manage, be the manager of.*

GIRO. *adj.* (Acad.) Aplícase al gallo de color oscuro que tiene amarillas o, a veces, plateadas las plumas del cuello y de las alas. *Streaked with yellow (a cock's plumage).* || **2.** (Acad.) Aplícase también al gallo matizado de blanco y negro. *Streaked with black and white (a cock's plumage).*

GLORIADO. *n.m.* (Acad.) Especie de ponche hecho con aguardiente. *Hot punch.*

GODO. *n.m.* (pey.) Español. *Spaniard (derog.)*

GOFIO. *n.m.* Harina gruesa de maíz, trigo o cebada tostados. *Toasted cornmeal.* || 2. •Comer GOFIO. Ser estúpido. *To be a fool.*

GOLFITO. *n.m.* Minigolf. *Mini-golf.*

GOLPEAR. *v.* •GOLPEAR a la puerta. Llamar a la puerta. *To knock on (at) the door.* Creo que oí alguien GOLPEAR (a la puerta). *I think I heard someone knocking at the door.* || **2. -se.** Cerrarse violentamente (puerta). *To bang.*

GOLPIZA. *n.f.* Paliza. *Beating.*

GOMERO. *n.m.* (Acad.) Arbol que produce goma. *Rubber plant.* || **2.** Recolector de caucho. *Rubber planter or worker on rubber plantation.*

GORJEAR. *v.* (Acad.) Hacer burla. *To make fun of.*

GORRERO. *n.m.* Gorrón, aprovechador. *Freeloader, parasite.*

GORRO. *n.m.* •Apretarse el GORRO. Echar a correr. *To get ready to run away, prepare for flight.*

GOTA. *n.f.* •GOTA de leche. Institución de asistencia y protección a la infancia. *Child welfare clinic, welfare food center.*

GOTERAS. *n.f.* (Acad.) Afueras, contornos, alrededores. *Outskirts.*

GOTERO. *n.m.* (Acad.) Cuentagotas. *Dropper.*

GRADIENTE. *n.m.* (Acad.) Pendiente, declive. *Slope, gradient.*

GRADO. *n.m.* •A tal GRADO. En tal GRADO. *To such a degree.*

GRAJO. *n.m.* (Acad.) Olor desagradable que se desprende del sudor. *Body odor.*

GRAMILLA. *n.f.* (Acad.) Césped, hierba menuda y túpida que cubre el suelo. *Grass, lawn, turf.*

GRANDE. *adj.* Niño, chico (en edad). *Older child.* ~Los más GRANDES pueden ir solos. *The older ones can go on their own.* ~Ya eres GRANDE y puedes comer solo. *You're a big boy now and you can feed yourself.* || **2.** Mayor. *Grown up.* ~Mis hijos ya son GRANDES. *My children are all grown up now.*

GRASOSO. *adj.* Grasiento. *Greasy.*

GRATIFICADOR. *adj.* Gratificante. *Rewarding, gratifying, pleasurable, satisfying.*

GRATO. *adj.* Agradecido. *Grateful.*

GREMIAL. *adj.* Sindical. *Pertaining to a labor union.* || **2.** Sindicato. *Labor union.*

GREÑA. *n.f.* •Agarrarse de las GREÑAS. Andar a la GREÑA. *To pull each other's hair, to have a heated argument.*

GRINGADA. *n.f.* Conjunto de gringos. *All gringos collectively.* || **2.** Acción típica de los gringos. *Typical thing a gringo or foreigner does.*

GRINGO. *n.m.* (Acad.) Norteamericano de los Estados Unidos. *Yank, yankee.* || **2.** Extranjero. *Foreigner from a non-Spanish speaking country.* || **3.** •Hablar en GRINGO. Decir tonterías, estupideces, disparates. *To talk nonsense.* || **4.** •Hacerse el GRINGO. Hacerse el tonto. *To play dumb.*

GRITO. *n.m.* Proclamación. *Proclamation.* ~El GRITO de independencia. *The proclamation of independence.* ~El GRITO de Dolores. *The proclamation of Mexican independence (1810).*

GRULLO. *n.m.* Peso, moneda. *Peso, dollar.*

GUA. *interj.* Exclamación que expresa temor, admiración, sorpresa o desdén. *Oh dear! (preocupation), well! (surprise), Get away! (Scorn).*

GUACA. *n.f.* (Acad.) Tesoro escondido o enterrado. *Buried treasure.* || **2.** Sepultura de los antiguos indios. *Tomb, funeral mound.* || **3.** Hucha, alcancía. *Piggy bank.*

GUACAL. *n.m.* (Acad.) Especie de cesta o jaula formada de varilla de madera, que se utiliza para el transporte de loza, cristal, frutas, etc. *Portable crate (generally carried on the back).*

GUACHIMÁN. *n.m.* (Acad.) Rondín, vigilante, guardián. *Watchman, guard.*

GUACHO. *adj.* (Acad.) Dícese de la cría que ha perdido la madre. *Motherless (animal).* || **2.** Dícese del animal sin dueño. *Stray, abandoned (animal).* || **3.** *n.m.* (Acad.) Huérfano, demadrado, expósito. *Orphan, foundling.* || **4.** Niño abandonado. *Abandoned, homeless child.* || **5.** Se dice del objeto que queda sin pareja. *Odd one (of a pair).* ~Guante GUACHO. *An odd glove.* || **6.** Solitario. *Lonely, forlorn.*

GUACO. *n.m.* (Acad.) Objeto de cerámica u otra materia que se encuentra en las guacas o sepulcros de los indios. *Ceramic vessel found in Indian burial grounds.*

GUAGUA. *n.f.* (Acad.) Rorro, niño de teta. *Baby.*

GUAICO. *n.m.* Hondonada. *Hollow, dip.*

GUANACO. *adj.* (Acad.) Tonto, simple. *Dumb.*

GUANO. *n.m.* (Acad.) Estiércol. *Manure, fertilizer.*

GUANTEAR. *v.* (Acad.) Dar guantadas, abofetar. *To smack, slap.*

GUANTÓN. *n.m.* Guantada, guantazo. *Slap, hit, blow.*

GUAPO. *adj.* Valiente. *Bold, brave, daring, courageous, gutsy.* || **2.** *n.m.* Machote. *Tough guy.*

GUAQUEAR. *v.* Buscar **guacas** o cementerios indígenas precolombianos en procura de objetos arqueologicamente valiosos. *To go in search of buried treasures or ancient Indian pottery.*

GUAQUERO. *n.m.* Buscador de **guacas**. *Person who digs for ancient Indian pottery.*

GUARACA. *n.f.* Honda, zurriaco. *Sling (for hurling missiles).*

GUARANDINGA. *n.f.* Cosa, cuestion, asunto, etc. (sustituyendo al nombre concreto de una persona o cosa). *Business, thing, thingamagig, whatitsname.* ~ ¿Qué GUARANDINGA es ésa que me dijiste? *What's that business you were telling me about?* || **2.** Enredo, problema. *Trouble.* ~ No sigas buscando GUARANDINGAS con esa gente. *Stop looking for trouble with those people.*

GUARANGO. *adj.* (Acad.) Incivil, mal educado, descarado. *Rude, uncouth, ill-bred.*

GUARAPO. *n.m.* (Acad.) Jugo de la caña dulce exprimida, que por vaporización produce el azúcar. *Sugar-cane liquor.*

GUARDAVALLAS. *n.f.* Portero. *Goalkeeper.*

GUASANGA. *n.f.* (Acad.) Bulla, algazara, barahunda. *Noise, din, uproar, hullabaloo.*

GUASCA. *n.f.* (Acad.) Ramal de cuero, cuerdo o soga, que sirve de rienda o látigo y para otros usos. *Leather strap, rawhide thong.* || **2.** •Dar GUASCAS. Azotar. *To whip, flog.*

GUASO. *adj.* Tosco, grosero, incivil. *Rude, coarse, vulgar.*

GUAYABA. *n.f.* (Acad.) Mentira, embuste. *Fib, lie.* || **2.** Tobillo. *Ankle.*

GUAYABERA. *n.f.* Blusa de tela muy liviana que usan los hombres. *Loose-fitting men's shirt.*

GUAYABERO. *n.m.* Mentiroso. *Liar.*

GUAYACA. *n.f.* Bolsa, talega. *Bag, goatskin bag.*

GUINEO. *n.m.* Nombre genérico de plátanos o bananas. *Banana.*

GURRUMINA. *n.f.* Molestia, cansera. *Bother, nuisance.*

GUSTAR. *v.* •GUSTAR de. Desear. ~GUSTAN de tomar algo? ¿Desea tomar algo? *Would you like something to drink?*

HABLADAS. *n.f.* Fanfarronada. *Bragging, boasting.*

HABLADERA. *v.* Habladuría. *Nasty, sarcastic remark.* || **2.** Rumor. *Rumor.*

HACENDADO. *n.m.* Estanciero, persona de campo que tiene hacienda, especialmente cuando se dedica a la cría de ganado. *Rancher, cattle dealer.*

HACER. *v.* Urinar. *Urinate, go to the bathroom.* ~ ¿HICISTE? *Did you go to the bathroom?* || **2.** •HACER de cuerpo (vientre). Evacuar el vientre. *To move one's bowels.* || **3.** HACER la mañanita. Desayunar con una copa pequeña de aguardiente. *To have a shot of liquor for breakfast.* || **4.** HACER compañía para jugar. *To pair up (in games).* || **5.** •No le HACE. No importa. *It doesn't matter.* || **6.** •HACE sed, sueño. Tengo sed, sueño. *I'm thirsty, sleepy.* || **7. -se.** Pasarle a. *To happen to.* ~No sé qué se habrá HECHO María. *I wonder what happened to María.* || **8.** •HACERSE la chanchita muerta o HACERSE el chancho rengo. Hacerse el bobo. *To pretend not to notice, to play dumb.* || **9.** •HACERSE a una cosa. Acostumbrarse a una cosa. *To get accustomed to something.* || **10.** •HACER mal. Sentarle mal algo a alguien. *To disagree with, to indispose.* ~Las gambas (camarones) que comí ayer me HICIERON mal. *The shrimps I had last night did not agree with me.* || **11.** •Se me HACE que. Me parece que. *I think that, I get the impression that.* || **12.** •HACERSE de. Adquirir. *To acquire.* ~Se HICIERON de mucho dinero. *They became wealthy.* ~Se HICIERON de gran fama. *They became famous.*

HACHAZO. *n.m.* Herida de gran tamaño producida por el golpe de un instrumento cortante (hacha, chuchillo, etc.). *Gash, open wound.*

HACHERO. *n.m.* Hachador. *Woodman, lumberjack.*

HACIENDA. *n.f.* Propriedad rural de gran extensión dedicada a la agricultura o a la ganadería. *County estate, large farm.*

HALAR. *v.* (Acad.) Tirar hacia sí de una cosa. *To pull.*

HALÓN. *n.m.* (Acad.) Tirón, acción y efecto de **halar**. *Pull, tug, yank.*

HAMACAR. *v.* (Acad.) Mecer. *To rock, swing.*

HAMAQUEAR. *v.* (Acad.) Mecer, columpiar, especialmente en hamaca. *To swing, rock.*

HAMBREADO. *adj.* Hambriento. *Hungry, starving.*

HARAS. *n.m.* Caballeriza, yeguada. *Stud farm.*

HARNEAR. *v.* Cribar, cerner. *To sieve, sift, screen.*

HARTO. *adv.* Sumamente, muy. *Very, extremely.* ~ Es un trabajo HARTO difícil. *It's a very difficult job.* || **2.** Mucho. *Much.* ~Esta película es HARTO mejor. *This movie is much better.* || **3.** *Pron.* Mucho. *Much.* ~Tenía HARTO trabajo que hacer. *He had a lot of work to do.* || **4.** Muchos. *Many.* ~¿Tienes amigos allí? -¡Sí, HARTOS!. *Do you have friends there? - yes, many.*

HATO. *n.m.* (Acad.) Hacienda de campo destinada a toda clase de ganado, y principalmente del mayor. *Cattle ranch.*

HECHIZO. *adj.* Fabricado en el país y a mano. *Home-made.*

HECHOR. *adj.* Garañón. Se dice en especial del burro. *Stud donkey, stallion jackass.*

HELADERO. *n.m.* Persona que vende helados. *Ice-cream vendor.*

HEMBRAJE. *n.m.* (Acad.) Conjunto de las hembras de una ganado. *Female stock (on cattle farm).*

HENDIJA. *n.f.* Rendija. *Spit, crack, device, slit.*

HENDIR. *v.* Hendir. *Cleave, split.*

HERMOSO. *adj.* Robusto, saludable. *Healthy, robust (said of children and youths).*

HERRETE. *n.m.* Hierro de marcar. *Branding iron.*

HERVIDO. *n.m.* (Acad.) Cocido u olla. *Stew.*

HICO. *n.m.* (Acad.) Cada una de las cuerdas que sostienen la hamaca. *Hammock clew (cord supporting hammock).* ‖ **2.** Cuerda, soga. *Cord.*

HIERRA. *n.f.* (Acad.) Acción de marcar con el hierro los ganados. *Branding.* ‖ **2.** (Acad.) Temporada en que se marca el ganado. *Branding period.* ‖ **3.** (Acad.) Fiesta que se celebra con tal motivo. *Branding celebration.*

HIERRE. *n.m.* (Acad.) Acción y efecto de marcar los ganados con el hierro. *Branding.*

HIJO. *n.m.* •Hijo de tigre sale pintado. *He's just like his mother (father).* ‖ **2.** •Hacerle a uno un hijo macho. Causarle a uno daño. *To do someone harm.*

HIJUELA. *n.f.* (Acad.) Fundo rústico que se forma de la división de otro mayor.

HILACHENTO. *adj.* Andrajoso. *Ragged, tattered.*

HILACHUDO. *adj.* (Acad.) Que tiene muchas hilachas. *Ragged, tattered, frayed.*

HILO. *n.m.* •Al hilo. Uno tras otro, seguido. *In a row.* ~Ganó tres partidos al hilo. Ganó tres partidos seguidos. *He won three games in a row.*

HISOPO. *n.m.* Brocha grande para blanquear paredes. *Paintbrush.*

HISTORIA. *n.f.* •Historia clínica. Historial clínico. *Medical record.* ‖ **2.** Embrollo, confusión. *Mix-up, messy business.*

HISTORIAR. *v.* (Acad.) Complicar, confundir, enmarañar. *To confound, complicate, confuse.*

HIT. *n.m.* Gran éxito (libro, canción, etc.). *Hit, popular success (of a book, play, song).*

HOBBY. *n.m.* Pasatiempo. *Hobby, pastime.*

HOCICÓN. *m.n.* Hablador, cuentista, chismoso. *Blabbermouth, big mouth.*

HOJALDA. *n.f.* Hojaldre. *Puff-pastry, flaky pastry.*

HOMBREAR. *v.* Ayudar, proteger. *To help, lend a hand.*

HOMENAJEAR. *v.* Agasajar, festejar. *To pay homage to someone with a banquet or a reception.*

HONGO. *n.m.* •Aburrise como un hongo. Aburrirse como una ostra. *To get bored stiff.*

HORA. *n.f.* •Hora pico. Hora punta. *Peak hour, rush hour.*

HORARIO. *n.m.* •Horario corrido. Horario intensivo. *Continuous working day (with no break for lunch).* ‖ **2.** •Llegar a horario (trenes, etc.). Llegar a la hora. *To arrive on time, be on schedule.*

HORCÓN. *n.m.* (Acad.) Madero vertical que en las casas rústicas sirve, a modo de columna, para sostener vigas o aleros de tejado. *Wooden post, prop, support.*

HORERO. *n.m.* Horario del reloj. *Hour hand (of the clock).*

HORMIGUILLAR. *v.* Revolver el mineral argentífero pulverizado con el magistral y la sal común para beneficiarlo. *To mix silver ore and salt.*

HORMIGUILLO. *n.m.* (Acad.) Movimiento que producen las reacciones entre el mineral y los ingredientes incorporados para el beneficio por almagamación. *Reaction between silver ore and a mixture of ferrous oxide and copper sulfate (in silver processing).*

HORNO. *n.m.* •Pollo al horno. Pollo asado. *Roast chicken.*

HORQUETA. *n.f.* (Acad.) Lugar donde se bifurca un camino. *Fork (road).* ‖ **2.** (Acad.) Parte donde el curso de un río o arroyo forma ángulo agudo, y terreno que este com-

prende. *Sharp turn (in river); fork of land.* ||
3. (Acad.) Parte del árbol donde se juntan
formando ángulo agudo el tronco y una rama
medianamente gruesa. *Fork (tree).*

HORRAR. *v.* (Acad.) Hablando de yeguas,
vacas, etc., malográrseles las crías. *To abort.*
|| **2.** (Acad.) Ahorrar. *To save.*

HOSPITALIZARSE. *v.* Acogerse a un hospital. *To go to the hospital.*

HOSTIGAR. *v.* (Acad.) Ser empalagoso un
alimento o bebida. *To surfeit, cloy.*

HOSTIGOSO. *v.* (Acad.) Empalagoso.
Sickly, cloying. || **2.** (Acad.) Fastidioso.
Annoying, tedious, irritating.

HOTELERÍA. *n.f.* Hostelería. *Inn, hostelry.*

HOYA. *n.f.* Cuenca de un río y el territorio
de esa cuenca. *River basin.*

HOYITO. *n.m.* Hoyuelo de la barba o de
las mejillas. *Dimple.*

HUASCA. *n.f.* (Acad.) Guasca. *Leather
strap; whip.* || **2.** Arandela. *Washer.*

HUERO. *adj.* Podrido, corrumpido (huevos). *Rotten (eggs).*

HUERTERO. Hortelano. *One who owns or
tends an orchard.*

HUESILLO. *n.m.* (Acad.) Durazno secado
al sol. *Dried peach.*

HUEVADA. *n.f.* Conjunto de huevos que un
ave está empollando. *Nest of eggs.*

HUEVO. *n.m.* •Costar una cosa un HUEVO.
Costar una cosa un ojo de la cara. *To cost an
arm and a leg.*

HUEVÓN. *ajd.* Lento, tardo, bobalicón, in-
genuo. *Stupid, simple-minded.*

HULERO. *n.m.* (Acad.) Trabajador que recoge el hule o goma elástica. *Rubber tapper,
rubber gatherer.*

HUMANARSE. *v.* Rebajarse, condens-
cender. *To condescend.*

HUMEAR. *v.* (Acad.) Fumigar. *To fumigate.*

HUMITA. *n.f.* (Acad.) Comido criolla hecha con pasta de maíz o granos de choclo
triturados, a la que se agrega una fritura de
cebollas, tomate y ají colorado molido. Se
sirve en pequeños envoltorios de chala, en
empanadas o en pote como un guiso.
Flavored corn paste wrapped in corn leaves.

HUMITERO. *n.m.* Persona que hace o vende **humitas.** *Humita vendor o maker.*

HUMO. *n.m.* •Hacerse HUMO. *To make
oneself scarce.* || **2.** •Irsele a HUMO a alguien.
Acometer de imprevisto a una persona. *To
jump someone.*

HURGÓN. adj. Se dice de la persona que
acostumbra **hurguetear**. *Said of the person
who likes to meddle in other people's affairs.*

HURGUETEAR. *v.* (Acad.) Hurgar, escu-
driñar, huronear. *To rummage through, pry
into, poke one's nose into.*

HUYÓN. *adj.* Que huye fácilmente, cobar-
de. *Coward.*

I

IDEÁTICO. *adj.* (Acad.) Venático, maniático. *Eccentric, odd, capricious, whimsical.* ~Es muy IDEÁTICO. *He's full of strange ideas.*

IDO. *adj.* Despistado, distraído. *Absent-minded.*

IGLESERIERO. *adj.* Se dice de quien frecuenta mucho las iglesías, rata de sacristía. *Church-going.*

IGLESIA. *n.f.* •Casarse por IGLESIA. *To have a church wedding.*

IGUAL. *adv.* De toda forma. *All the same.* ~IGUAL no puedo ir mañana. *All the same I can't go tomorrow.* ~IGUAL no tenemos dinero. *It doesn't really matter since we don't have the money.*

IGUALITO. *adj.* Idéntico. *Exactly the same, identical.* ~Los dos están IGUALITOS. *These two are identical.*

IMBORNAL. *n.m.* •Irse por los IMBORNALES. Irse por los cerros de Úbeda. *To go off at a tangent, wander, digress (in a conversation).*

IMPACTADO. *adj.* Atónito, pasmado, anonadado. *Stunned, shocked.* ~Quedó IMPACTADO por las noticias. *He was stunned by the news.*

IMPACTANTE. *adj.* Que impacta. *Shocking (news), powerful (book, image), stunning, impressive (program, movie, etc.), crushing (defeat).*

IMPAGO. *adj.* (Acad.) Dícese de la persona a quien no se le ha pagado. *Unpaid, still to be paid (person).* || **2.** Se dice de la cuenta no pagada. *Unpaid, outstanding (debt, taxes).* || **3.** Hecho de no pagar lo que se debe. *Defaulting.* || **4.** Omisión del pago de la deuda debida y vencida. *Non-payment, default.*

IMPAVIDEZ. *n.m.* Descaro, frescura. *Impertinence, insolence.*

IMPÁVIDO. *adj.* Descarado, fresco, insolente. *Sassy, insolent, fresh.*

IMPLEMENTO. *n.m.* Herramienta, equipo. *Tool, implement.* ~IMPLEMENTOS deportivos. *Sport equipment.*

IMPLICANCIA. *n.f.* (Acad.) Consecuencia, secuela. *Implication.*

IMPONENCIA. *n.f.* (Acad.) Calidad de imponente, grandeza, majestad. *Imposing character, impressiveness, grandeur.* ~La IMPONENCIA de esta cadena de montañas. *The grandeur of that mountain range.*

IMPOSIBLE. *adj.* Desaseado. *Slovenly, dirty.* || **2.** Repugnante. *Repulsive.*

INACTUAL. *adj.* Falto de vigencia o de valor en la actualidad. *Lacking present validity, old-fashioned, out-of-date.*

INCÁSICO. *adj.* Incaico. *Inca (used as adjective).*

INCONDICIONAL. *adj.* Servil. *Servile, fawning.* || **2.** *n.m.* Adulador. *Toady, yes-man.*

INCONDICIONALISMO. *n.m.* Servilismo. *Toadyism, servility.*

INCONOCIBLE. *adj.* Cambiado, desconocido. *Unrecognizable.*

INCUMPLIDO. *adj.* Informal, que no cumple con sus obligaciones. *Unreliable.*

INCUMPLIR. *v.* No cumplir, dejar de cumplir. *To break (contract), fail to keep (promise, appointment).*

INCURSIONAR. *v.* (Acad.) Hablando de un escritor o de un artista, hacer una obra de género distinto del que cultiva habitualmente. *To make incursions into, broach a subject* ~Aunque INCURSIONÓ algunas veces en la novela, fue sobre todo un ensayista. *Although he made various incursionary attempts into the novel, he was primarily an essayist.*

INDIADA. *n.f.* Acción propia de indios. *Typically Indian thing to do.*

INDÍGENA. *adj.* Indio. *Indian.* || **2.** *m.m.* Indian. *Indian.*

INDIGESTARSE. *v.* Preocuparse, turbarse. *To get worried, to get alarmed.*

INDIO. *n.m.* (Acad.) •Subírsele a uno el IN-DIO. Montar en cólera. *To get out of hand, fly off the handle.*

INFALTABLE. *adj.* Que no falta o que no puede faltar. *Not to be missed.*

INFLADOR. *n.m.* Bomba (para inflar las ruedas de una bicicleta). *Bicycle pump.*

INFORMAL. *adj.* •Economía INFORMAL. Economía sumergida. *Black, underground economy.*

INFRASCRITO. *n.m.* Voz con que una persona que habla ante un público se refiere a sí mismo. *The present speaker, yours truly.*

INFUNDIA. *n.f.* Enjundia. *Fat.*

INGENIERO. *n.m.* Licenciado. *Graduate.* ~El INGENIERO Pérez. *Dr. Pérez.*

INGRESAR. *v.* Entrar, introducirse. *To gain entrance to, break into.* ~Los ladrones INGRE-SARON a su casa. *The thieves broke into his house.*

INGRESO. *n.m.* Entrada. *Entrance, entry.* ~Fue difícil el INGRESO al estadio. *Access to the stadium was difficult.*

ÍNGRIMO. *adj.* (Acad.) Solitario, abandonado, sin compañía. *All alone, all by one's self.* || **2.** Desierto (lugar). *Lonely, deserted, solitary.*

INOFICIOSO. *adj.* Inútil. *Useless.*

INQUILINATO. *n.m.* (Acad.) Casa de vecindad. *Tenement, tenement house.*

INSTALAR. *v.* Crear, establecer (comisión). *To set up, establish (committee).*

INSULTADA. *n.f.* (Acad.) Insulto o serie de insultos. *Insult, string of insults.*

INSUMOS. *n.m.* Bienes consumibles. *Consumption, consumables, supplies.*

INTEGRAR. *v.* Pagar una cantidad que se debe. *To hand over, pay up.*

INTENCIONALMENTE. *adv.* Intencionadamente. *Intentionally.*

INTERINATO. *n.m.* Interinidad, tiempo que dura el desempeño interino de un cargo. *Period of temporary employment.* || **2.** Cargo o empleo interino. *Temporary post of position.*

INTERIOR. *n.m.* (Acad.) En algunos países de América, todo lo que en ellos no es la capital o las ciudades principales. *Provinces.* ~En el INTERIOR. *In the provinces, away from the capital (or the main cities).*

INTERIORIZAR. *v.* Informar. *To imform.* || **2.** Informarse. *To familiarize oneself with.*

INTERREGNO. *n.m.* Intérvalo. *Interval, intervening period.* || **2.** •En el INTERREGNO. Entre tanto. *In the meantime.*

INTERTANTO. *n.m.* •En el INTERTANTO. Mientras tanto. *In the meantime.*

INTERVENCIÓN. *n.f.* Acción y efecto de INTERVENIR. *Government takeover.*

INTERVENIR. *v.* Interponer el gobierno su autoridad. *To take control of, to install government appointees in.*

INTRIGAR. *v.* Llevar a cabo una acción de modo que el desenlace sea una sorpresa. *To conduct in a surprising way.* || **2.** -se. Quedar intrigado. *To be intrigued, be puzzled.*

INUNDADIZO. *adj.* Se dice de terrenos que suelen inundarse. *Liable to flooding.*

INVERNADA. *n.f.* (Acad.) Invernadero para el ganado. *Winter pasture (for cattle).*

INVERNAR. *v.* Pastorear el ganado en los invernaderos. *To pasture in winter pasture.*

INVOLUCRAR. *v.* Conllevar. *Involve.* ~Este nuevo negocio INVOLUCRA la inversión de mucho dinero. *The new venture involve a substantial monetary investment.*

INYECTADO. *adj.* Encarnizado (hablando de los ojos). *Blood-shot (eyes).*

IR. *v.* •Que le VAYA bien. Adios, hasta luego. *Goodbye.*

IRIS. *n.m.* •Hacer un IRIS. Guiñar el ojo. *To wink.*

IRRESTRICTO. *adj.* Ilimitado. *Unrestricted, unlimited, unconditional.*

ITEMIZAR. *v.* Detallar, enumerar. *To itemize.*

IZADA. *n.f.* Acción de izar. *Raising, lifting.*

J

JABA. *n.f.* Cesto o jaula de varillas para el envase y transporte de objetos. *Light cage-like crate (used for transporting fragile objects).* || **2.** Haba. *Bean.*

JABÓN. *n.m.* Susto, miedo. *Fright, scare.*

JABONADA. *n.f.* Jabonadura. *Soaping, lathering.* || **2.** Reprimenda. *Dressing down, reprimend.*

JACARÉ. *n.m.* Caimán. *Alligator.*

JAGÜEL (variante de **jagüey**).

JAGÜEY. *n.m.* (Acad.) Balza, pozo o zanja llena de agua, artificialmente, ya por filtraciones naturales del terreno. *Large pool or basin.*

JAHUEY (variante de **jagüey**).

JAI. *n.f.* Alta sociedad. *High society.* ~Se codea con la JAI. *She rubs shoulders with the rich and the famous.*

JAIBA. *n.f.* Cangrejo. *Crab, crayfish.*

JALADO. *adj.* Borracho. *Tight.*

JALADOR. *n.m.* Tirador (puerta). *Door-handle.*

JALAR. *v.* (Acad.) Andar o correr muy de prisa. *To hurry up, get a move on.* || **2.** Tirar de, atraer hacia sí, arrastrar. *Tu pull, haul.* ~Todos tenemos que JALAR parejo. *We all have to pull together.* || **3. -se.** Emborracharse. *To get drunk.* || **4.** Largarse, irse. *Go off, hurry up, clear out.* ~JÁLALE, que van a cerrar. *Get a move on, they're closing.* || **5.** Ir. *To go.* ~Estaba tan oscuro que no sabía por donde JALAR. *It was so dark, I didn't know which way to go.*

JALÓN. *n.m.* (Acad.) Tirón. *Pull, tug, yank.* || **2.** Trecho, jornada. *Distance, stretch.*

JARDÍN. *n.m.* •JARDÍN infantil. Jardín de infancia. *Kindergarten, nursery school.*

JARDINAJE. *n.m.* Arte y oficio del jardinero. *Gardening.*

JARRADA. *n.f.* Lo que cabe en una jarra. *Jugful.*

JARRO. *n.m.* Tazón. *Mug, beer mug, stein.* || **2.** •A boca de JARRO. A quemarropa. *At point-blank range.*

JEBE. *n.m.* (Acad.) Hevea (planta del caucho). *Rubber plant.*

JEBERO. *n.m.* Cauchero. *Rubber plantation worker.*

JEDENTINA. *n.f.* Hedor, hediondez. *Foul smell.*

JEDER. *v.* Heder. *To reek, stink.*

JEFE. *n.m.* ¡Sí, (mi) JEFE!. ¡Si, señor! *Yes sir, boss!*

JEREMIQUEAR. *v.* (Acad.) Lloriquear, gimotear. *To whine, moan, snivel, whimper.*

JERGA. *n.f.* Manta de caballo. *Horse blanket.*

JERINGA. *n.f.* (Acad.) Molestia, pejiguera, importunación. *Annoyance, nuisance.*

JERINGAR. *v.* Molestar, enfadar. *To bug, pester.*

JERINGÓN. *adj.* Fastidioso, jeringador. *Annoying.* || **2.** *n.m.* Persona fastidiosa, molesta. *Pest, nuisance.*

JERINGUEAR (variante de **jeringar**).

JERÓNIMO. *n..m.* •Sin GERÓNIMO de duda. *Without the shadow of a doubt.*

JERSEY. *n..* Tejido de punto. *Jersey (textile).*

JESUITISMO. *n.m.* Comportamiento hipócrita y disimulado. *Hypocritical conduct.*

JETA. *n.f.* Boca. *Mouth, trap (coll.).* ~¡Cállese la JETA! *Shut your trap!*

JETÓN. *adj.* De boca grande. *Big-mouthed.* || **2.** De labios gruesos. *Thick-lipped.*

JÍBARO. *adj.*(Acad.) Campesino, silvestre. Dícese de las personas, los animales, las costumbres, las prendas de vestir y algunas otras cosas. *Rural, rustic.*

JÍCARA. *n.f.* (Acad.) Vasija pequeña de madera, ordinariamente hecha de la corteza del fruto de la güira, y usado como la loza del mismo nombre en España. *Gourd cup or bowl (made from a calabash gourd).*

JINETA. *n.f.* (Acad.) Mujer que monta a caballo. *Horsewoman, rider.*

JINETEAR. *v.* (Acad.) Domar caballos cerriles. *To break in a horse.*

JIPATO. *adj.* Pálido, anémico. *Pale, wan.*

JODA. *n.f.* Fastidio, molestia. *Annoyance, bother, drag (coll.).* || **2.** Broma. *Joke, joking.* ~Te lo digo en JODA. *I'm just joking.* || **3.** Juerga. *Partying, reveling.* ~Está de JODA. *He's in a reveling mood.*

JODIDO. *adj.* De trato difícil, exigente. *Demanding, tough (coll.).* || **2.** Egoísta. *Selfish.*

JODIENDA. *n.f.* Molestia, fastidio. *Nuisance.*

JODÓN. *adj.* Fastidioso, pesado. *Annoying, irksone, tedious.*

JOL. *n.m.* Vestíbulo. *Hall, lobby.*

JONRÓN. *n.m.* Cuadrangular. *Home run.*

JORA. *n.f.* (Acad.) Maíz germinado para hacer chicha. *The type of corn used for making chicha.*

JOROBÓN. *adj.* Fastidioso. *Annoying.*

JOTA. *n.f.* (Acad.) Especie de sandalia, ojota. *Indian sandal.*

JOYERO. *n.m.* Orfebre. *Goldsmith.*

JUDAS. *n.m.* Mirilla. *Peephole.*

JUEGO. *n.m.* Aparato (en un parque de diversiónes o atracciones). *Fairground attraction, ride.*

JUGAR. *v.* •JUGAR a. Jugar (tenis, golf, póquer). *To play (tennis, golf, poker).* || **2.** Moverse una cosa dentro de otra por no estar muy ajustada. *To have room to move about.*

JULEPE. *n.m.* (Acad.) Susto, miedo. *Fright, scare.* || **2.** Ajetreo, trabajo. *Work, strenuous activity, hustle and bustle.*

JUMADO. *ajd.* Borracho. *Drunk.*

JUMARSE. *v.* (Acad.) Embriagarse, emborracharse. *To get plastered.*

JUMO (variante de **jumado**).

JUNTAR. *v.* Coleccionar. *To collect (stamps, coins).*

JUNTO. *adv.* •JUNTO suyo. Junto a él. *Together with him.*

LABERINTO. *n.m.* Griterío. *Shouting, uproar.* || **2.** Ruido, escándalo. *Row, racket.*

LABIOSO. *adj.* Hablador. *Talkative.* || **2.** Lisonjero, adulador. *Flattering.* || **3.** Ladino, taimado. *Sly.* || **4.** Persuasivo. *Persuasive.*

LABORISMO. *n.m.* Sistema social o de partido político que se apoya en los obreros. *Labor movement, worker's movement.* || **2.** Obrerismo (se aplica casi exclusivamente al partido político inglés llamado *Labour Party*). *Labour Party.*

LACEADOR. *n.m.* Peón encargado de echar el lazo a las reses y caballos. *Lasso er (of animals).*

LACIAR. *v.* Poner lacio el pelo rizoso. *To uncurl, straighten (hair).*

LACRA. *n.f.* Úlcera, llaga. *Sore, ulcer.* || **2.** Vicio físico o moral que marca a quien lo tiene. *Blot, blemish.* La prostitución es una LACRA social. *Prostitution is a cancer on society.*

LACRE. *adj.* (Acad.) De color rojo. *Bright red.*

LADILLA. *n.f.* Persona molesta, pesada. *Bore, pain, pest.*

LADINO. *n.m.* (Acad.) Mestizo que sólo habla español. *Spanish-speaking Indian.* ||**2.** *adj.* Mestizo. *Spanish-speaking (Indian).*

LADRILLERA (variante de **ladrillería**).

LADRILLERÍA. *n.f.* Ladrillar. *Brickworks, place where bricks are made.*

LADRILLO. *n.m.* •De LADRILLO a la vista. Fachada a ladrillo visto. *Brick facade.*

LAICIDAD. *n.f.* Laicismo. *Laicism (doctrine of the independence of the State, etc. from interference).*

LALO. *n.m.* Forma familial de Eduardo.

Nickname for Eduardo.

LAMA. *n.f.* (Acad.) Musgo, planta briofita. *Moss.* || **2.** (Acad.) Moho, cardenillo. *Mold.*

LAMBEPLATOS. *n.m.* Pordiosero, servil. *Bootlicker.* || **2.** Pobre diablo. *Poor wretch.*

LAMBER. *v.* (Acad.) Lamer. *To lick.* || **2.** Adular servilmente. *To suck up to (coll.).*

LAMBETEAR. *v.* Lamer. *To lick.* || **2.** Lamer algo insistentemente y con delectación. *To lick greedily, noisily.* || **3.** Adular. *To suck up to, flatter.*

LAMBIDO. *adj.* Sinvergüenza, descarado. *Brazen, shameless.* || **2.** Presumido. *Cocky, conceited.*

LAMBISCONEAR (variante de **lambisquear**).

LAMBISCONERÍA. *n.f.* Gula. *Greediness, gluttony.* || **2.** Adulación. *Flattering, fawning.* || **3.** Presunción. *Cockiness.*

LAMBISQUEAR. *v.* Lamer aprisa y con ansia. *To lick avidly.*

LAMENTABLEMENTE. *adv.* Desafortunadamente. *Unfortunately.*

LAMIDA. *n.f.* Lamedura. *Lick.*

LAMPA. *n.f.* (Acad.) Azada. *Shovel, spade.*

LANA. *n.f.* Dinero. *Dough, bread (coll.).* Tiene mucha LANA. *He's loaded.*

LANCETA. *n.f.* Aguijada. *Goad.* || **2.** Aguijón (insecto). *Sting.*

LANZA. *n.f.* Estafador. *Shark (coll.).* || **2.** (Acad.) •Ser una LANZA. Ser hábil y despejado. *To be on the ball, to be sharp.*

LANZAMIENTO. *n.m.* •LANZAMIENTO de bala. Lanzamiento de peso. *Shot put.*

LAPIDAR. *v.* Tallar o labrar piedras preciosas. *To work, carve (precious stones).*

LARGA. *n.f.* •Dar la(s) LARGA(s). Poner la(s) larga(s). *To put the lights on main or full beam.*

LARGAR. *v.* Lanzar, arrojar (pelota). *Throw, hurl.* || **2.** (Acad.) Seguido de palabras como bofetada, portazo, propina, etc., dar. *To give.* || **3.** •LARGARSE a. Ponerse a. *To start to.* ~Se LARGÓ a llorar. Se puso a llorar. *He started to cry.*

LARGO. *adj.* •Seguir de LARGO. No parar. *To keep on going.*

LARGUCHO. *adj.* Larguirucho. *Lanky.*

LARGURUCHO (variante de **largucho**).

LASTIMADURA. *n.f.* Herida. *Wound, injury.* || **2.** Moretón. *Bruise, graze.*

LASTIMÓN. *n.m.* Herida. *Wound, injury.*

LATA. *n.f.* Plomo, pelmazo. *Drag (coll.).*

LATEAR. *v.* Dar (la) lata. *To be a nuisance, be annoying.* || **2.** Hablar mucho y sin sustancia. *To chatter away pointlessly.* ||**3.** Acariciar. *To caress.*

LATEAZO. *n.m.* Caricia. *Petting.*

LATERÍA. *n.f.* (Acad.) Hojalatería. *Tinworks; tinsmith's workshop.*

LATERO. *n.m&f.* (Acad.) Hojalatero. *Tinsmith.*

LATIGUDO. *adj.* Correoso. *Leathery.*

LATIGUEADA. *n.f.* Azotaina. *Whipping, thrashing.*

LATIGUEAR. *v.* Azotar. *To whip, thrash.*

LATINOAMÉRICA. *n.f.* Iberoamérica (palabre preferida en España), Hispanoamérica (palabra preferida en Hispanoamérica). *Latin America.*

LAVADA. *n.f.* Lavado. *Wash.* ~Necesito darle una LAVADA a esta ropa sucia. *I need to give these soiled clothes a wash.* || **2.** Ropa de casa que se ha de lavar y que se está lavando. *Laundry.*

LAVADERO. *n.m.* (Acad.) Paraje del lecho de un río o arroyo donde se recogen arenas auríferas y se lavan allí mismo agitándolas en una batea. *Place or river bank where gold is obtained by washing gold-bearing deposits, gold-panning site.*

LAVAPLATOS. *n.m.* (Acad.) Fregadero, pila dispuesta para lavar la vajilla. *Sink.*

LAVATORIO. *n.m.* (Acad.) Jofaina, palangana. *Washbowl.* || **2.** (Acad.) Lavabo, mueble especial donde se pone la palangana. *Washstand.* || **3.** (Acad.) Lavabo, pieza de la casa dispuesta para el aseo. *Washroom.*

LAZARIENTO. *adj.* Lazarino. *Leprous.*

LECHADA. *n.f.* Acción de lechar. *Milking.*

LECHAR. *v.* Ordeñar. *To milk.*

LECHE. *n.f.* Buena suerte. *Good luck.* || **2.** Negocio productivo. *Successful business.*

LECHERA. *n.f.* Vaca lechera. *Cow.*

LECHERO. *adj.* Afortunado. *Lucky.* || **2.** Lácteo. *Dairy.* ~Productos LECHEROS. Productos lácteos. *Dairy products.*

LECHOSA. *n.f.* Papaya. *Papaya.*

LECHUDO. *adj.* Persona de mucha suerte. *Lucky.*

LEGAJAR. *v.* Formar legajos. *To file.*

LEGISLATURA. *n.f.* Congreso o asamblea legislativa. *Legislature, legislative body.*

LEGISTA. *n.m.* •Médico LEGISTA. Médico forense. *Forensic expert.* || **2.** Médico que se ocupa de los aspectos legales de la medicina. *Criminal pathologist.*

LENGUA. *n.f.* •LENGUA larga. Chismoso, hablador. *Gossip.* || **2.** •LENGUA de trapo. Chismoso, hablador. *Gossip.* || **3.** •LENGUA sucia. Hablador maldiciente. *Foul-mouthed person.*

LENGÜETA. *n.f.* Hablador, charlatán. *Chatterbox.* || **2.** Chismoso. *Gossip.*

LENGÜETEAR. *v.* Lamer. *To lick.*

LENGÜETERÍAS. *n.f.* Chismes, habladurías. *Gossip.*

LENGÜÓN. *adj.* Chismoso. *Gossiping.* || **2.** Calumniador. *Slanderer.*

LENTES. *n.m.* Gafas. *Eyeglasses.*

LEÓN. *n.m.* (Acad.) Especie de tigre de pelo leonado, puma. *Puma, cougar.*

LERDEAR. *v.* (Acad.) Tardar, hacer algo con lentitud. *To be slow in doing things.* ||**2.** (Acad.) Moverse con pesadez o torpeza.*To* *move sluggishly or awkwardly.* || **3.** (Acad.) Retardarse, llegar tarde. *To be late.*

LERDÓN. *adj.* Excesivamente lerdo. *Extremely clumsy.*

LEVANTAR. *v.* •Levantar la mesa. Quitar la mesa. *To clear the table.* || **2.** -se. Ligar con. *To pick up, have an affair with.* || **3.** Acostarse con. *To go to bed with, to score with (coll.).*

LIBERAL. *n.m.* Miembro del Partido Liberal. *Member of the Liberal Party.*

LIBERTADOR. *n.m.* •El Libertador. Simón Bolívar. *Simon Bolivar.*

LIBERTARIO. *adj.* Libertador. *Liberating.* Guerra libertaria. *War of liberation.*

LIBRANZA. *n.f.* •Libranza postal. Giro postal. *Money order.*

LIBRETISTA. *n.m.* Guionista. *Scriptwriter.*

LIBRETO. *n.m.* Guión. *Script.*

LICENCIA. *n.f.* •Licencia de manejar. Licencia de conducir. *Driver's license.*

LICITACIÓN. *n.f.* (com.) Propuesta. *Tender (bus.).* ~Se llamará a licitación para la construcción del puente. *The construction of the bridge will be put out to tender.* || **2.** Presentarse a una licitación. Presentar una propuesta. *To submit a tender.* || **3.** Ganar una licitación. Aceptarse una propuesta. *To win a contract.*

LICITAR. *v.* Llamar a concurso. *To invite tenders.* || **2.** Presentar una propuesta. *To submit a tender, to bid.*

LICORERÍA. *n.f.* Fábrica de licores. *Distillery.*

LICORERO. *n.m.* Licorista. *Distiller.*

LIENCILLO. *n.m.* Tela ordinaria de algodón. *Thick cotton fabric.*

LIGA. *n.f.* Gomita. *Rubber band.*

LIGERO. *adj.* Rápidamente. *Rapidly, swiftly.* ~No andes tan ligero. *Don't walk so rapidly.* || **2.** Pronto, sin tardanza. *Soon, immediately.* ~Vamos ligero, que se está haciendo tarde. *Let go right away, it's getting late.*

LIMATÓN. *n.m.* Madero que se coloca en

el ángulo que forman otras piezas de un techo. *Crossbeam, roofbeam.*

LIMÓN. *n.m.* Limonero. *Lemon tree.* || **2.** Pasamanos. *Handrail.*

LIMOSNEAR. *v.* Mendigar. *To beg for alms.*

LIMOSNERO. *n.m.* Mendigo. *Beggar.*

LIMPIADA. *n.f.* Limpieza. *Cleaning.*

LIMPIAR. *v.* Pegar, golpear. *To hit, beat.* || **2.** Robar, hurtar (casa). *To steal, clean out.* ~Le limpiaron la casa. *They cleaned out his house.*

LIMPIAVENTANAS. *n.m.* Líquido para limpiar las ventanas. *Window cleaner (liquid).*

LIMPIAVÍAS. *n.m.* Rastrillo delantero, quitapiedras. *Cowcatcher.*

LIMPIAVIDRIOS. *n.m.* Persona encargada de limpiar las ventanas. *Window cleaner (person).*

LIMPIO. *adj.* •Estar (quedar) en limpio. Estar pelado, tronado. *To be broke.*

LIMPITO. *adj.* Diminutivo de limpio. *Clean.*

LINDEZA. *n.f.* Amabilidad. *Niceness.* || **2.** Excelencia. *Excellence, high quality.*

LINDO. *adj.* •Este vestido de queda muy lindo. Este vestido te queda muy bonito. *This dress suits you very well.* || **2.** Magnífico. *Wonderful.* ~Fue una linda ceremonia. *It was a wonderful ceremony.* || **3.** Bueno, excelente. *Good, excellent.* ~Son lindas empanadas. *These are excellent meat pies.* ~Logró lindos asientos. *He picked out very good seats.* || **4.** Bien parecido (hombre). *Good-looking.* || **5.** *adv.* Bien. *Well, beautifully.* ~Canta muy lindo. *She sings beautifully.*

LINO. *n.m.* Linaza. *Linseed, flaxseed.*

LIPE. *n.m.* Caparrosa. *Vitriol.* || **2.** Sulfato de cobre. *Copper sulphate.*

LIQUIDAR. *v.* Destruir, inutilizar. *To destroy, ruin, make useless.* || **2.** Matar. *To kill.* ~La policía liquidó a los bandidos. *The police killed the criminals.*

LÍQUIDO. *adj.* Solo, único, exacto. *Exact,*

accurate, right, correctly measured. ~4 varas LÍQUIDAS. *Exactly 4 yards.*

LIRISMO. *n.m.* Sueño, fantasía, utopía. *Fantasy, dream, Utopian ideal.* || **2.** Manera de ser de las personas que imaginan utopías o acciones desinteresadas. *Fancifulness, dreaminess.*

LISO. *adj.* (Acad.) Desvergonzado, atrevido, insolente, respondón. *Brazen, shameless.*

LISTO. *interj.* •Y LISTO. ¡Y ya está! *And that's it!* || **2.** Muy bien, de acuerdo. *Alright, okay.*

LISURA. *n.f.* Descaro, desvergüenza. *Shamelessness, brazenness, impudence.*

LIVIANDAD. *n.f.* Ligereza, levedad, poco peso. *Lightness.*

LIVIANO. *adj.* Ligero. *Light.* ~Me gustan estas maletas porque son LIVIANAS. *I like these suitcases because they're light.* ~Necesito comprarme un vestido de tela LIVIANA para el verano. *I need to buy a light material dress for the summer.*

LIVING. *n.m.* Sala de estar. *Living-room.*

LLAMADO. *n.m.* Llamada telefónica. *Telephone call.* ~Usted tiene un LLAMADO. *There's a telephone call for you.* || **2.** Llamamiento. *Call (made to the population).*

LLAMARÓN. *n.m.* Llamarada. *Flare-up, sudden blaze.*

LLANTA. *n.f.* Neumático. *Tire.* || **2.** •LLANTA de repuesto. Rueda de recambio. *Spare tire.* || **3.** Rollo. *Spare tire (coll.).*

LLAVE. *n.m.* Grifo. *Tap, faucet.*

LLEVARSE. *v.* •LLEVARSE a uno por delante. Atropellar a uno. *To run someone over.* || **2.** Atropellar a uno en sus derechos. *To trample on someone's rights.*

LLORONA. *n.f.* Fantasma, alma en pena que, según la superstición popular, aparece por las noches en algunos lugares para pedir sufragios que la rescaten del purgatorio. *Ghost of woman said to roam the streets wailing).*

LLOVIDA. *n.f.* Lluvia. *Rain, rain shower.*

LO. *pron.* •A LO que. Tan pronto como. *As soon as.* ~A LO que me vio me saludó. *As soon as he saw me he said hello.*

LOCATARIO. *n.m.* Inquilino. *Tenant.*

LOCERÍA. *n.f.* Fábrica de loza. *China shop, crockery shop.*

LOCO. *adj.* •Ser LOCO. Estar loco. *To act crazy.* ~¡Ustedes están LOCOS!. *You must be crazy!* || **2.** •LOCO de remate (o rematado). Loco de atar. *Insane, crazy, out of one's mind.*

LOCRO. *m.n.* (Acad.) Plato de carne, patatas, maíz y otro ingredientes. *Meat and vegetable stew.*

LOGRERO. *n.m.* (Acad.) Persona que procura lucrarse por cualquier medio. *Sponger, parasite.*

LOMADA. *n.f.* Loma. *Hillock, low ridge.*

LOMBRICIENTO. *adj.* Se dice del que tiene lombrices. *Suffering from worms.*

LOMILLERÍA. *n.f.* (Acad.) Taller donde se hacen lomillos, caronas, riendas, lazos, etc. *Harness maker's.* || **2.** (Acad.) Tienda donde se venden, que suele ser en el mismo taller. *Harness shop.*

LOMILLO. *n.m.* (Acad.) Pieza del recado de montar, consistente en dos almohadas rellena de junco o de totora, afianzada en una lonja de suela, que se aplica sobre la carona. *Pads of a pack saddle.*

LOMO. *n.m.* Solomillo. *Sirloin steak.*

LONA. *n.f.* Arpillera, tela barata. *Sackcloth.*

LONCHAR. *v.* Almorzar. *To have lunch.*

LONCHERA. *n.f.* Fiambrera. *Lunch box.*

LONCHERÍA. *n.f.* Restaurante. *Restaurant.*

LONETA. *n.f.* Especie de lona que se emplea para hacer toldos, etc. *Canvas.*

LOQUEAR. *v.* Hacer payasadas. *To horse or clown around.*

LOQUERA. *n.f.* Privación de la razón, locura. *Madness.*

LORA. *n.f.* (Acad.) Loro. *Female parrot.* || **2.** (Acad.) Mujer charlatana. *Chatterbox.*

LOTE. *n.m.* Terreno. *Lot, plot.*

LOTERÍA. *n.f.* •Sacar la LOTERÍA. *To have a stroke of luck, to hit the jackpot (coll.).*

LUCIR. *v.* Aparecer, mostrarse. *To look.*

~La paciente LUCE mucho mejor hoy. *The patient looks* much *better today.* ~La catedral LUCÍA esplenderosa. *The cathedral stood out in all its splendor.*

LUEGO. *adv.* De vez en cuando. *From time to time.*

LUEGUITO. *adv.* En seguida. *Right away, immediately.*

LUJAR. *v.* (Acad.) Dar lustre al calzado. *To shine, polish (shoes).*

LUMINARIA. *n.f.* Lumbrera, persona brillante. *Genious, wiz.* || **2.** Estrella. *Celebrity, prominent figure.*

LUNA. *n.f.* •Esta con (de) LUNA. Estar de mal humor. *To be in a bad mood.*

LUNAREJO. *adj.* Persona que tiene uno o más lunares en la cara. *Spotty-faced.*

LUNES. •Hacer de San LUNES. Dejar de trabajar los lunes. *To have a long weekend.*

(hum.).

LUSTRABOTAS. *n.m.* (Acad.) Limpiabotas. *Bootblack.*

LUSTRADA. *n.f.* Acción de lustrar el calzado. *Shoe shine.*

LUSTRADOR. *n.m.* Limpiabotas. *Shoeblack, bootblack.*

LUSTRAR. *v.* Sacar brillo. *To polish, shine.* || **2. -se.** Sacar brillo a los zapatos *To polish, shine (shoes).* ~Si quieres venir conmigo vas a tener que LÚSTRARTE los zapatos. *If you wish to come with me, you will have to polish your shoes.*

LUSTRÍN. *n.m.* Cajon de limpiabotas. *Bootblack's box.* || **2.** Quiosco o cobertizo donde se lustran los zapatos. *Shoeshine stand.*

LUZ. *n.f.* •Prender la LUZ. Encender la luz. *To turn on the light.* ~No dejes la LUZ prendida. *Don't forget to turn off the light.*

M

MACACO. *adj.* Feo, deforme. *Ugly, misshapen, deformed.* || **2.** *n.m.* Nombre despectivo que dan al colono chino. *Chinese settler (derog.).*

MACANA. *n.f.* (Acad.) Garrote grueso de madera dura y pesada. *Billy club.*

MACANEAR. *v.* (Acad.) Decir desatinos o embustes. *To talk nonsense, exaggerate wildly, tell tall stories.*

MACANUDO. *adj.* (Acad.) Bueno, magnífico, extraordinario, excelente en sentido material o moral. *Excellent, wonderful, fine, fabulous, grand.*

MACETA. *n.f.* (Acad.) Dícese del caballo viejo, de cascos crecidos y que, por esa causa, anda con dificultad. *Old horse.* || **2.** Martillo grande de madera. *Large wooden hammer.*

MACHA. *n.f.* Mujer fuerte. *Mannish woman.*

MACHAJE. *n.m.* Conjunto de animales machos. *Male animals (collectively).*

MACHETAZO. *n.m.* Machete grande. *Large machete.* || **2.** Golpe que se da con el machete. *Blow or slash with a machete.*

MACHETE. *n.m.* (Acad.) Cuchillo grande de diversas formas, que sirve para desmontar, cortar la caña de azúcar y otros usos. *Machete, cane knife, big knife.*

MACHETEAR. *v.* Cortar con un machete (caña). *To cut down with a machete (sugar cane).*

MACHETERO. *n.m.* (Acad.) El que en los ingenios de azúcar corta las cañas. *Cane cutter.*

MACHOTE. *n.m.* Modelo, borrador. *Rough draft, sketch.* || **2.** Patrón. *Pattern.*

MACHUCÓN. *n.m.* Moretón. *Bruise.*

MACIZA. *n.f.* Madera prensada, aglomerado. *Chipboard.*

MACOLLO. *n.m.* (Acad.) Cada uno de los brotes de un pie vegetal. *Bunch, cluster (of flowers, roots).*

MACUCO. *n.m.* (Acad.) Muchacho grandullón. *Overgrown boy, big lad.* || **2.** Astuto, taimado. *Crafty, cunning.*

MADRE. *n.f.* •La MADRE Patria. España. *Spain.*

MADRINA. n.f. (Acad.) Yegua que sirve de guía a una piara de ganada caballar. *Lead mare.*

MADRUGAR. *v.* •MADRUGARLE a uno. Adelantarse a uno. *To get ahead of someone.* ~Iba yo mismo a contar este chiste, ¡Me MADRUGASTE!. *I was going to tell that joke myself. You beat me to it!*

MADURO. *n.m.* Especie de plátano duro. *Plantain.*

MAGNIFICAR. *v.* Ampliar. *To magnify.* || **2.** Engrandecer, exagerar (problema). *To exaggerate, blow out of proportion.*

MAGUEY. *n.m.* (Acad.) Pita (planta). *Maguey (kind of agave).*

MAGULLÓN. *n.m.* Moretón. *Bruise.*

MAICENA. *n.f.* Harina fina de maíz. *Cornstarch, corn flour.*

MAICERO. *n.m.* Persona que se dedica al cultivo o comercio del maíz. *Corn grower or vendor.* || **2.** Perteneciente o relativo al maíz. *Pertaining to corn.*

MAJADEREAR. *v.* (Acad.) Molestar, incomodar uno a otra persona. *To bother, annoy.* || **2.** Insistir con terquedad importuna en una pretensión o negativa. *To be a nuisance or a pest.*

MAL. *n.m.* Ataque de epilepsia. *Epileptic fit.*

MALA. *adj.* •MALA palabra. Palabrota. *Dirty word.* || **2.** •En las MALAS. Cuando no andan bien las cosas, en momentos difíciles. *In rough times, when things are bad.* || **3.** •Estar de MALAS. Estar desafortunado. *To be unlucky.*

MALACRIANZA. *n.f.* Descortesía. *Rudeness.*

MALAGRADECIDO. *adj.* Desagradecido, ingrato. *Ungrateful, unappreciative.*

MALAS. *adj.* •A las MALAS. Por las malas. *By force, unwillingly.*

MALCRIADEZ. *n.f.* (Acad.) Cualidad de malcriado, grosería, indecencia. *Rudeness, bad manners, ill-breeding.*

MALCRIADEZA (variante de **malcriadez**).

MALECÓN. *n.m.* Paseo marítimo. *Seafront.*

MALETA. *n.f.* Lío de ropa. *Bundle of clothes.* || **2.** *adj.* Travieso. *Naughty, mischievous.* || **3.** Bribón, perverso. *Wicked.* || **4.** Perezoso. *Lazy.* || **5.** Estúpido, inhábil. *Stupid, useless.*

MALEZA. *n.f.* (Acad.) Cualquier hierba mala. *Weed.*

MALGENIOSO. *adj.* (Acad.) De mal genio. *Bad-tempered.*

MALHAYA. *interj.* •¡MALHAYA sea! ¡Maldito sea! *Damn!*

MALOCA. *n.f.* (Acad.) Invasión de hombre blancos en tierra de indios, con pillaje y exterminio. *Raid on Indian territory.* || **2.** Ataque inesperado de los indios contra poblaciones de españoles o de otros indios, **malón.** *Indian raid.*

MALÓN. *n.m.* (Acad.) Irrupción o ataque inesperado de indios. *Indian raid.*

MALTÓN. *adj.* Animal o persona joven de desarrollo precoz. *Young child or animal.*

MALTRAÍDO. *adj.* (Acad.) Mal vestido, desaliñado. *Untidy, disheveled.*

MALVÓN. *n.m.* (Acad.) Geranio. *Geranium.*

MAMÁ. *n.f.* •MAMÁ grande. Abuela. *Grandmother.* || **2.** •MAMÁ señora. Abuela. *Grandmother.*

MAMACITA. *n.f.* Madre. *Mother.* || **2.** Mujer atractiva. *Attractive woman.* ~¡Hola, MAMACITA rica! *Hi, gorgeous!*

MAMADA. *n.f.* (Acad.) Embriaguez, borrachera. *Drunkenness.* || **2.** Ganga o ventaja conseguida a poca costa. *Cinch, bargain.* || **3.** Empleo o posición que proporciona tal ventaja. *Soft job, sinecure.*

MAMADERA. *n.f.* (Acad.) Utensilio para la lactancia artificial, biberón. *Feeding bottle, baby bottle.* || **2.** Tetilla. *Rubber nipple (of baby's bottle).*

MAMADO. *adj.* Borracho. *Drunk.*

MAMANDURRÍA. *n.f.* (Acad.). Sueldo que se disfruta sin merecerlo, sinecura, ganga permanente. *Sinecure, soft job.*

MAMARSE. *v.* Aguantar, resistir. *To bear, endure, manage (to do something).*

MAMELUCO. *n.m.* Pijama de una sola pieza para bebés o niños y que les cubre hasta los pies. *Romper-suit, all-in-one.* || **2.** Mono. *Overalls.*

MAMITA. *n.f.* Madrecita. *Mommy.*

MAMÓN. *adj.* Se dice de cualquier animal mamífero de poca edad. ~Ternero MAMÓN, chivito MAMÓN. *Yearling calf.*

MAMPUESTO. *n.m.* (Acad.) Cualquier objeto en que se apoya el arma de fuego para tomar mejor la puntería. *Support for firearms (when taking aim).*

MANA. *n.f.* (Acad.) Maná. *Manna.*

MANCAR. *v.* Fallar, errar. *To miss (shot).*

MANCORNA. *n.f.* Gemelos. *Cufflinks.*

MANCUERNA. *n.f.* (Acad.) Gemelos de los puños de la camisa. *Cufflink.*

MANDADERO. *n.m.* Chico de los mandados. *Office boy.*

MANDADO. *n.m.* Compra. *Purchase.* || **2.** •Ir de MANDADOS. *To go shopping.*

MANDAR. *v.* (Acad.) Con algunos verbos

en infinitivo, como cambiar, largar, mudar, etc., cumplir o hacer cumplir lo significado por el verbo. *To have someone do something.* ~Mis padres me MANDARON llamar. *My parents sent for me.* ~MANDÓ decir que no podía venir. *She sent word that she couldn't come.* ~¿Por qué no MANDAS a arreglar esos zapatos? *Why don't you have those shoes mended?* || **2.** Arrojar, lanzar. *To throw, hurl.* ~MANDÓ la pelota fuera de la cancha. *He sent the ball out of play.* || **3.** Hacer algo de mérito. *To pull off.* ~¡Se MANDÓ una casa! *He built such a beautiful house!* || **4.** Hacer una cosa con poco esfuerzo. *To do or perform something with the greatest of ease.* ~Se MANDÓ un discurso de dos horas. *He reeled off a two-hour speech.* || **5.** Engullir. *To polish off.* ~Se MANDÓ todo el postre. *He polished off all the desert.* || **6. -se.** MANDARSE a mudar. Irse, marcharse. *To go away, leave.* || **7.** •¡MÁNDESE a mudar! *Please leave immediately!*

MANDARÍN. *adj.* Mandón. *Bossy, domineering.*

MANDINGA. *n.m.* (Acad.) Nombre del diablo en el lenguaje de los campesinos. *The devil.* || **2.** •Es obra de MANDINGA. *It's the devil's doing.*

MANEADOR. *n.m.* Tira larga de cuero que sirve para atar el caballo, apiolar animales y otros usos. *Long strap used for hobbling horses or cattle.*

MANECO. *adj.* || **1.** De manos contrahechas o lesionadas. *Having deformed hands.* || **2.** De pies deformes. *Having deformed feet.*

MANEJAR. *v.* (Acad.) Conducir, guiar un automóvil. *To drive.*

MANEJO. *n.m.* (aut.) Conducción. *Driving.*

MANGA. *n.f.* (Acad.) Espacio comprendido entre dos palanqueras o estacadas que van convergiendo hasta la entrada de un corral en las estancias, o hasta un embarcadero en las costas. *Narrowing gangway or lane (leading cattle to a corral or loading platform).* || **2.** Partida de gente o animales. *Crowd, gang, mob.* ~Una MANGA de ladrones. *A bunch of thieves.*

MANGANZÓN. *adj.* Holgazán, mangón.

Lazy. || **2.** *n.m.* Holgazán. *Lazy-bones, layabout.*

MANGONEADOR. *n.m.* Sujeto aprovechador. *Corrupt official, grafter.*

MANGONEAR. *v.* || **1.** Explotar una situación ventajosa para fines de utilidad personal (empleo público, etc.). *To profit illicitly from public office.* || **2.** Manejar los negocios o asuntos ajenos en beneficio propio. *To defraud.*

MANGONEO. *n.m.* Chanchullo, manipulación. *Graft, fixing.*

MANGUEAR. *v.* (Acad.) Acosar el ganado mayor o menor para que entre en la **manga**, espacio comprendido entre dos palangueras o estacadas. *To force (the cattle) to enter the gangway.*

MANÍ. *n.m.* Cacahuete. *Peanut.*

MANICURISTA. *n.m&f.* Manicuro o manicura. *Manucurist.*

MANILARGO. *adj.* Se dice de la persona propensa a tomar lo ajeno. *Light-fingered, thievish.*

MANO. *n.m.* (Acad.) Tratándose de bananas, rácimo. *Bunch of bananas.* || **2.** Conjunto de cuatro, cinco o seis objetos de la misma clase. *Cluster, group of objects.* || **3.** Percance, trance desfavorable. *Misfortune, mishap.* || **4.** Caso inesperado, imprevisto. *Unexpected event.* || **5.** Suerte. *Luck.* ~¡Qué MANO! ¡Qué suerte! *What luck!* || **6.** Desgracia. *Mishap, misfortune.* ~¡Qué MANO! ¡Qué mala suerte! *What bad luck!* || **7.** •Estar o quedar a MANO. Estar en paz, no deberse nada dos personas. *To be even.* || **8.** •Dar una MANO. Echar una mano. *To give a hand.* || **9.** •Estar con una MANO atrás y otra adelante. Estar en la mayor pobreza. *To be broke.* || **10.** •Pasarle la MANO a uno. Adular, halagar. *To flatter.* || **11.** •MANO única. De sentido único. *One-way street.*

MANOPLA. *n.f.* (Acad.) Llave inglesa, arma de hierro en forma de eslabón. *Spanner.* || **2.** Puño de hierro. *Brass knuckles.*

MANOSEAR. *v.* Acariciar importunadamente a una mujer. *Caress, pet, fondle.*

MAÑOSEAR. *v.* Dicho de los niños, ponerse **mañoso**. *To be finicky, difficult, fussy, especially about food (applied mostly to children)*

MANOSEO. *n.m.* Acción de manosear. *Petting, fondling, caressing, pawing (coll.).*

MAÑOSO. *adj.* || **1**. Dicho de los niños, que no quieren alimentarse sino de golosinas o dulces. *Difficult, fussy, especially about food. Preferring sweets to regular meals (said of children).* || **2**. Terco (animal). *Obstinate (animal).* || **3**. Resabiado (animal). *Vicious (animal).*

MANOTADA. *n.f.* Porción que cabe en la mano cerrada. *Handful, fistful.*

MANOTEADOR. *n.m.* Bolsista. *Bagsnatcher.* || **2**. Estafador. *Swindler.* || **3**. Ladrón. *Thief.* || **4**. Persona que mueve mucho las manos al hablar. *Gesticulator.*

MANQUE. *conj.* Aunque. *Although.*

MANQUEAR. *v.* Cojear. *To limp.*

MANTEADO. *n.m.* Toldo o cobertizo de mantas, lonas, etc., para dar sombra. *Awning, canopy.*

MANTENIDA. *adj.* Concubina. *Kept woman.*

MANTENIDO. *adj.* Persona que vive a expensas de otra. *Gigolo.*

MANTEQUILLERA. *n.f.* (Acad.) Vasija en que se tiene o se sirve la manteca, mantequillero. *Butter dish.*

MANTEQUILLERO. *n.m.* (Acad.) El que hace o vende manteca, mantequero. *Person who makes or sell butter.*

MANUDO. *adj.* Se dice de la persona de manos grandes y gruesas. *Having big hands.*

MANYAR. *v.* (fest.) Comer. *To eat.*

MANZANA. *n.f.* (Acad.) Nuez de la garganta. *Adam's apple.* || **2**. •Manzana de Adán. Nuez de la garganta. *Adam's apple.*

MÁQUINA. *n.f.* •Máquina registradora. Caja registradora. *Cash-register.*

MARACA. *n.f.* Instrumento músical de los guaraníes, que consiste en una calabaza con granos de maíz en su interior para acompa-

ñar el canto. *Maraca, percussion instrument, made of a dry gourd.*

MARAQUEAR. *v.* Sacudir, hacer mover de un lado a otro. *To shake, rattle.*

MARCHANTAJE. *n.m.* Clientela. *Clientele.*

MARCHANTE. *n.m.* (Acad.) Parroquiano, persona que suele comprar en una misma tienda. *Client, customer.*

MARIMBA. *n.f.* (Acad.) Instrumento musical en que se percuten con un macillo blando tiras de vidrio, como en el timpano. *Marimba (type of xylophone).*

MARLO. *n.m.* Espiga de maíz desgranada. *Grainless stalk of corn.*

MAROMA. *n.f.* (Acad.) Volatín, voltereta o pirueta de un acróbata. *Stunt, trick, somersault, tumble.* || **2**. (Acad.) Función de circo en que se hacen ejercicios de acrobacia, volatines, etc. *Acrobatic performance.* || **3**. (Acad.) Voltereta política. *Change in one's political allegiance.*

MAROMEAR. *v.* Bailar el volatín en la maroma. *To walk a tightrope, to perform acrobatic stunts.* || **2**. Balancear, tratando de estar bien con todos, especialmente en política. *To do a political balancing act.*

MAROMERO. *n.m.* (Acad.) Acróbata, volatinero. *Tightrope walker, acrobat.* || **2**. (Acad.) Político astuto que varia de opinión o partido según las circunstancias. *Clever politician, politician who manages to be on good terms with all parties.* || **3**. (Acad.) Versátil. *Changeable, fickle, unstable.*

MARTAJAR. *v.* Quebrar el maíz en la piedra. *To crush corn on a stone.*

MARTILLERO. *n.m.* (Acad.) Dueño o encargado de un martillo, establecimiento para las subastas públicas. *Auctioneer.*

MARTINGALA. *n.f.* Ardid, treta, combinación para ganar en un juego. *Trick, scheme.*

MÁS. *prep.* •No más (seguido del verbo). || **1**. En oraciones exortivas, añade énfasis a la expresión. Por favor..., sírvase... *Please, go right ahead, feel free to... (used to invite someone to do or carry on doing something).*

Entre (pase) no MÁS. *Please (do) come in.* Sírvase no MÁS. *Please help yourself.* Firme aquí no MÁS. *Please sign here.* || **2.** No MÁS. Apenas. *As soon as.* || **3.** En cuanto. *No sooner... than.* ~No MÁS llegué me echaron. *No sooner had I arrived than they threw me out.* || **4.** •Así no MÁS. Así como así. *Just like that.* ~A ella no le vas a convencer así no MÁS.*You're not going to convince her that easily (just like that).* || **5.** •Pruébelo no MÁS. *Just try it.* || **6.** Solamente. *Only.* ~Ayer no MÁS lo vi pasar por la calle. *Only yesterday I saw him walking down the street.* || **7.** •Espera no MÁS que venga tu padre.*Just you wait till you father arrives.* || **8.** •No MÁS rogar. Basta de rogar. *Please stop your pleading.* || **9.** •Siga leyendo no MÁS. ~Siga leyendo (no se haga problema). *Please go on reading (don't mind me).* || **10.** •MÁS que nunca. Con mayor razón. *All the more.* || **11.** •¡Cómo NO! Con mucho gusto. *Certainly, with pleasure.* || **12.** •Aqui no MÁS. Aquí mismo. *Right here.* ~Aquí está la llave no MÁS. Aquí mismo está la llave. *The key is right here.* || **13.** Pronto, en seguida.*Shortly.* ~Ahora no MÁS viene Teresa. Ahora mismo viene Teresa. *Teresa will be here any minute now.* || **14.** •Así no MÁS. Así así, medianamente. *So-so.*

MASCADA. *n.f.* (Acad.) Porción de tabaco que se toma de una vez para mascarlo. *Plug of chewing tobacco.*

MASITA. *n.f.* (Acad.) Pasta o pastecillo dulce. *Pastry, cookie.*

MASITERO. *n.m.* Pastelero, repostero. *Pastrycook.*

MASTICAR. *v.* Masticar tabaco. *To chew tobacco.*

MATADERO. *n.m.* Casa de citas. *Brothel.*

MATAMBRE. *n.m.* Carne aderezada, dispuesta en forma de rollo con relleno y sancochada. *Meat roulade filled with vegetables and hard-boiled eggs.*

MATAZÓN. *n.m.* (Acad.) Matanza de personas, masacre. *Massacre, slaughter.*

MATE. *n.m.* Infusión que se hace con las hojas del árbol-arbusto llamado**yerba mate**. *Maté (herb and drink similar to tea).* || **2.** *n.m.* (Acad.) Calabaza que, seca, vaciada y

convenientemente abierta y cortada, sirve para muchísimos usos domésticos. *Gourd, drinking vessel.*

MATERIAL. *n.m.* •De MATERIAL. Se dice de las construcciones de adobe o de ladrillos. *Made of brick, brick-built.*

MATERO. *adj.* (Acad.) Aficionado a tomar **mate**. *Fond of drinking mate.*

MATINÉ, MATINÉE. *n.f.* (Acad.) Función de espectáculo, teatro, cine, circo, etc., que se ofrece en las primeras horas de la tarde. *Matinée.*

MATRERO. *adj.* Fugitivo, vagabundo, que buscaba el campo para escapar de la justicia. *Fugitive from justice.* ~Un gaucho MATRERO. *A gaucho on the run from the law.*

MATURRANGO. *adj.* Dícese del mal jinete. *Poor rider, incompetent horseman.*

MAULA. *adj.* (Acad.) Cobarde, despreciable, taimado. *Good-for-nothing, unreliable.* || **2.** Se dice del animal remolón, bellaco, flojo para el trabajo. *Useless, vicious, lazy (animal).*

MAYOREO. *n.m.* (Acad.) Venta al por mayor. *Wholesale (trade).*

MAZA. *n.f.* Cubo de la rueda. *Hub (of wheel).*

MAZAMORRA. *n.f.* Comida a base de maíz hervido. *Milky pudding made with corn.* || **2.** Ampolla. *Blister.*

MEAR. *v.* •MEAR fuera del tarro. Obrar desacertadamente o inoportunamente. *To be wrong, do the wrong thing.*

MECATE. *n.m.* || **1.** Cualquier fibra de corteza vegetal usada para atar. *Strip of pita fiber.* || **2.** Cuerda de fibras retorcidas o trenzadas usada para ataduras. *Rope, string, cord.* || **3.** Bramante o cordel. *Twine.* || **4.** Persona tosca e inculta. *Boor.* || **5.** •Caerse del MECATE. **a)** Quedar en evidencia. *To be caught in the act.* **b)** Quedar cesante. *To loose one's job.* || **6.** •No aflojar el MECATE. No perder de vista una asunto. *Not loose sight of.* || **7.** •Tener a uno a MECATE corto. No ceder en su autoridad, no dejar obrar a otro a su albedrío. *To hold someone on a tight rope, to give him little room to act freely.*

MECHA. *n.f.* Mechón. *Lock of hair.*

MECHUDO. *adj.* (Acad.) Que tiene mechas de pelo, mechones o greñas. *Tousled, umkempt.*

MEDIA. *n.f.* m. (Acad.) Calcetín. *Socks.* || **2.** Contador de agua, gas o energía eléctrica. *Meter.*

MEDIDOR. *n.m.* (Acad.) Contador de agua, gas o energía eléctrica. *Meter.*

MEDIO. •Día de (por) MEDIO. Un día sí y un día no. *Every other day.*

MEDIR. *v.* •MEDIR las calles. Holgazanear, callejear. *To loaf around.* || **2.** -se. Competir con alguien en fuerza, habilidad o inteligencia. *To match one's ability, wit, etc.* || **3.** En los deportes, competir un equipo con otro. *To play each other, meet.* || **4.** Reñir. *To quarrel, come to blows.* || **5.** •MEDIRSE la ropa. *To try on (clothes).*

MEJOR. *adv.* •MEJOR que. Es mejor que. *It's preferable that.* ~MEJOR que lo haga Ud. *You'd better do it yourself.* || **2.** *adj.* •A lo MEJOR. Posiblemente. *Probably, maybe; with any luck.* ~¿Crees que lo hará? A lo MEJOR. Do you think he'll do it? *Possibly.*

MEJUNJE. *n.m.* Enredo, confusión, lío. *Mess, mix-up.*

MELADO. *n.m.* (Acad.) En la fabricación del azúcar de caña, jarabe que se obtiene por la evaporación del jugo purificado de la caña antes de concentrarlo a punto de cristalización en los tachos. *Syrup.*

MELGA. *n.f.* (Acad.) Faja de tierra que se marca para sembrar, amelga. *Plot of land prepared for sowing.*

MELLAR. *v.* (Acad.) Menoscabar, disminuir, minorar una cosa no material. Mellar la honra, el crédito. *To damage, soil (one's reputation).*

MEMBRESÍA. *n.f.* Participación en una asociación, partido, etc. *Membership.*

MEMORISTA. *adj.* (Acad.) Que tiene feliz memoria. *Having a retentive memory.* || **2.** Se aplica a la persona que aprende las cosas de memoria y que no tiene capacidad para razonar. *To learn something parrot-fashion.*

~No es tan brillante, es un MEMORALISTA. *He's not so brillant, he just learns by rote (memory).*

MEMORIZACIÓN. *n.f.* Esfuerzo y método para recordar lo que uno aprende. *Memorization.*

MEMORIZAR. *v.* (Acad.) Aprender de memoria. Fijar en la memoria. *To learn by heart, memorize, commit to memory.*

MENEQUEAR. *v.* Mover reiteradamente una cosa hacia un lado y otro sin mudarla de lugar. *To shake, wag.*

MENEQUEO. *n.m.* Acción de mover una cosa de un lado a otro; sacudir con frecuencia. *Shaking, wagging.*

MENEQUETEO. *n.m.* Meneo afectado y repetido. *Prolonged shaking and wagging.*

MENSO. *adj.* Tonto, necio. *Stupid.* || **2.** *n.m.* Tonto, necio. *Fool.*

MENSURA. *n.f.* Acción de medir un terreno. *Act of measuring a piece of land.*

MENUDEAR. *v.* Abundar un cosa. *To abound, be plentiful.* ||**2.** Crecer en número, aumentar. *To increase, grow in number.*

MENUDENCIA. *n.f.* (Acad.) Menudillo de las aves. *Giblets.*

MENUDEO. *n.m.* (Acad.) Venta al por menor. *Retail trade.* || **2.** •Al MENUDEO. Al por menor. *Retail sales.*

MESADA. *n.f.* Mensualidad. *Monthly allowance; pocket money.* || **2.** Meseta. *Plateau, tableland.*

MESERO, RA. *adj.* (Acad.) Camarero o camarera de café o restaurante. *Waiter, waitress.*

META. *n.f.* Portería. *Goal (place where a goalkeeper stands in soccer).*

METALIZADO. *adj.* Se dice de la persona que vive dedicada a ganar dinero por cualquier medio, que todo lo valora o tasa conforme a su costo en dinero. *Mercenary, dedicated to making money; who sees everything in terms of money.*

METATE. *n.m.* Piedra cuadrilonga sostenida en tres pies, sobre la cual se muele el maíz y otros granos con un cilindro. *Stone* with a concave upper surface used for grinding and pulping seeds, vegetables, etc.

METER. v. •¡MÉTELE! Interjección usada para exhortar a alguien a que se dé prisa, a que trabaje con brío, a que se decida a hacer algo o a continuar en una empresa. *Let's go!, let's get with it!*

METICHE. adj. Entrometido. *Meddling, meddlesome, nosey.*

METIDA. n.f. •METIDA de pata. Metedura de pata. *Blunder.*

METIDO. adj. (Acad.) Dícese de la persona entrometida. *Meddling, interfering.*

MEXICANO. adj. Mejicano. *Mexican*

MÉXICO. n.m. Méjico. *Mexico.*

MEZQUINAR. v. (Acad.) Regatear, escatimar alguna cosa, darla con mezquindad. *To skimp on, be stingy with.*

MEZZANINA. n.f. Entresuelo, entrepiso. *Mezzanine.*

MICA. n.f. Cristal, vidrio (de un reloj). *Crystal.*

MICHI. n.m. Gato. *Pussy cat.*

MIENTRAS. adj. •MIENTRAS más... más... Cuanto más... más... *The more... the more...* ~MIENTRAS más se le da, más pide. *The more you give him, the more he wants.*

MILICO. n.m. (Acad.) Militar, soldado (pey.). *Soldier.*

MILITAROTE. n.m. Militar inculto, autoritario y de maneras bruscas y torpes. *Rough soldier, blustering soldier.*

MIMETIZARSE. v. Adquirir el color, apariencia, etc. de las cosas del contorno. *To change color, camouflage oneself.*

MINA. n.f. Mujer cualquiera. *Girl, chick.*

MINESTRÓN. n.m. Minestrone. *Minestrone.*

MINGA. n.f. (Acad.) Reunión de amigos y vecinos para hacer algún trabajo en común, sin más renumeración que la comilona que les paga el dueño cuando lo terminan. *Work carried out in exchange for food.*

MIÑÓN. adj. Se dice de la cosa o persona pequeña y bonita. *Sweet, cute.*

MIRAR. v. •MIRAR vidrieras. Mirar escaparates. *To go (out) window-shopping.*

MITOTE. n.m. (Acad.) Fiesta casera. *House party.* || **2.** (Acad.) Melindre, aspaviento. *Finickiness, fussiness.*

MITOTERO. adj. (Acad.) Que hace **mitotes** o melindres. *Finicky, fussy.*

MOCHO. adj. Mutilado. *Mutilated.*

MOCIONAR. v. Presentar una moción. *To move, propose.*

MODO. n.m. •De mal MODO. De mala manera. *Rudely.* || **2.** •Ni MODO. De ninguna manera. *Not a chance.*

MOHOSEARSE. v. Enmohecerse. *To get moldy or rusty.*

MOJARRA. n.f. (Acad.) Cuchillo corto y ancho. *Short, broad knife.*

MOLDE. n.m. (costura) Patrón. *Pattern.*

MOLESTOSO. adj. (Acad.) Que causa molestia. *Annoying.*

MOLOTE. n.m (Acad.) Riña, alboroto. *Riot, commotion.*

MONDONGO. n.m. (cul.) Callos. *Tripe.*

MONEAR. v. Jactarse. *To boast.*

MOÑO. n.m. Lazo. *Bow.*

MONORRIEL. n.m. Monocarril, monorail. *Monorail.*

MONTEPÍO. n.m. Casa de empeños. *Pawnshop.*

MONTONERA. n.f. (Acad.) Grupo o pelotón de gente a caballo que intervenían como fuerza irregular en las guerras civiles de algunos países suramericanos. *Band of guerrilla fighters, troop of mounted rebels.*

MONTONERO. n.m. Guerillero. *Guerrilla fighter.*

MONTUNO. adj. (Acad.) Rudo, rústico, montaraz. *Wild, untamed, rustic.*

MORDIDA. n.f. (Acad.) Provecho o dinero obtenido de un particular por un funcionario o empleado, con abuso de las atribuciones de su cargo, soborno. *Bribe, kickback.*

MORDISCÓN. n.m. Mordisco. *Bite.*

MORETEAR. v. Amoratar, acardenalar. *To*

bruise.

MORGUE. *n.m.* Depósito de cadáveres, instituto anatómico forense. *Morgue.*

MORLACO. *n.m.* Dinero. *Buck, peso (any national coin).*

MOROCHO. *adj.* Moreno, trigueño. *Dark-complexioned.* || **2.** (Acad.) Tratándose de personas, robusto, fresco, bien conservado. *Strong, robust.*

MORTAJA. *n.f.* (Acad.) Hoja de papel con que se lía el tabaco del cigarrillo. *Cigarette paper.*

MOSQUERO. *n.m.* (Acad.) Hervidero o abundancia de moscas. *Swarm of flies.*

MOTA. *n.f.* (Acad.) Mechón de cabellos cortos y crepos. *Tight curls.*

MOTE. *n.m.* (Acad.) Maíz desgranado y cocido con sal, que se emplea como alimento en algunas partes de América. *Boiled corn.*

MOTONETA. *n.f.* Escúter, Vespa®. *Scooter, motor scooter.*

MOTORISTA. *n.m.* Conductor, chofer. *Driver.*

MOTUDO. *adj.* (Acad.) Dícese del pelo dispuesto en forma de mota y de la persona que lo tiene. *Kinky, frizzy.*

MOVER. *v.* •De no te MUEVAS. Firme, contundente. *An open and shut case.*

MUCAMO-A. *n.m.* (Acad.) Criado, servidor. *Servant (masc.), maid (fem.).*

MUDADA. *n.f.* (Acad.) Mudanza de casa. *Moving, change of domicile.* || **2.** Muda de ropa. *Change of clothes.*

MUDAR. *v.* •MANDARSE a mudar (ver **Mandar**).

MUERTE. *n.m.* Cada MUERTE de obispo. Muy de vez en cuando. *Once in a blue moon.*

MUJERERO. *adj.* Dícese del hombre dado a mujeres, mujeriego. *Womenizer, women chaser.*

MUNICIONERA. *n.f.* Perdigonera. *Shot pouch or bag.*

MURALLA. *n.f.* Pared. (Any) *wall.*

NACIENCIA. *n.f.* (Rur.) Nacimiento. *Birth.*

NACO. *n.m.* (Acad.) Andullo de tabaco. *Plug of tobacco.*

NADA. *n.f.* Pequeña cantidad. *A small quantity of, little.* ~Le puse una NADA de sal. *I added a pinch of salt.* Ganó por una NADA. *He won by a wisker.* ‖ **2.** *adj.* De ningún modo. *At all (in negative sentences).* No me gustó NADA esta película. *I didn't like that movie at all.* ‖ **3.** •A cada NADA. En cada momento, en cada paso. *Constantly, all the time, at every step.* ‖ **4.** •Más NADA. Nada más. *Nothing else.* No quiero más NADA. *I don't want anything else.*

NALGÓN. *adj.* Que tiene gruesas las nalgas, nalgudo. *Big-bottomed, big-buttocked.*

NANA. *n.f.* Niñera. *Nanny, nurse.*

NARIGADA. *n.f.* Polvo o pulgarada, porción de rapé. *Pinch of snuff.*

NATA. *n.f.* (min.) Escoria de la copelación. *Slag, scoria, scum (of metals).*

NAVAJA. *n.f.* Cortaplumas. *Penknife.*

NEGOCIADO. *n.m.* Negocio de importancia, ilícito y escandaloso. *Illegal transaction, shady deal.*

NEGOCIO. *n.m.* Casa de negocios, firma. *Firm, company.* ‖ **2.** Tienda o despacho donde se compra y vende. *Place of business, shop, store.*

NEGRADA. *n.f.* Conjunto de negros. *Group of negroes.* ‖ **2.** Dicho o hecho propio de negros. *Remark or act typical of a negro.*

NEGRILLO. *n.m.* Mineral de plata cuprífera de color muy oscuro. *Black cupriferous silver ore.*

NEGRO, -GRA. *n.m&f.* Voz de cariño que se usan entre casados, novios y personas que se quieren bien. *Dear, sweetheart, honey.*

NEUTRAL. *adj.* n.m. (auto.) •Estar en NEUTRAL. Estar en punto muerto. *To be in neutral.*

NEVADO. *n.m.* Montaña cubierta de nieves perpétuas. *Snow-capped mountain.*

NEVAZÓN. *m.f.* Nevada, nevazo. *Snowstorm, blizzard.*

NIEVE. *n.f.* Helado. *Ice-cream.* ‖ **2.** Sorbete. *Sorbet, water-ice.*

NIGUA. *n.f.* Insecto americano parecido a la pulga. *Jigger flea.*

NIGUATERO. *adj.* Que tiene los pies llenos de **niguas**. *Contaminated with jigger fleas.*

NIGÜENTO (variante de **niguatero**).

NIGÜERO. *n.m.* Lugar donde hay **niguas**. *Place where **niguas** abound.*

NIÑO, -ÑA. *n.m&f.* *Young master, young lady, mistress.*

NIQUEL. *n.m.* Moneda de níquel, generalmente de poco valor. *Small coin, nickel.* ‖ **2.** dinero. *Money.*

NOCAUT. *n.m.* (dep.) K.O., queo. *Knockout.*

NOCHE. *n.f.* •En la NOCHE. Por la noche. *At night.*

NOCHECITA. *n.f.* Crepúsculo vesperino. *Dusk, nightfall, twilight.* ‖ 2. •A la NOCHECITA. Al oscurecer. *At nightfall.*

NOCHERO. *adj.* Nocherniego, que anda de noche. *Given to wandering at night*

NOMAS (variante de **no más**).

NÓMINA. *n.f.* Lista de nombres. *List of names.*

NORMAL. *adj.* •Escuela NORMAL. Escuela en que se forman los maestros de primeras letras. *Teacher's training college (primary).*

NORMALISTA. *n.m&f.* Alumno o alumna de una escuela normal. *Student teacher, school teacher.*

NORMAR. *v.* Establecer normas para algo. *To lay down rules, establish norms.*

NORTINO. *adj.* Norteño. *Northern.* ‖ **2.** *n.m.* Norteño. *Northerner.*

NOTICIERO. *n.m.* Noticias, boletín informativo. *News bulletin, newscast.*

NOTICIOSO. *n.m.* Boletín informativo. *Newscast, news bulletin.*

NOVEDOSO. *adj.* (Acad.) Que implica novedad. *Novel, original.*

NOVIAR. *v* (intr.). Galantear, estar de novio. *To go out together, to date, to go steady.* ‖ **2.** *v* (trans.) *To court, date, go out with someone.*

NUBLAZÓN. *n.f.* Nublado. *Storm cloud, black cloud.*

NURSE. *n.f.* Enfermera de un hospital o clínica. *Nurse.*

ÑA. *n.f.* (Acad.) En algunas partes de America tratamiento vulgar de *doña. Shortened form of* doña, *Mrs.* ~ÑA Berta. Sra. Berta. *Mrs. Berta.*

ÑANDÚ. n.m. (Acad.) Avestruz de America. *American Ostrich.*

ÑANDUBAY. *n.m.* (Acad.) Árbol de madera rojiza muy dura e incorruptible. *Nandubay tree; a kind of hardwood.*

ÑANDUTÍ. *n.m.* (Acad.) Tejido muy fino que hacían principalmente las mujeres del Paraguay, hoy muy generalizado en la America del Sur para toda clase de ropa blanca. *Fine lace common to Paraguay and South America.*

ÑAÑO. *adj.* (Acad.) Unido por amistad íntima. *Close (friend).*

ÑAPA. *n.f.* (Acad.) Añadidura, propina. yapa. *Gratuity, tip, bonus, something extra.* || **2.** •De ÑAPA. De añadidura. *In addition, to boot, besides.*

ÑATA. *n.f.* Nariz. *Nose.*

ÑATO. *adj.* (Acad) De nariz corta y aplastada, chato. *Pug-nosed, flat-nosed.*

ÑAU. *excl.* Miau. *Mew, miaow.*

ÑAUAR. *v.* Maullar el gato. *To miaow.*

ÑEQUE. *adj.* (Acad.) Fuerte, vigoroso. *Strong, vigorous.* || **2.** (Acad.) Fuerza, energía. *Strength, energy, vigor.* || **3.** Valor. *Courage.* || 4. •Estar ÑEQUE. Ser valiente. *To be courageous.*

ÑISCA. *n.f.* Pizca, pedacito. *Bit, small piece.*

ÑO. *n.f.* (Acad.) En alguna partes de America tratamiento vulgar de *don. Mr.* ~ÑO Bernardo. Señor Bernado. *Mr. Bernardo.*

ÑOCO. *adj.* (Acad.) Dícese de la persona a quien le falta un dedo o una mano. *Lacking a finger or a hand*

ÑOÑO. *adj.* Caduco, pasado de moda. *Outmoded, old-fashioned.*

ÑOQUI. *n.m.* (Acad.) Masa hecha con patatas (papas) mezcladas con harina de trigo, matequilla, leche, huevo y queso rallado, dividida en trocitos, que se cuecen en agua hirviente con sal. *Gnocchi.*

OBISPO. *n.m.* •A cada muerte de OBISPO. Muy de vez en cuando. *Once in a blue moon.*

OBJETO. *n.m.* •OBJETO volador no identificado. Objeto volante no identificado. *UFO*

OBLEA. *n.f.* Sello medicinal. *Capsule (med.).*

OBLITERAR. *v.* (Acad.) Anular, tachar, borrar. *To obliterate.*

OBRA. *n.f.* •OBRAS viales. Obras de vialidad. *Roadworks.*

OBRERO. *n.m.* •OBRERO calificado. Obrero cualificado. *Skilled worker.*

OBSEQUIAR. *v.* OBSEQUIAR con. *To present someone with a gift.* ~Le OBSEQUIARON con un reloj. *They presented him with a watch.*

OBSERVAR. *v.* •OBSERVAR algo a uno. Hacer una advertencia u observación. *To point something out to someone.* || **2.** Observar buena conducta, comportarse bien. *To be well-behaved.*

OBSTETRA. *n.m.* Obstétrico, togólogo. *Obstetrician.*

OBSTINADO. *adj.* Porfiado, terco, testarudo. *Obstinate, stubborn.*

OCASIÓN. *n.f.* Rebajas. *Bargain, sale.* || **2.** De OCASIÓN. De rebaja. *On sale, at reduced prices.*

OCIOSEAR. *v.* Holgazanear. *To idle, loaf about.*

OCUPAR. *v.* Emplear. *To use.* ~¿Estás OCUPANDO esta silla? *Are you using this chair?*

ODIOSIDAD. *n.f.* Fastidio, molestia. *Irksomeness, annoyance.*

ODIOSO. *adj.* Fastidioso, molesto. *Irksome, annoying.*

OFERTAR. *v.* (Acad.) Ofrecer, prometer algo. *To offer, promise someone something.*

OFF. *adv.* •Hablar en OFF. En el lenguaje del cine, teatro, televisión o radiofusión, se dice del hablar un actor lejos del micrófono, para dar idea de lejanía. *To speak offstage or off mike in order to convey the idea of distance.*

OFFSIDE. *adj.* •Estar OFFSIDE. Estar fuera de juego. *To be offside.* || **2.** •Pescar a uno en OFFSIDE. *To catch someone red-handed.* || **3.** •Estar en OFFSIDE. Estar distraído, estar en la luna. *To be daydreaming.*

OFICIALADA. *n.f.* Oficialidad. *Officers (collectively).*

OFICIALISMO. *n.m.* (Acad.) Conjunto de hombres de un gobierno. *Representative of the ruling or governing party.* || **2.** (Acad.) Conjunto de tendencias o fuerzas políticas que apoyen al gobierno. *Pro-government political forces.*

OFICIALISTA. *n.m.* (Acad.) Dícese de la persona que es partidaria del oficialismo o pertenece a él. *Member or supporter of the governing party.* || **2.** Relacionado con el gobierno. *Governmental, pro-government.* ~Un periódico OFICIALISTA. *A pro-government newspaper.*

OJALÁ. *adv.* Aunque. *Although.* ~OJALÁ llueva, voy a viajar. *Although it may rain, I will still travel.*

OJALATERO. *n.m.* Hojalatero. *Tinsmith.*

OJO. *n.m.* •OJO de agua. Manantial. *Spring.* || **2.** •Pelar el OJO. Estar alerta. *To be on the alert.* || **3.** •OJO mágico. *Peephole, spyhole.*

OJÓN. *n.m.* De ojos grandes. *Big-eyed.*

OJOTA. *n.f.* (Acad.) Calzado a manera de sandalia, hecho de cuero o filamento vegetal, que usaban los indios del Perú y de Chile, y que todavía usan los campesinos de algunas regiones de América del Sur. *Sandal.* || **2.** Cuero de piel curtida de llama. *Tanned llama leather.*

OKEY. *interj.* Muy bien, de acuerdo. *OK!, Okay!*

OLOR. *n.m.* •¡Qué rico OLOR!. ¡Qué olor agradable, qué buen olor! *What a lovely smell!*

OMELETTE. *n.f.* Toratilla. *Omelet.*

ONDA. *n.f.* •Agarrarle la ONDA a algo. Entender. *To understand, get the point.*|| **2.** ¡Qué ONDA! Qué hay de nuevo? *What's new?* || **3.** ¡Qué buena ONDA! ¡Qué bien! *That's great (fantastic)!* || **4.** •¡Qué mala ONDA! ¡Es una lástima!. *That's terrible!*

ONOMÁSTICO. *n.m.* Cumpleaños. *Birthday.* || **2.** Día del Santo. *One's saint's day, one's name day (celebrated in Spain and Latin America as equivalent as one's birthday.*

OPA. *adj.* (Acad.) Tonto, idiota. *Dummy.* || **2.** Sordomudo. *Deaf and dumb.* || **3.** ¡Hola! *Hello, hi!*

OPACARSE. *v.* Oscurecerse, nublarse. *To cloud over.* || **2.** Perder brillo, ponerse opaca una cosa. *To loose its shine, become tarnished.* || **3.** Empañarse. *To mist up.* || **4.** Superar a una persona en alguna cualidad. *To outshine, overshadow, eclipse.* || **5.** Deslucir. *To mar.* ~Su actuación se vio OPACADA por algunas fallas técnicas. *Her performance was marred by technical problems.*

OPERATIVO. *n.m.* Operacion. *Operation.* ~Se llevó a cabo un OPERATIVO de vigilancia. *A surveillance operation was carried out.*

OPORTUNIDAD. *n.f.* Vez, circunstancia. *Occasion.* ~En aquella OPORTUNIDAD tuvo que ceder. *On that occasion he had to give in.* || **2.** •En otras OPORTUNIDADES. En otras ocasiones. *On other occasions.*

OPOSITOR. *n.m.* (Acad.) Partidario de la oposición en política. *Member of the opposition.*

ORDEN. *n.f.* Pedido. *Order.* || **2.** •¡A la ORDEN! **a)** Con mucho gusto, para servirle. *You're welcome, not at all, with pleasure.* ~Estamos a la ORDEN para cualquier cosa que necesite. *Let us know if there is anything else we can do for you.* **b)** (en la tienda). ¿En qué puedo servirle? *What can I do (get) for you?* **c)** No hay de que. *You're welcome, don't mention it.*

ORDEÑA. *n.f.* Ordeño. *Milking.*

ORDENAMIENTO. *n.m.* Organización. *Organization.*

ORDENAR. *v.* Encargar. *To order.*

OREJA. *n.f.* •Parar la OREJA. Escuchar atentamente. *To pay close attention.* ~Para bien la OREJA que esto es muy importante. *Pay attention, this is very important.* || **2.** •Arderle la OREJA a alguien. Tener mucha curiosidad. *To prick one's ears.*

OREJANO. *adj.* Se dice de las personas o animales de temperamento arisco o huraño. *Unbranded, ownerless (animal), unsociable (person).*

OREJEAR. *v.* Dar tirones de orejas a una persona. *To pull someone's ears.* || **2.** Escuchar con disimulo. *To eavedrop.* || **3.** Desconfiar. *To be distrustful.*

OREJERO. *adj.* Receloso. *Suspicious.*

OREJÓN. *adj.* Tosco. *Coarse, rough.*

ORFANATORIO. *n.m.* Casa de huérfanos. *Orphanage.*

ORILLAS. *n.f.* Afueras. *Outlying districts.*

ORILLERO. *adj.* (Acad.) Arrabalero. *Vulgar, common.*

ORO. *n.m.* •Guardar algo como ORO en polvo. *To treasure something as if it were gold.*

OVEROL. *n.m.* (Acad.) Mono, traje de faena de una sola pieza. *Overalls.*

P

PACHAMAMA. *n.f.* La tierra entendida como una divinidad en las creencias de los antiguos aborígenes y cuyo culto todavía se practica por ciertos indios y mestizos. *The good earth, Mother Earth.*

PACHANGA. *n.f.* (Acad.) Alboroto, fiesta, diversión bulliciosa. *Partying.* ~Esta noche nos vamos de PACHANGA. *Tonight we're going partying.*

PACHANGUERO. *adj.* Amigo de diversión bulliciosa, fiestero. *Fond of parties.*

PACHO. *adj.* Rechoncho. *Chubby.*

PACHOCHA. *n.f.* (Acad.) Flema, tardanza, indolencia. *Sluggishness, slowness.*

PACHÓN. *adj.* (Acad.) Peludo, lanudo. *Shaggy, hairy, wooly.*

PACHORRADA. *n.f.* Patochada. *Blunder, stupidity, coarse remark.*

PACHORREAR. *v.* Proceder con flema, indolencia. *To be slow or sluggish.*

PACHORRIENTO. *adj.* Que en todo procede con demasiada lentitud y flema, pachorrudo. *Slow, sluggish.*

PACHORRO. *adj.* Indolente, pachorrudo. *Slow, sluggish.*

PACO. *n.m.* Gendarme, policía. *Cop, policeman.* || **2.** Color bayo, bermejo o rojizo. *Reddish.*

PACOTILLA. *n.f.* Chusma, grupo de gente maleante. *Rabble, crowd, mob.*

PACOTILLERO. *adj.* (Acad.) Buhonero o mercader ambulante. *Peddler, street vendor (generally selling shoddy goods).*

PADRE. *adj.* Muy grande, en superior grado. *Very big.* ~Se armó un lío PADRE. *There was quite a commotion.*

PADRILLO. *n.m.* (Acad.) Caballo padre. *Stallion.*

PADRÓN. *n.m.* Caballo semental. *Stallion.* || **2.** •PADRÓN electoral. Registro electoral. *Electoral roll (register).*

PADROTE. *n.m.* (Acad.) Macho destinado en el ganado para la generación y procreación. *Stallion.*

PAGANINI. *n.m.* •Ser el PAGANINI. Ser el que paga. *To be the one who gets stuck with the bill.*

PAICO. *n.m.* Pazote. *Wormseed, Mexican tea.*

PAILA. *n.m.* (Acad.) Sartén, vasija. *Large copper frying pan.*

PAILERO. *n.m.* Persona que hace o vende pailas (sartenes). *Pan maker or peddler.* || **3.** Persona que atiende las pailas (sartenes) en los ingenios de azúcar. *Workman in charge of sugar pans (in sugar mills).* || **4.** Trabajador en cobre, cobrero. *Coppersmith.* || **5.** Calderero. *Tinker.*

PAILÓN. *n.m.* Hondonada de perímetro circular. *Hollow ground in the form of a bowl.*

PAJAREAR. *v.* (Acad.) Oxear, espantar a las aves. *To scare birds away.* || **2.** (Acad.) Espantar a las caballerías. *To shy (horse).* || **3. -se.** Estar distraído. *To have one's head in the clouds, to daydream.*

PAJARERO. *adj.* (Acad.) Espantadizo, hablando de las caballerías. *Nervous (horse).* || **2.** Brioso (caballo). *Spirited (horse).* || **3.** (Acad.) *n.m.* Muchacho encargado de espantar a los pájaros en los sembrados. *Bird chaser.*

PAJILLA. *n.f.* Sombrero de paja. *Straw hat.*

PAJÓN. *n.m.* (Acad.) Gramínea silvestre,

muy rica en fibra, que en época de escasez sirve de alimento al ganado. *Scrub, stubble.*

PAJONAL . *n.m.* (Acad.) Herbazal. *Scrubland.*

PAJUELA. *n.f.* Mondadientes. *Toothpick.*

PALABREAR. *v.* Apalabrar, concertar una cosa de palabra. *To give one's word.* || **2.** Dar palabra de matrimonio. *To promise to marry someone.*

PALACETE. *n.m.* Palacio pequeño. *Small palace.*

PALANGANA. *n.m.* Fanfarón, charlatán. *Boaster, braggart.* || **2.** Fuente o plato ancho y de poco fondo. *Dish, platter.*

PALANGANADA. *n.f.* Fanfarronada. *Bragging, boasting.*

PALANGANEAR. *v.* (Acad.) Fanfarronear. *To brag, show off.*

PALANQUEAR. *v.* Hacer avanzar una embarcación con la palanca. *To punt, pole along (boat).*

PALEAR. *v.* Robar. *To steal, swipe (coll.).*

PALENQUE. *n.m.* Poste que sirve para atar animales. *Tethering-post.*

PALETA. *n.f.* Palmeta con que se golpea la ropa al lavarla. *Washing paddle (for beating clothes).* || **2.** (Acad.) Dulce o helado en forma de pala, que se chupa cogiéndolo por un palito que sirve de mango; chupetín. *Popsicle©, ice lolly.*

PALLADA (variante de **payada**).

PALLADOR. (variante de **payador**).

PALLAR. *n.m.* Haba, frijol de gran tamaño. *Lima bean.* || **2.** Judía. *Haricot bean.* || **3.** (variante de **payar**).

PALMADA. *n.f.* Golpe, azote. *Smack, slap.*

PALMERO. *n.m.* Palmera. *Palm tree.*

PALMISTA. *n.m&f.* Quiromántico. *Palmist.*

PALO. *n.m.* (Acad.) PALO ensebado. Palo enjabonado. *Greasy pole.* || **2.** Arbol. *Tree.* || **3.** Notable, excelente, digno de admiración. *Splendid, marvelous.* Es un PALO de hombre. *He's a great guy.* || **4.** •Ni a PALO(s). *No way (coll.).* ~Ni a PALO retiro lo que he di-

cho. *There's no way you will make me take back what I said.* || **5.** Un millón (pesos, soles). *A million pesos, soles, etc.* || **6.** •PALO de agua. Aguacero fuerte. *Downpour.*

PALOMILLA. *n.f.* (Acad.) Plebe, vulgo, gentuza, pandilla de vagabundos o matones. *Gang, rabble, mob.* || **2.** Grupo de muchachos vagabundos. *Mob of kids.* || **3.** Muchacho travieso. *Little devil, urchin.*

PALOMINO. *adj.* Caballo de color muy blanco. *Palomino (white horse).*

PALPAMIENTO. *n.m.* Examen minucioso de una persona (en busca de alguna arma). *Frisking, body-search.*

PALPAR. *n.m.* Registrar. *To frisk, search (a person).*

PALPITARSE. *v.* •PALPITARSE una cosa. Prever, presentir, sospechar algo. *To have a hunch (feeling) about something.* ~Eso me lo PALPITABA yo. *I could see that happening all along.*

PÁLPITO. *n.m.* Presentimiento, corazonada, intuición. *Hunch, feeling.*

PALTA. *n.f.* (Acad.) Aguacate, fruto. *Avocado.*

PALTO. *n.m.* Arbol del aguacate. *Avocado tree.*

PALTÓ. *n.m.* Saco, chaqueta. *Jacket.*

PAMPEAR. *v.* (Acad.) Recorrer la pampa. *To travel over the pampas.*

PAMPERO. *adj.* (Acad.) Natural de las pampas. *Of or from the pampas.* || **2.** (Acad.) Dícese del viento impetuoso, precedente de dicha región, que suele soplar en el Río de la Plata. *Strong wind blowing over the pampas from the Andes.*

PAMPLONADA. *n.f.* Pamplinada. *Triviality, silly thing, piece of nonsense.*

PAN. *n.m.* •Ser más bueno que un PAN de Dios. *To be the salt of the earth.*

PANCA. *n.f.* (Acad.) Hoja que cubre la mazorca de maíz. *Dry leaf of corn.*

PANCITO. *n.m.* Panecillo. *Roll, bread.*

PANDILLERO. *n.m.* Que forma parte de una pandilla. *Gang member.*

PANECITO (variante de **pancito**).

PANELA. *n.f.* Masa preparada con azúcar o miel, de diversas maneras. *Brown sugarloaf.* || **2.** Pesado, antipático. *Bore, drag.* || **3.** Zalamero. *Flatterer.*

PANETELA. *n.f.* Especie de bizcocho. *Spongecake.*

PANOCHA. *n.f.* Especie de pan o torta grande hecho de maíz tierno. *Large corn pancake with corn and cheese.*

PANQUEQUE. *n.m.* Crepe. *Pancake.*

PANQUEQUERÍA. *n.f.* Lugar donde se hace o vende **panqueques**. *Pancake house.*

PANTALETA. *n.f.* Pantalones bombachos de mujer. *Bloomers, drawers.*

PANTALLA. *n.f.* (Acad.) Instrumento para hacer o hacerse aire, paipay, soplillo. *Fan.* || **2.** Guardaespaldas. *Bodyguard.*

PANTEÓN. *n.m.* (Acad.) Cementerio. *Cemetery.*

PANTEONERO. *n.m.* (Acad.) Sepultero. *Gravedigger.*

PAPA. *n.f.* Patata. *Potato.* || **2.** •**PAPA** dulce. Patata dulce. *Sweet potato.* || **3.** •**PAPAS** fritas. Patatas fritas. *French fries.* || **4.** Comida. *Food.* ~Rica **PAPA**. *Tasty food.* || **5.** •**PAPÁ** grande. Abuelo. *Granfather.* || **6.** •**PAPÁS**. Padres. *Parents.*

PAPAL. *n.m.* (Acad.) Terreno sembrado de papas. *Potato field.*

PAPEL. *n.m.* Envoltura de papel en que se venden dosis de polvos medicinales. *Paper containing a dose of medicine.* || **2.** •**PAPEL** de arroz. El papel blanco fino de los cigarrillos. *Kind of paper used in making cigarrettes.* || **3.** •**PAPEL** de oficio. Papel para escribir de catorce pulgadas de largo, usado preferentemente para asuntos oficiales. *Official foolscap paper.*

PAPELERÍO. *n.m.* (Acad.) Papelería, conjunto de papeles desordenados. *Mass, heap of paper.*

PAPELISTA. *n.m.* Picapleitos. *Troublemaker, quarrelsome person.* || **2.** Mal abogado. *Pettyfogging lawyer.*

PAPELÓN. *n.m.* (Acad.) Pan de azúcar sin refinar. *Sugar loaf made from unrefined sugar.* || **2.** •Pasar (hacer) un **PAPELÓN**. Hacer un papel desairado y ridículo. *To make a fool of oneself.*

PAPERO. *adj.* Se dice de la persona que cultiva o vende papas. *Said of the person who grows or sell potatoes.*

PAQUETA (variante de **paquete**).

PAQUETE. *n.m.* Persona inapta. *Useless person.* ~El nuevo lanzador es un **PAQUETE**. *The new pitcher is useless.* || **2.** *adj.* Se dice de la persona bien vestida o de las cosas o locales bien puestas. *Elegant, chic.*

PAQUETEAR. *v.* Presumir, mostrarse ante los demás bien vestido. *To show off (clothes).*

PAQUETUDO (variante de **paquete**).

PAQUÍN. *n.m.* Periódico. *Rag.*

PARA. *prep.* •Son las cinco **PARA** las diez. Son las cinco menos diez. *It's ten minutes to five.*

PARACA. *n.f.* (Acad.) Viento muy fuerte del Pacífico. *Strong wind from the Pacific.*

PARACAIDISTA. *n.m.* Que llega sin ser invitado. *Gatecrasher, squatter.*

PARADA. *n.f.* Apuesta. *Bet.* || **2.** Desfile, procesión cívica. *Parade.* || **3.** Fanfarronada. *Presumption, boastfulness.* || **4.** Orgullo, engreimiento. *Vanity, pride.* || **5.** •Hacer (la) **PARADA** a uno. Desafiar a uno. *To challenge someone.*

PARADERO. *n.m.* Parada de taxis u otros vehículos colectivos. *Bus stop.*

PARADO. *adj.* (Acad.) Derecho o en pie. *Standing.* ~Estar **PARADO**. *To be standing (up), to be on one's feet.* ~Estuve **PARADO** dos horas. *I stood for two hours.* || **2.** Erguido (cabello). *Stiff, straight (hair).* || **3.** Recto, en posición vertical. *In an upright posición.* || **4.** •Estar bien **PARADO**. Tener buena posición, apoyos o influencias. *To be well-placed, have influence.*

PARAFINA. *n.f.* Combustible. *Kerosene.*

PÁRAMO. *n.m.* Llovizna. *Drizzle.*

PARAR. *v.* (Acad.) Poner de **PIE**. *To stand.*

~PÁRALO en la silla para que vea mejor. *Stand him on the chair so he can see better.* || **2.** Poner en una posición vertical. *To stand...up.* ~El perro PARÓ las orejas. *The dog pricked up his ears.* || **3.** Hacer (declararse en) huelga. *To go on strike.* || **4.** Apostar. *To bet.* ~¡Cuánto quiere PARAR? ¿Cuánto quiere apostar? *How much do you want to bet?* || **5.**•PA-RARLE a uno el gallo. Pararle a uno el macho. *To shut somebody up, put a halt to.* ||**6.** Prestar atención. *To lend an ear.* || **7. -se.** Ponerse de pie. *To stand up.* ~PÁRATE derecho. *Stand up straight.* || **8.** •PARÁRSELE el pelo a uno. *To stand on end.* || **9.** Prosperar, enriquecerse. *To get rich.*

PARCHADO. *n.m.* Remiendo. *Repair, patching.*

PARCHAR. *v.* Remendar, arreglar. *To repair, patch up, mend.*

PARECIMIENTO. *n.m.* Parecido, semejanza. *Similarity, likeness, resemblance.*

PAREJA. *n.f.* Par de animales. *Team of animals.* || **2.** Yunta. *Yoke of oxen.*

PAREJERO. *adj.* (Acad.) Dícese del caballo de carrera y en general de todo caballo excelente y veloz. *Fast race horse.* || **2.** Presumido, vanidoso. *Vain, presumptuous.*

PAREJO. *adj.* Equitativo. *Impartial.* Siempre ha sido muy PAREJO con nosotros. *He has always treated us impartially.* ||**2.** Raso, plano. *Flat, level.* || **3.** A un tiempo, al igual. *At the same time, together.* ~Todos necesitan tirar PAREJO. *All must pull at the same time.* || **4.** •Ir PAREJOS. *To be neck and neck.*

PARICIÓN. *n.f.* (Acad.) Parto, acción de parir. *Childbirth.*

PARIHUELA. *n.f.* Fuente para mariscos. *Seafood platter.*

PARLANTE. *n.m.* Altavoz. *Loudspeaker*

PARO. *n.m.* Huelga. *Strike.* || **2.** •Hacer un PARO. Hacer (declararse en) huelga. *To go on strike.* || **3.** •Estar de PARO. Estar de huelga. *To be on strike.* || **4.** •Paro general. *General strike.*

PARQUEADERO. *n.m.* Aparcamiento. *Parking lot.* || **2.** Lugar para aparcar. *Parking space.*

PARQUEAR. *v.* Aparcar. *To park.*

PARQUEO. *n.m.* Aparcamiento. *Parking.*

PARRANDA. *n.f.* Multitud, montón de cosas, especialmente si son viejas o en desuso. *Lot, group, heap.* ~Una parranda de sillas. *A heap of old chairs.*

PARTIDA. *n.f.* •Confesar uno la PARTIDA. Decir la verdad que se estaba ocultando. *To tell the truth, come clean.*

PARTIDO. *n.m.* Partida. *Game.* || **2.** •Dar PARTIDO. Conceder ventaja. *To yield as a handicap, to spot (points, etc.).*

PARVADA. *n.f.* Bandada de aves. *Flock.*

PASABLE. *adj.* Se dice de un río o arroyo que se puede vadear. *Fordable.* ~El río es PASABLE a la altura de Melo. *You can cross the river at Melo.*

PASAJE. *n.m.* Calle sin salida. *Cul-de-sac.*

PASAR. *v.* Engañar. *To put one over on.* ~Se cree que me va a PASAR a mí. *He thinks he can put one over on me.* ||**2.** Caerle antipático una persona. *To dislike a person.* ~No lr PASO a este tipo. *I can't stand that guy.*

PASCANA. *n.f.* (Acad.) Etapa o parada en un viaje. *Stage, stop (during a journey).* ||**2.** Posada, mesón, paradero. *Wayside inn.*

PASEANDERO. *n.m.* (Acad.) Paseador, persona que pasea mucho y con frecuencia. *Fond of strolling.*

PASEO. *n.m.* Excursión. *Outing, trip.* ~No vivo aquí, estoy de PASEO. *I don't live here, I'm just visiting.*

PASMADO. *adj.* Infectado (herida). *Infected (wound).* || **2.** Enfermo, en especial si sufre de infecciones. *Sick, swolen (from infections).*

PASMARSE. *v.* Infectarse una herida. *To become infected.* || **2.** Enfermarse una persona. *To fall ill.*

PASMAZÓN. *n.m.* Pasmo, malestar general. *Illness.*

PASO. *n.m.* Vado en un río. *Ford.* || **2.** •Marcar el PASO. Obedecer sumisamente. *To toe the line.* ~Mira que cuando ingreses en el ejército te van a hacer marcar el PASO. *You just wait till you get into the army, they'll really make you toe the line.* || **3.** •Sacar del PASO. Sacar de apuro. *To get someone out of a jam.* || **4.** •A PASO de oca. A paso de ganso. *Goose step.*

PASOSO. *adj.* Poroso. *Porous, permeable, absorbent.*

PASPARSE. *v.* Agrietarse la piel por efecto del frío. *To crack, become cracked (in the lips or the skin).*

PASTA. *n.f.* •Las PASTAS. La pasta. *Pasta.* ~Las PASTAS engordan. La pasta engorda. *Pasta is fattening.*

PASTAJE. *n.m.* Pastizal. *Pasture, grazing land.* || **2.** Pasto. *Grass.* || **3.** Derecho que se paga para que pasten los animales en algún lugar. *Grazing fee.* || **4.** El hecho de pastar los animales en algún lugar. *Grazing.*

PASTAL. *n.m.* Pastizal. *Pasture, grazing land.*

PASTO. *n.m.* Hierba. *Grass.*

PASTOREAR. *v.* Apacentar, pastar. *To graze, pasture.* || **2.** Acechar. *To lie in wait for.*

PASTOSO. *adj.* (Acad.) Dícese del terreno que tiene buenos pastos. *Grassy.*

PASUDO. *adj.* Se dice del pelo ensortijado. *Kinky (hair).*

PATA. *n.f.* (Acad.) •Bailar en una PATA. Estar muy contento. *To jump with joy, to be overjoyed.* || **2.** PATA arriba.*On one's back.* || **3.** •Estirar la PATA. *To kick the bucket (coll.).* || **4.** •Tener PATA. Tener influencias. *To have contacts.*

PATADA. *n.f.* •Caerle a uno como una PATADA (una cosa). *To produce a disagreable effect on someone.* ~Este vino blanco me cayó como unaPATADA. *The white wine really disagreed with me.* ~Lo que me dijo de Juan me cayó como una PATADA. *What he said about John really disturbed me (was like a kick in the teeth).* || **2.** Retroceso de una arma de fuego al ser disparada. *Kick, recoil.* || **3.** Descarga, golpe de corriente. *Shock, jolt.* •Toqué el cable y me dio tremenda PATADA.

I touched the cable and it gave me a real shock. || **4.** •Andar a las PATADAS. *Not to get along, to fight like cats and dogs.* || **5.** •En dos PATADAS. Con facilidad, sin esfuerzo, en un santiamén. *In a flash, in no time.*

PATAGRÁS. *n.m.* Cierto queso blando y mantecoso. *A type of soft cheese.*

PATASCA. *n.f.* Guisado de maíz con carne de cerdo. *Pork and corn stew.*

PATEAR. *v.* Hacer daño una comida o un licor. *To disagree with.* ~Me patean las CEBOLLAS. *Onions disagree with me.* || **2.** Cocear un animal. *To kick (animal).* || **3.** Retroceder con fuerza y súbitamente una arma de fuego a ser disparada. *To kick, recoil (firearm).* || **4.** Subirse a la cabeza los vapores de un licor. *To go to one's head (liquor).* || **5.** Caminar a pie largas distancias. *To walk a long distance.*

PATIMOCHO. *adj.* Cojo. *Lame.*

PATINADA. *n.f.* Patinazo. *Skid.* ~El coche dio una PATINADA. *The car skidded (went into a skid).*

PATITO. *n.m.* •Hacer PATITOS. Hacer cabrillas. *To play ducks and drakes.*

PATO. *n.m.* Orinal. *Bedpan.* || **2.** Marica. *Homosexual.* || **3.** •Pagar el PATO. Pagar los vidrios rotos. *To take the rap, to be the scapegoat, to get the blame.* || **4.** •Ser uno el PATO de la boda. *To be a laughing stock.*

PATOJEAR. *v.* Caminar moviéndose de un lado para otro como los patos. *To waddle in walking.*

PATÓN. *adj.* Patudo. *Having large feet.* ~¡Que niño tan PATÓN! *What enormous feet this child has!*

PATOTA. *n.f.* Pandilla de jóvenes que se divierten cometiendo desmanes en los lugares públicos. *Mob, street gang.* || **2.** Grupo de amigos. *Mob, crowd of friends.*

PATRONO. *n.m.* Santo elegido como protector de una congregación religiosa o laica. *Patron saint.*

PATULECO. *adj.* (Acad.) Persona que tiene un defectio físico en los pies o en las piernas. *Bowlegged, bandy-legged.*

PAVA. *n.m.* (Acad.) Recipiente de metal, o hierro esmaltado, con asa en la parte superior, tapa y pico, que se usa para calentar agua, hervidor. *Kettle.*

PAVO. *n.m.* (Acad.) Pasajero clandestino, polizón. *Stowaway.* || **2.** (Acad.) •Comer PAVO. En un baile, quedarse sin bailar una mujer, por no haber sido invitada a ello. *To be a wallflower.* || **3.** Sufrir un desengaño. *To be disappointed.*

PAY. *n.m.* Torta. *Pie.*

PAYA. n.f. Composición poética dialogada que improvisan los payadores. *Improvised song, poetic composition improvised by strolling singers.*

PAYADA (variante de **paya**).

PAYADOR. *n.m.* Cantor popular errante. *Traveling country singer who accompanies himself on the guitar.*

PAYAR. *v.* Cantar **payadas**. *To improvise songs.*

PAYASEAR. *v.* Hacer el payaso. *To clown around.*

PAZOTE. *n.m.* Hierba arómatica usada en la medicina popular. *Wormseed, Mexican tea.*

PEAL. *n.m.* (Acad.) Lazo que se arroja a un animal para derribarlo. *Lasso.*

PECHADA. *n.m.* (Acad.) Golpe, encontrón dado con el pecho o con los hombros. *Push, shove.* || **2.** (Acad.) Golpe que da el jinete con el pecho del caballo. *Bumping contest between two riders.* || **3.** Sablazo. *Touch for a loan.*

PECHADOR. *n.m.* (Acad.) Sablista, estafador. *Sponger, one who borrows from friends.*

PECHAR. *v.* (Acad.) Sablear, estafar. *To scrounge money off, to touch someone for a loan.* || **2.** Dar **pechadas**. *To shove, jostle.*

PECHAZO. *n.m.* (Acad.) Sablazo, estafa. *Sponging, scrounging.* ||**2.** Empujón. *Push, shove.*

PECHUGA. *n.m.* (Acad.) Enfado que se le causa a una persona. *Trouble, annoyance.* || **3.** Abuso de confianza. *Abuse of trust.* || **4.**

Desenfado, cinismo. *Nerve, audacity, gall, impudence.*

PECHUGÓN. *adj.* (Acad.) Indelicado, sinvergüenza, gorrón. *Shameless individual, impudent person, sponger.*

PECHUGONA. *adj.* Se dice de la mujer de pechos abultados. *Big-breasted.*

PEDIDERA. *n.f.* Petición. *Petition.*

PEDILÓN (variante de **pedinche**).

PEDINCHE. *m.* Pedigüeño. *Scrounger.*

PEDIR. *v.* •PEDIR para. Pedir, solicitar. *To request.* ~PIDIÓ para salir temprano. *He asked if he could leave early.*

PEDREGÓN. *n.m.* Pedrejón. *Rock, boulder.*

PEGA. *n.f.* (Acad.) Trabajo, ocupación retribuida. *Work, occupation.* ~Tengo mucha PEGA. *I'm snowed under with work.* ||**2.** •Buscar PEGA. *To look for work.*

PEGADA. *n.f.* Golpe (boxeo). *Punch.* ~Tiene buena PEGADA. *He packs a good punch.*

PEGAJOSO. *adj.* Pegadizo. *Catchy (music, song).*

PEGAPEGA. *n.m.* Cualquier materia que sirve para pegar. *Glue.* || **2.** Adulador. *Flatterer.* || **3.** Liga para cazar pájaros. *Birdlime.*

PEGAR. *v.* •PEGARLA. Tener suerte. *To be lucky.* || **2.** Lograr lo que se desea. *To get what one wants.* || **3.** •PEGÁRSELE a uno las sábanas. Levantarse tarde. *To get up late.*

PEGOSTE. *n.m.* Pegote. *Sticking plaster.*

PEGUAL. *n.m.* (Acad.) Cincha con argollas para sujetar los animales cogidos con lazo o para transportar objetos pesados. *Saddle cinch.*

PEINADOR. *n.m.* Peluquero. *Hairdresser, stylist.* || **2.** Tocador. *Dressing table.*

PEINILLA. *n.f.* (Acad.) Peine alargado y angosto de una sola hilera de dientes. *Comb.*

PELA. *n.f.* Paliza. *Beating, thrashing.*

PELADA. *n.f.* Corte de pelo. *Haircut.* || **2.** Cabeza calva o cortada al rape. *Baldness, bald head; head of close-cropped hair.* ||**3.** Error, equivocación. *Blunder, mistake.*

PELADERA. *n.f.* Murmuración. *Gossip.*

PELADERO. *n.m.* (Acad.) Terreno pelado, desprovisto de vegetación. *Wasteland.* ‖ **2.** (Variante de **pelador**).

PELADOR. *n.m.* Pelapatatas. *Peeler.*

PELAPAPAS. *n.m.* Pelapatatas. *Peeler.*

PELAR. *v.* Desacreditar. *To slander, run down.* ‖ **2.** Dar una paliza. *To beat up.*

PELEADO. *adj.* Enemistado. *On bad terms with someone.* Juan y María están PELEADOS. *John and Mary are not talking to each others.*

PELECHO. *n.m.* Piel que mudan los animales. *Sloughed skin.* ‖ **2.** Ropa pobre o raída. *Old clothing.*

PELERO. *n.m.* Sudadero de las caballerías. *Horse blanket.*

PELLEJERÍA. *n.f.* Trance apurado, dificultad, contratiempo. *Jam, fix, trouble, difficulty.*

PELLÓN. *n.m.* Pelleja curtida que se usa sobre la silla de montar. *Sheepskin saddle blanket.*

PELO. *n.m.* •Por un PELO. *By the skin of one's teeth.* ~Me salvé por un PELO. *I escaped by the skin of my teeth.* ~Perdí el autobus por un PELO. *I missed the bus by a few seconds.* ‖ **2.** •Venir una cosa al PELO. Convenir, venir a propósito. *To suit someone just fine, to be just what one wanted.* ~Esta vacación nos vino al PELO. *This vacation was just what we needed.* ‖ **3.** •De medio PELO. Que aparenta tener una educación y una posición social más elevada de la que en realidad tiene. *Of no social standing, socially unimportant.* ‖ **4.** •Dejarlo a uno en PELO. Arruinar a una persona, dejarlo sin dinero. *To leave penniless.*

PELOTA. *n.m.* Imbécil. *Jerk.* ‖ **2.** •PELOTA de fútbol. Balón (fútbol). *Football (in soccer).* ‖ **3.** Pasión por una persona o cosa. *Passion for someone or something.* ‖**4.** •Tener PELOTA por. Estar muy enamorado de una persona. *To have a passion for, be madly in love with.* ‖ **5.** Manceba. *Mistress.* ‖ **6.** •Tener PELOTAS. Ser audaz. *To have guts.*

PELOTERO. *n.m.* Jugador de béisbol. *Baseball player.*

PELOTUDEZ. Estupidez. *Stupidity.*

PELOTUDO. *n.m.* Imbécil. *Jerk.* ~Este tipo es un PELOTUDO. *What a jerk this guy is!*

PELUQUEADA. *n.f.* (Acad.) Acción y efecto de **peluquear** o **peluquearse**. *Hair cutting.*

PELUQUEAR. *v.* (Acad.) Cortar el pelo a una persona. *To give a haircut.* ‖ **2.** Cortarse el pelo una persona. *To have a haircut.*

PENA. *n.f.* (Acad.) Vergüenza. *Embarrassment.* ~Me da PENA molestarle a esta hora de la noche. *I feel embarrassed disturbing you at that time of the night.*

PENAL. *n.m.* (dep.) Falta, infracción. *Foul (in the penalty area), penalty (kick).*

PENCA. *n.f.* Racimo (de plátanos). *Bunch (of bananas).* ‖ **2.** •A la pura PENCA. Harapiento, casi desnudo. *Nude, naked.*

PENDEJADA. *n.f.* Estupidez, tontería. *Stupidity.*

PENDEJEAR. *v.* Hacer o decir necedades o tonterías. *To act the fool, to behave irresponsibly.*

PENDEJO. *adj.* Estúpido. *Dumb.* ‖ **2.** *n.m.* Estúpido. *Dummy.* ‖ **3.** •Hacerse el PENDEJO. Hacerse el tonto. *To act dumb.*

PENDIENTE. *adj.* •Estar PENDIENTE de (un problema). Tener alguna preocupación o aprehension. *To be preocupied.*

PENDOLEAR. *v.* Escribir mucho. *To write a lot.*

PENITENCIADO. *n.m.* Presidario. *Convict*

PENOSO. *adj.* (persona) Encogido, vergonzoso. *Bashful, timid, shy.*

PENSIÓN. *n.f.* (Acad.) Pena, pesar. *Sorrow.* ~Tiene PENSIÓN. *She's down in the dumps.* ~Dicen que murió de PENSIÓN. *They said he died from a broken heart.*

PEÓN. *n.m.* (Acad.) Jornalero cuyo trabajo no requiere arte ni habilidad. *Agricultural laborer, farmhand.* ‖ **2.** Peón de albañil. *Mason's helper.*

PEONADA. *n.f.* (Acad.) Conjunto de peones que trabajan en una obra. *Gang of laborers.*

PEONÍA. *n.f.* Obra que un peón puede hacer en un día. *Day's plowing.*

PEPA. *n.f.* (Acad.) Semilla, grano, almendra. *Seed (of an apple, melon, etc.).* || **2.** Hueso, carozo. *Pit, stone (of an avocado, pear, etc.).*

PEPAZO. *n.m.* Tiro en el blanco. *Shot, hit, throw; accurate shot.*

PEPENA. *n.f.* (Acad.) Acción y efecto de **pepenar.**

PEPENAR. *v.* (Acad.) Recoger del suelo, rebuscar. *To pick up.* || **2.** Escarbar, hurgar. *To scavenge, scour the rubbish.*

PERCUDIRSE. *v.* (Acad.) Penetrarse de suciedad una cosa de manera que ya no puede quedar completamente limpio. *To become ingrained with dirt.*

PERCUTIDO. *adj.* Penetrado de suciedad un cosa de manera que ya no puede quedar completamente limpio. *Ingrained with dirt.*

PERFILARSE. *v.* Adelgazar. *To get slim.*

PERFORMANCE. *n.f.* (aut.mec.) Comportamiento. *Performance.* || **2.** (dep.) Desempeño. *Performance.*

PERICA. *n.f.* Borrachera. *Drunkenness.*

PERICO. *n.m/f.* Charlatán, hablador, locuaz. *Talkative, gossipy.* || **2.** •Echar PERICOS. Hablar locuazmente. *To to in a speaking mood.*

PERICOTE. *n.m.* (Acad.) Ratón, roedor pequeño (nota: en la previa edición decía «Rata grande», y así aparece en la mayoría de los diccionarios). *Large rat.* || **2.** •Mientras los gatos duermen, los PERICOTES se pasean. Cuando los jefes se descuidan, los subalternos no cumplen con sus obligaciones. *While the cat's away, the mice will play.*

PERJUICIADO. *adj.* Perjudicado. *Prejudiced.*

PERMISIONARIO. *n.m.* Persona o institución que tiene un permiso o concesión oficial para algo. *Official agent or agency; concessionaire.*

PERRADA. *n.f.* (Acad.) Mala jugada, mala pasada. *Dirty trick.*

PERSONERO. *n.m.* Representante. *Representative.*

PERUÉTANO. *adj.* || **1.** Molesto, pesado. *Boring, tedious.* || **2.** *n.m.* Persona molesta, pesada. *Bore.*

PESA. *n.f.* Carnicería, tienda donde se vende carne. *Butcher's shop.*

PESADOR. *n.m.* Carnicero. *Butcher.*

PESAR. *v.* Vender carne. *To sell meat.*

PESCADO. *n.m.* Pez. *Fish.*

PESCOCEAR. *v.* Dar pescozones. *To slap on the back of the neck.*

PESCUEZÓN. *adj.* Pescozudo. *Thick-necked, fat in the neck.* || **2.** De cuello largo. *Long-necked.*

PESEBRE. *n.m.* Nacimiento, belén. *Nativity scene, crib.*

PESEBRERA (variante de **pesebre**).

PESERO (variante de **pesador**).

PESETADA. *n.f.* Treta, chasco. *Joke, trick.*

PESETERO. *n.m.* Se dice de la persona que suele pedir dinero prestado. *Sponging, cadging.*

PESOR. *n.m.* (Acad.) Pesantez. *Weight, heaviness.*

PESTAÑAR. *v.* Pestañear. *To blink, wink.*

PETACA. *n.f.* Persona gruesa de baja estatura. *Short fat person.* || **2.** Baúl de cuero. *Leather-covered chest.* || **3.** Haragán, vago. *Lazy person.* || **4.** Joroba. *Hump.* || **5.** •Echarse con las PETACAS. Aflojar, desmayar. *To loose heart, get down-hearted.*

PETACÓN. *adj.* Rechoncho. *Tubby, fat, chubby.*

PETATE. *n.m.* Colchón hecho con hojas de palma. *Straw sleeping mat.* || **2.** Esterilla de palma con la que se confeccionan cestos, canastas, sombreros, etc. *Straw matting used to make baskets, hats, etc.* || **3.** Persona insignificante. *Poor devil.*

PETICIONAR. *v.* Elevar una petición. *To petition.*

PETISO (variante de **petizo**).

PETIZO. *adj.* (Acad.) Pequeño, bajo, de poca altura, estatura o alzada. *Small, short.* || **2.** *n.m.* Persona de baja estatura. *Shorty* (coll.). || **3.** Caballo de poca alzada. *Small* horse, pony. || **4.** Rechoncho. *Stocky, chubby.*

PIAL (variante de **peal**).

PIALAR. *v.* Enlazar un animal por las patas. *To hobble a horse.*

PIALE. *n.m.* Acción de tirar el lazo para enlazar un animal por las patas. *Throw of the lasso.*

PIANO. *n.m.* •PIANO a PIANO. Sin prisa. *Calm down, take it easy.* || **2.** •Tocar el PIANO. Robar, hurtar. *To rob, steal.*

PIBE. *n.m.* Chiquillo (tiene matiz afectuosa). *Youngster, kid.*

PICA. *n.f.* (Acad.) Camino o senda abierta por el hombre a través de le espesura del monte. *Path, trail.*

PICADA. *n.f.* (Acad.) Camino o senda abierta por el hombre a través de le espesura del monte. *Path, trail.* || **2.** Aperitivo. *Nibbles, snack.* || 3. •Bajar en PICADA. Bajar en picado. *To nose-dive, plummet, take a nose-dive.*

PICADO. *adj.* (Acad.) Achispado, calamocano. *Typsy.*

PICAFLOR. *n.m.* Colibrí. *Hummingbird.* || **2.** Galanteador, donjuan. *Womenizer, flirt.*

PICANA. *n.f.* (Acad.) Aguijada de los boyeros. *Cattle prod, goad.* || **2.** Espuela. *Spur.*

PICANEAR. *v.* (Acad.) Aguijar a los bueyes. *To goad, prod.*

PICANTE. *n.m.* Guisado de mondongo y otros ingredientes, con much ají picante. *Very hot sauce, highly seasoned sauce or stew.*

PICAR. *v.* Moler o desmenuzar una cosa. *To grind, crush.* || **2.** -se. Embriagarse a medias. *To get high.*

PICARÓN. *n.m.* Especie de buñuelo. *Fritter.*

PICHANA. *n.f.* Escoba rústica hecha con un manojo de ramitas. *Bass broom.*

PICHICATO. *adj.* Mezquino, cicatero. *Mean, stingy.*

PICHINCHA. *n.f.* Ocasión, ganga. *Bargain.* || **2.** precio bajo que se paga por algo valioso. *Bargain price.* || **3.** Negocio muy bueno. *Good deal.* || **4.** Suerte. *Lucky break.*

PICHINCHERO. *adj.* Se dice de la perso-

na que busca **pichinchas** o lo que se vende por debajo del precio normal. *Bargain-hunter.*

PICHÓN. *n.m.* Muchacho inexperto, novicio, aprendiz. *Novice, greenhorn.* || **2.** Pollo de ave, excepto el de la gallinas. *Chick, young bird.*

PICHONEAR. *v.* || **1.** Ganar en el juego a un jugador inexperto. *To win easily (game).* || **2.** Engañar. *To deceive, trick.*

PICHULEAR. *v.* Hacer negocios de poca monta. *To be a small-time businessman.*

PICHULEO. *n.m.* Negocio de poca monta. *Small-time dealing.*

PICHULÍN. *n.m.* Pene de los niños. *Weenie.*

PICORETO. *n.m.* Charlatán, indiscreto. *Loose-tongued, indiscreet.*

PICOSO. *adj.* Picante. *Hot, spicy.*

PICOTÓN. *n.m.* Picotazo. *Peck.*

PIE[1]. *n.m.* •Ganado en PIE. El ganado menor o mayor que se vende vivo. *Livestock, cattle on the hoof.* || **2.** •Leche al PIE de la vaca. Leche recién extraída de la vaca. *Fresh milk from the cow.*

PIE[2] (se pronuncia *pai*). Pastel. *Pie.*

PIEDRA. *n.f.* (Acad.) •Piedra de MOLER. La de buen tamaño, con una cara cóncava o plana sobre la cual una persona desliza otra piedra llamada manol, para triturar diversos tipos de granos. *Stone for grounding a variety of grains.*

PIEL. *n.f.* •Ser la PIEL de Judas. Ser muy travieso y revoltoso. *To be a little monster or devil.*

PIEZA. *n.f.* •Ser de una sola PIEZA. Ser recto, probo. *To be an upright citizen.* || **2.** •PIEZA redonda. Cuarto de alquiler independiente con puerta a la calle. *Rented room with private entrance.* || **3.** Dormitorio. *Bedroom.* || **4.** Cuarto (hotel). *Hotel room.*

PIFIA. *n.f.* Burla, escarnio, rechifla. *Booing and hissing, catcalls.*

PIFIAR. *v.* (Acad.) Burlar, escarnecer, hacer bromas pesadas. *To joke about, mock.* || **2.** Llevarse un chasco. *To be disappointed, to suffer a setback.*

PIJOTEAR. *v.* Regatear. *To haggle.*

PIJOTERÍA. *n.f.* Mezquindad, tacañería. *Meanness.* || **2.** Pequeña cantidad. *Insignificant amount.* || **3.** Bagatela. *Trifle.*

PIJOTERO. *adj.* Tacaño, mezquino. *Mean.*

PILA. *n.f.* Gran cantidad o número. *A lot, heaps.* ~Hace una PILA de años. *A great many years ago.* || **2.** •Tener PILAS. *To have a lot, heaps of.*

PILATUNA. *n.f.* Pillería, jugarreta. *Prank, dirty trick.*

PILATUNO. *adj.* Se dice de lo notoriamente injusto. *Manifestly unjust.*

PILCA. *n.f.* (Acad.) Pared de piedra en seco, pirca. *Stone wall.*

PILCHA. *n.f.* (Acad.) Prenda de vestir, particularmente si es elegante y cara. *Clothes.*

PILOTEAR. *v.* Pilotar (avión). *To pilot, fly (an airplane).* || **2.** Ayudar a alguien, dirigiéndolo en un asunto. *To guide, direct.* || **3.** Patrocinar o dirigir una empresa o una iniciativa cualquiera. *To run, manage.*

PIÑA. *n.f.* Trompada, torta. *Blow, punch.* || **2.** •Darse PIÑAS. *To fight, exchange blows.*

PIÑAL. *n.m.* Plantación de piñas o **ananás**. *Pineapple plantation.*

PINCHE, *adj.* Maldito. *Lousy, damn, bloody.* ~Todo por unos PINCHES centavos. *All for a few lousy pennies.* ~¿Por qué no nos vamos de este PINCHE sitio? *Let's get out of this God-forsaken place.*

PINEDO. *n.m.* (Acad.) Pinar. *Pine forest.*

PINGANILLA. *n.m.* Persona pobre que se las da de elegante. *Poor man with pretensions of elegance.*

PININO. *n.m.* Pinito. •Hacer PININOS. Hacer pinitos. *To take one's first steps.*

PINTA. *n.f.* Aire o señal de casta o linaje. *Lineage trait or characteristic.* ~Este muchacho tiene la PINTA de los Hernández. *This boy is a true Hernandez, you can't deny he's an Hernandez.* || **2.** Ausencia del escolar. *Absence from school, truancy.*

PINTADO. *adj.* Parecido, semejante. *Like, identical.* ~Este niño sale PINTADO al padre.

The boy looks exactly, is the spitting image of his father.

PINTAR. *v.* Dar señales de que va a salir bien o mal una cosa. *To appear to be going well or badly.* ~El negocio PINTA bien. *It looks as though the business will be a success.* ~La cosa no PINTA nada bien. *Things don't look good at all.*

PINTO (variante de **pintado**).

PINTOR. *adj.* Fachendoso, pinturero. *Boasting, showing-off.*

PINZA. *n.f.* •Tratar a alguien con PINZA. *To treat someone with kid gloves.*

PIOCHA. *n.f.* Azadón. *Pickaxe.*

PIOLA. *n.f.* Soga. *Cord.*

PIOLÍN. *n.m.* (Acad.) Cordel delgado de cáñamo, algodón u otra fibra. *Parcel twine, string.*

PIPA. *n.f.* Barriga. *Belly.*

PIPIRIPAO. *adj.* Mediocre, de escaso valor. *Of little value.*

PIPÓN. *adj.* Barrigón. *Paunchy, pot-bellied.* || **2.** Harto, repleto de comer. *Full, replete (to have had too much to eat).*

PIQUE. *n.m.* Bote que da la pelota al tocar el suelo. *Rebound, bounce.* ~La pelota dio tres PIQUES. *The ball bounced three times.*

PIQUETAZO. *n.m.* Picotazo. *Peck.*

PIQUETEAR. *v.* Formar un piquete frente a. *To picket.*

PIQUIÑA. *n.f.* Picazón, comezón. *Itching.*

PIQUININO. *n.m.* Niño, chiquillo. *Child, youngster.* || **2.** Se dice de la persona de baja estatura. *Short (person).*

PIRCA. *n.f.* (Acad.) Pared de piedra en seco. *Dry-stone wall.*

PIRCAR. *v.* (Acad.) Cerrar un lugar con muro de piedra en seco. *To erect a dry-stone wall.*

PIRULO. *n.m.* Niño de cuerpo delgado. *Slim child.*

PISCO. *adj.* Presuntuoso, vano. *Conceited, vain.* || **2.** Pavo. *Turkey.*

PISO. *n.m.* Suelo. *Floor.* ~No entres, que

está el PISO mojado. *Don't go in, the floor's wet.*

PISÓN. *n.m.* Pisotón. *Stamp on the foot.*

PISTERO. *adj.* (Acad.) Dícese de la persona muy aficionada al dinero. *Mercenary, fond of money.*

PISTO. *n.m.* (Acad.) Dinero. *Money.*

PISTÓN. *n.m.* Corneta. *Buggle.*

PITADA. *n.f.* Fumada. *Puff (of a cigarette).*

PITADOR. *n.m.* Fumador. *Smoker.*

PITAR. *v.* (Acad.) Fumar cigarrillos. *To smoke.*

PITEAR. *v.* Hacer sonar un pito. *To wistle, blow a wistle.*

PITO. *n.m.* •Tocar PITO. *To be out of place, not to belong.* ~¿Qué PITO toca este tipo aquí? *What on earth is this fellow doing here?* ~Nosotros aquí no tocamos un PITO. *That's nothing to do with us.* || **2.** Pene. *Weenie.* || **3.** Pipa de fumar. *Pipe (for smoking).* || **3.** Garrapata. *Tick.*

PITÓN. *n.m.* Tubo de metal con que se remata la manga de riego. *Nozzle of a hose pipe.*

PITRE. *adj.* Elegante con afectación. *Extravagantly dressed.*

PITUCO. *adj.* (Acad.) Dícese del petimetre. *Elegantly dressed, dashing young man or woman.* ~Vienes muy PITUCO esta noche. *I can see you're all dressed up tonight.*

PIYAMA. *n.m.* (Acad.) Pijama. *Pajamas.*

PIZARRÓN. *n.m.* (Acad.) Pizarra. *Blackboard.*

PLACA. *n.f.* Mancha en la piel producida por alguna enfermedad. *Spot caused by a throat or mouth infection.*

PLAGADO. *adj.* Lleno o cubierto (de). *Full (of).* ~Este libro esta PLAGADO de errores. *This book if full of mistakes.*

PLAGIAR. *v.* (Acad.) Apoderarse de una persona para obtener recate por su libertad, secuestrar. *To kidnap.*

PLAGIARIO. *n.m.* Secuestrador. *Kidnapper.*

PLAGIO. *n.m.* Secuestro. *Kidnap, kidnap-*

ping.

PLAN. *n.m.* Llano, planicie. *Plain, plateau.* || **2.** Parte plana de la hoja de las armas blancas. *Flat (of a sword).* || **3.** Fondo plano de algo. *Flat bottom.* El plan de un barco. *The flat bottom of a boat.*

PLANAZO. *n.m.* Golpe dado con la parte plana de las armas blancas. *Blow with the flat of a sword.*

PLANCHADA. *n.f.* Planchado. *Ironing.* ~Dale una PLANCHADITA al cuello. *Just run the iron over the collar.*

PLANCHADO. *adj.* Sin dinero. *Broke.*

PLANCHAR. *v.* No ser invitada una mujer a bailar. *To sit out a dance, to be a wallflower.* || **2.** Cometer un error o indiscreción que le deje uno en ridículo. *To make a fool of oneself.*

PLANILLA. *n.f.* (Acad.) Estado de cuentas, liquidación, ajuste de gasto. *Expense account, statement of account.* || **2.** Nómina, planilla (de sueldos). *Payroll.* || **3.** •Estar en PLANILLA. *To be on the payroll.* || **4.** Personal. *Staff.* || **5.** Impreso, formulario. *Form, application form.*

PLANTARSE. *v.* Engalanarse. *To doll oneself up.*

PLANTEL. *n.m.* Personal. *Staff.*

PLASTA. *adj.* Cachazudo. *Lazy, slow, sluggish, laid-back.* || **2.** *n.m.* Cachaza. *Laid-back attitude, slowness.* || **3.** Persona cachazuda. *Slow or laid-back person.* || **4.** Persona aburrida. *Bore.* || **5.** Persona fea. *Ugly mug.*

PLATA. *n.f.* Dinero. *Money.* || **2.** •Estar podrido en PLATA. *To be stinking rich, to be rolling in money.*

PLATAL. *n.m.* Dineral. *Fortune.* ~Nos salió un PLATAL. *It cost us a fortune.*

PLÁTICA. *n.f.* Conversación. *Talk.*

PLATICAR. *v.* Conversar. *To talk, chat.* ~PLATICARON de muchas cosas. *They talked about many things.*

PLATILLO. *n.m.* •PLATILLO volador. Platillo volante. *Flying saucer.*

PLATO. *n.m.* •Ser un PLATO. Ser notable por

algo gracioso o raro. *To be a scream.* ‖ **2.** •¡Qué PLATO! Exclamación que puede ser de admiración, de sorpresa o bien de disgusto. *What a scream!, what a character!*

PLATÓN. *n.m.* Fuente o plato grande para el servicio de mesa. *Large dish, serving dish.* ‖ **2.** Palangana. *Washbasin.*

PLATUDO. *adj.* (Acad.) Que tiene mucho dinero, rico, adinerado. *Rich, well-off.*

PLAYA. *n.f.* (Acad.) Espacio plano, ancho y despejado, destinado a usos determinados en los poblados e industrias de mucha superficie. PLAYA de estacionamiento, PLAYA de maniobras, etc. *Flat open space.* ‖ **2.** •PLAYA de estacionamiento. Aparcamiento. *Parking lot.*

PLAYO. *adj.* Que tiene poco fondo. *Shallow.* Un río PLAYO, un plato PLAYO. *A shallow river, a shallow plate.*

PLAZA. *n.f.* Mercado. *Market.* ~Un producto de lo mejor que hay en PLAZA. *One of the best product on the market.*

PLEGARSE. *v.* Unirse. *To join in.* ~Mucha gente se fue PLEGANDO al desfile. *Many people joined the procession.*

PLEITEAR. *v.* Discutir. *To argue.*

PLEITO. *n.m.* Discusión. *Argument.* ‖ **2.** Pelea. *Fight, boxing match.* ‖ **3.** Disputa. *Quarrel.*

PLOMERÍA. *n.f.* Fontanería. *Plumbing.*

PLOMERO. *n.m.* Fontanero. *Plumber.*

PLOMO. *n.m.* Bala. *Bullet, shot.* ‖ **2.** De color de plomo, plomizo. *Lead grey, lead-colored.*

PLUMA. *n.f.* •Pluma FUENTE. Pluma estilográfica. *Fountain pen.* ‖ **2.** Grifo o llave de agua. *Faucet.* ‖ **3.** Prostituta. *Prostitute.*

PLUSCAFÉ. *n.m.* Trago de licor que se suele tomar después del café. *Liqueur (taken after a meal).*

POBLACIÓN. *n.f.* •POBLACIÓN flotante. Población de tránsito que siempre tienen las ciudades grandes. *Floating population, people not permanently living in a city.*

POBLADA. *n.f.* (Acad.) Multitud, gentío, turba, populacho, en especial cuando está levantisca o agresiva; motín, asonada, tumulto. *Crowd, multitude; revolt, armed rising.*

POBLANO. *adj.* (Acad.) Lugareño, campesino. *Rustic, rural.* ~Una reunión POBLANA. *A town meeting.* ‖ **2.** Aldeano. *Villager.*

POCILLO. *n.m.* Taza pequeña. *Small coffee cup.*

PODER. *n.m.* •Casarse por PODER. Casarse por poderes. *To get married by proxy.*

PODRIDO. *adj.* •Olor a PODRIDO. Mal olor. *Foul odor.* ~Aquí hay olor a PODRIDO. *Something must be rotting in this place.* ‖ **2.** •Estar PODRIDO en plata. Tener mucho dinero. *To be stinking (filthy) rich.*

POEMA. *n.m.* •Ser un POEMA. Ser divino, bonito, exquisito. *To be lovely, divine, exquisite.*

POLITIQUEAR. *v.* (Acad.) Hacer política de intrigas y bajezas. *To indulge in politicking.*

POLLA. *n.f.* (Acad.) Apuesta, especialmente en carreras de caballos. *Bet, gambling pool.* ‖ **2.** (Acad.) Carrera de caballos donde se corre la **polla.** *Horse race.*

POLLERA. *n.f.* (Acad.) Falda externa del vestido femenino. *Skirt.*

POLLERO. *n.m.* Jugador. *Gambler.*

POLLO. *n.m.* •Listo el POLLO. Y se acabó. *And that's that.* ~Nos tomamos un taxi y listo el POLLO. *We'll take a taxi and that's that!*

POLOLEAR. *v.* Molestar, importunar. *To annoy.* ‖ **2.** Coquetear. *To flirt with.*

POLOLEO. *n.m.* Coqueteo. *Flirting.*

POLTRONEAR. *v.* Holgazanear. *To loaf around.*

POLVERO. *n.m.* Polvareda. *Cloud of dust.*

POLVORILLA (variante de **polvorín**).

POLVORÍN. *n.m.* Persona de mal genio que se enfada fácilmente. *Quick-tempered person.*

POLVORÓN. *n.m.* Especie de bizcocho dulce. *Cake.*

POMADA. *n.f.* •Hacer POMADA a alguien. Darle una paliza a alguien. *To give someone a thrashing.*

POMELO. *n.m.* Toronja. *Grapefruit.*

PONCHADA. *n.f.* Lo que cabe en un poncho. *Ponchoful, content of a poncho.* || **2.** Gran cantidad de cosas. *Large quantity (of anything).*

PONER. *v.* •PONLE. Cosa de, unos. ¿Cuánto se tarda en llegar? -PONLE dos horas. *How long does it take to get there? -About two hours.*

PONGO. *n.m.* Criado indio. *Indian servant.*

PONTAJE. *n.m.* Pontazgo. *Bridge toll.*

POPOLEAR. *v.* (Acad.) Molestar, importunar. *To annoy.*

POQUITO. *adj.* •Ser uno muy POQUITO. Ser apocado o tímido. *To be timid, have little confidence in oneself.*

POROTO. *n.m.* (Acad.) Especie de alubias de la cual se conocen muchas variedades en color y tamaño. *Green bean; kidney bean.* || **2.** Guiso que se hace con este vegetal. *Bean dish.* || **3.** •Apuntarse un POROTO. Anotarse o apuntarse un tanto en el juego, o un acierto en cualquier actividad. *To score, make a hit.* ~Te apuntaste (anotaste) un POROTO. *Well done!, congratulation!*

PORQUERÍA. *n.f.* •De PORQUERÍA. Asqueroso, malísimo. *Crummy, lousy.* ~Una película de PORQUERÍA. *A rotten film.* ~La novela es una PORQUERÍA. *That novel is rubbish.*

PORRAZO. *n.m.* •De un PORRAZO. De una sola vez, en un solo acto. *In one go, at one blow.*

PORTACIÓN. *n.f.* •PORTACIÓN de armas. Acción de llevar arma. *The carrying of arms.* ~Lo detuvieron por PORTACIÓN de armas. *He was arrested for carrying a firearm.*

PORTADOCUMENTOS. *n.m.* Portafolio. *Briefcase, attaché case.*

PORTAL. *n.m.* Belén, nacimiento. *Nativity scene.*

PORTALIGAS. *n.m.* (Acad.) Liguero de las mujeres. *Garter belt.*

POSTA. *n.f.* Carrera de relevos. *Relay, relay race.*

POSTEMILLA. *n.f.* Postema que sale en la encía. *Gumboil, abscess.*

POSTERGAR. *v.* Aplazar, retrasar. *To postpone, put off.* ~POSTERGÓ su decisión. *He put off (deferred) making a decision.* || **2.** Demorar. *To delay.*

POSTERGACIÓN. *n.f.* Retraso o aplazamiento. *Postponement, deferment, deferal.*

POSTULACIÓN. *n.f.* El hecho de proponer a un ciudadano como candidato para un puesto electivo. *Nomination, proposal.*

POSTULANTE. *n.m.* Candidato. *Candidate.*

POSTULAR. *v.* Proponer a un ciudadano como candidato para un puesto electivo *Nominate, propose.* || **2.** -se. Presentarse como candidato. *To stand, run for.*

POTEAR. *v.* (golf) Golpear la bola. *To putt.*

POTO. *n.m.* Trasero. *Bottom, backside.* || **2.** Parte posterior de una cosa. *Lower end.* || **3.** Vasija. *Earthenware jug.*

POTRANCO. *n.m.* Potrillo. *Colt, young horse.*

POTRERAJE. *n.m.* Precio que se paga por tener un animal pastando en un **potrero**. *Fee paid for use of grazing ground.*

POTRERO. *n.m.* (Acad.) Finca rústica, cercada y con árboles, destinada principalmente a la cría y sostenimiento de toda especie de ganado. *Cattle ranch.* || **2.** Terreno cercado. *Field.*

POTRO. *n.m.* Hernia, tumor. *Hernia, tumor.*

POTROSO. *adj.* Hernioso, que tiene una hernia. *To have a rupture o hernia.*

PRECISADO. *adj.* Obligado. *Forced, obliged.* ~Se vieron PRECISADOS a abandonar el barco. *They had (were obliged) to abandon ship.*

PRECISAR. *v.* Necesitar algo o alguien. *To need.* ~PRECISO herramientas. *I need tools.*

PREDICAMENTO (Angl.) *n.m.* Situación difícil. *Predicament.*

PREDIO. *n.m.* Terreno, propiedad, hacienda. *Estate, land, property.* || **2.** Local. *Premises, site, grounds.* ~En los PREDIOS de la universidad. *In the university grounds, on the university campus.*

PRELIMINAR. *n.m.* Partido eliminatorio. *Qualifying or preliminary game or competition.*

PREMIACIÓN. *n.f.* Entrega de premios. *Awarding of prizes.* || **2.** Ceremonia de entrega de premios. *Award ceremonies.* ~Se hizo el sorteo y PREMIACIÓN del concurso. *The draw was held and the prizes awarded.*

PREMUNIRSE. *v.* Precaverse. *To take precautions.*

PRENDEDOR. *n.m.* Broche. *Brooch.*

PRENDER. *v.* Encender (radio, luz, horno). *To turn on.*

PREOCUPACIÓN. *n.f.* Atención preferente que se da a algo. *Special consideration, preference, priority.*

PREOCUPARSE. *v.* Conceder atención preferente a algo. *To give special attention to something, give something priority.*

PRESA. *n.f.* Trozo de carne. *Piece of meat.* || **2.** Pieza (pollo). *Piece (of chicken): wing, breast, etc.*

PRESCINDENTE. *adj.* Se dice de quien se mantiene alejado por su propia voluntad de una disputa, lucha o competencia. *Nonparticipating.*

PRESENTACIÓN. *n.f.* Escrito dirigido a una autoridad, en que se pide alguna cosa. *Petition.*

PRESERVAR. *v.* Conservar, mantener. *To maintain.* ~PRESERVAR el salario real. *To maintain real wage levels.*

PRESIDENCIABLE. *adj.* Apto para ser presidente. *Capable of becoming president.* || **2.** Posible candidato a la presidencia. *Potential presidential candidate.*

PRESTAR. *v.* Pedir prestado. *To borrow (from).*

PRESTIGIADO. *adj.* Prestigioso. *Prestigious.*

PRESUPESTÍVORO. *n.m.* Empleado público. *Public employee.*

PRESUPUESTAL. *adj.* Presupuestario. *Budgetary.*

PRETENCIÓN. *n.f.* Presunción, vanidad. *Presumption, arrogance.*

PRETENCIOSO. adj. Presumido. *Vain, conceited.*

PRIMERA. *Adj.* •De PRIMERA. *In a high degree.* ~Es un mentiroso de PRIMERA. *He is quite a liar.*

PRINGAR. *v.* Lloviznar. *To drizzle.*

PROCER. *n.m.* Héroe nacional (en especial de la lucha por la independencia). *National hero (especially of a struggle for independence).*

PROCURA. *adj.* Acción de procurar, tratar de obtener algo que se desea. *Procuring, obtaining.* || **2.** •Andar en PROCURA de algo. Hacer diligencias para procurar algo. *To be trying to do or get something.*

PROCURADOR. *n.m.* •PROCURADOR general de la Nación. Ministro de Justicia. *Attorney general.*

PROCURADURÍA. *n.f.* •PROCURADURÍA general. *Attorney general's office.*

PRODUCIRSE. *v.* Acontecer, ocurrir. *To take place, occur.* ~El accidente se PRODUJO en la carretera de Mar de Plata. *The accident took place on the Mar de Plata highway.*

PRONTO. *adv.* •De PRONTO. A lo mejor. *Perhaps, maybe.* ~De PRONTO no se han enterado. *Perhaps they haven't heard.*

PRONUNCIADO. *adj.* Muy perceptible o acusado. *Pronounced, marked.*

PROPICIADOR. *n.m.* Patronizador. *Sponsor.*

PROPICIAR. *v.* Patrocinar. *To sponsor.*

PROSA. *n.f.* (Acad.) •Echar (tirar) PROSA. Darse importancia, tomar actitudes de superioridad. *To get on one's high horse (coll.).* || **2.** Altanería, presuntuosidad. *Affectation, pomposity.*

PROSECRETARIO. (Acad.) *n.m.* Vicesecretario. *Under secretary, assistant secretary.*

PROSUDO. *adj.* Que habla con arrogancia; que afecta pompa y gravedad. *Affected, pompus.*

PROVISIORIAMENTE. *adj.* Provisionalmente. *Temporarily.*

PROVISORIO. *adj.* Provisional. *Provisional, temporary.*

PRUDENCIARSE. *v.* Ser prudente. *To be cautious.* || **2.** Moderarse, dominarse, soportar con paciencia. *To hold back, control oneself.*

PRUEBA. *n.f.* Acrobacia que ejerce el acróbata de un circo. *Circus act.*

PRUEBISTA. *n.* Gimnasta de circo. *Acrobat.* || **2.** Mago. *Magician.*

PUBLICISTA. *n.m.* (Acad.) Persona que ejerce la publicidad, **publicitario.** *Publicity agent.*

PUBLICITARIO (variante de **publicista**).

PUCHA. •¡La PUCHA! Expresión para demostrar disgusto, asombro o admiración. *Wow! Oh, no!, I'l be damned!*

PUCHO. *n.m.* (Acad.) Resto, residuo, pequeña cantidad sobrante de alguna cosa. *Scrap, left-overs, remnant.* ~Queda un PUCHO de sopa. *There's a drop of soup left.* || **2.** (Acad.) Colilla del cigarro. *Cigarrette but, cigar stub.* || **3.** •A PUCHOS. En pequeñas cantidades. *Bit by bit, a little at a time.* ~Me está pagando a PUCHOS. *He's paying me a little at a time.* || **4.** •No valer un PUCHO. No valer nada. *To be worthless.* || **5.** •Sobre el PUCHO. Inmediatemente, en seguida. Right away. ~Tomó la decisión sobre el PUCHO. *He took his decision right there and then.*

PUCO. *n.m.* Olla, tinaja. *Bowl.*

PUEBLADA. *n.f.* Motín, tumulto, rebelión popular. *Riot, mutiny, popular uprising.*

PUEBLERO. *adj.* Perteneciente o relativo a una ciudad o pueblo. *Pertaining to, or characteristic of a town or city.* || **2.** Habitante de una ciudad o pueblo. *Townsman, city dweller.*

PUERCADA. *n.f.* Porquería, cochinada; dicho obsceno. *Obscene remark or action.*

PUERTA. *n.f.* •De puertas para AFUERA. De puertas para fuera. *In public.*

PUESTERO. *n.m.* (Acad.) Hombre que vive en una de las partes en que se divide una estancia y que está encargado de cuidar los animales que en esta parte se crían. *Farmer responsible for the managing of part of a large ranch.* || **2.** Persona que tiene o atiende un puesto de venta. *Stall-holder, market vendor.*

PUJAR. *v.* •PUJAR para adentro. Soportar, tolerar. *To endure, to put up with.*

PULGA. *n.f.* •Ser de pocas PULGAS. *To have little patience, be irritable.*

PULGUIENTO. *adj.* Pulgoso. *Flee-ridden, flee-bitten.*

PULÓVER. *n.m.* Suéter. *Pullover, sweater.*

PULPERÍA. *n.f.* (Acad.) Tienda donde se venden diferentes géneros para el basto. *Local store.*

PULPERO. *n.m.* (Acad.) El que tiene o atiende una **pulpería.** *Local storekeeper.*

PULQUE. *n.m.* Bebida espiritosa que se obtiene haciendo fermentar el aguamiel que brota del rizoma de la pita. *Fermented juice of the of the agave or maguey plant.*

PULSEADA. *n.f.* (Acad.) Acción y efecto de pulsear. *Arm-wrestling.*

PUNA. *n.f.* (Acad.) Páramo. *High barren plateau.* || **2.** (Acad.) Angustia que se sufre en ciertos lugares elevados, **soroche.** *Mountain or altitude sickness.*

PUNTA. *n.f.* •A PUNTA de. A fuerza de. *By dint of.*

PUNTADA. *n.f.* •No dar PUNTADA sin nudo (hilo). No hacer nada que no resulte en beneficio propio. *To look after oneself.*

PUNTAJE. *n.m.* Puntuación. *Score.* ~Sacó el PUNTAJE más alto de la clase. *She received the highest grades in the class.*

PUNTAL. *n.m.* (Acad.) Tentempié, refrigerio. *Snack.*

PUNTAZO. *n.m.* Golpe que se tira de punta, con arma blanca. *Stab, jab.* || **2.** Herida poca profunda, causada con este golpe. *Stab, knife wound.*

PUNTEAR. *v.* (Acad.) Remover la capa superior de la tierra con la punta de la pala. *To turn over, dig up.* || **2.** (Acad.) Marchar a la cabeza de un grupo de personas o animales. *To lead, head.* ~Herrera PUNTEÓ toda la etapa de ayer. *Herrera was in the lead throughout yesterday's stage.*

PUNTERO. *n.m.* Persona o animal que va delante de los demás componentes de un grupo. *Leading animal, leader.* || **2.** (Acad.) En algunos deportes, el que juega en primera fila, delantero. *Winger.* || **3.** Equipo que lleva la mayor ventaja en un partido. *Leading team.*

PUNTILLAZO (variante de **puntazo**).

PUNTUDO. *adj.* Puntiagudo. *Sharp.*

PUPO. *n.m.* (Acad.) Ombligo, cicatriz. *Belly button.*

PUPÓN. *adj.* Satisfecho, repleto (comida). *Stuffed, full (food).* || **2.** Barrigón. *Pot-bellied, paunchy.*

PUQUIO. *n.m.* (Acad.) Manantial de agua. *Spring, fountain.*

PURO. *adj.* Solo. *One, single.* ~Queda una PURA vela para esta noche. *There's only one candle left for tonight.* || **2.** *adv.* Sólo. *Only.* ~En esta oficina trabajan PURAS mujeres. *The only people working in this office are women.*

|| **3.** Muy, tan. *Sheer.* ~Se murió de puro vieja. *She died of sheer old age.*

PUTEADA. *n.f.* (Acad.) Acción y efecto de **putear**, injuriar. *Insult, swearword.*

PUTEAR. *v.* (Acad.) Injuriar, dirigir palabras soeces a alguien. *To insult.* ~La PUTEÓ de arriba a abajo. *He called her every name under the sun.* || **2.** Decir palabrotas. *To swear, curse.* ~Cuando se enteró se puso a PUTEAR. *When he found out he began swearing.*

PUYAR. *v.* (Acad.) Herir con la puya. *To jab, wound, prick with a goad or sharp point.* || **2.** (Acad.) Incitar con ahinco. *To upset, needle.*

PUYAZO (variante de **puyonazo**).

PUYÓN. *n.m.* Brote de las plantas. *Shoot, bud.* || **2.** Púa del trompo. *Metal point of spinning top.*

PUYONAZO. *m.m.* Herida que se hace con puya. *Wound caused by a goad or sharp point.* || **2.** Herida dolorosa causada por una espina grande. *Painful prick of a large thorn.*

QUE. *conj.* •¡A mí, QUÉ! ¡A mí, qué me importa! *What do I care?* ‖ **2.** Expresión que denota amenaza o desafío. ~¡A QUE te doy un palo! Te advierto que te voy a dar un palo. *You better mind or I'll smack you.* ‖ **3.** •¡QUÉ esperanza! De ninguna manera. *Not on your life!* ‖ **4.** •¿QUÉ hubo? Frase con la que se saludan los amigos en la sociedad sin etiqueta. *What's up?*

QUEBRACHO. *n.m.* Arbol de madera muy dura, una de cuyas variedades posee una corteza rica en tanino. *Quebracho (South American hardwood tree).*

QUEBRADA. *n.f.* (Acad.) Arroyo o riachuelo que corre por una quiebra. *Mountain stream, rivulet.*

QUEBRANTAR. *v.* Domar un caballo. *To break in a horse.*

QUEBRAR. *v.* Romper. *To break (Glass, dish).* ‖ **2.** Rajar. *To crack.* ‖ **3.** •ROMPERSE la cabeza. Preocuparse mucho por algo. *To rack one's brain.*

QUEBRAZÓN. *n.f.* Destrozo grande de objetos de loza o vidrio. *Crashing, breaking, shattering (of glass, china, etc.).*

QUEDADA. *n.f.* Solterona. *Old maid, spinster.*

QUEDADIZO (variante de **quedado**).

QUEDADO. *adj.* Lento, tardo, indolente. *Lazy.*

QUEDAR. *v.* •No QUEDAR (de) otra. *Not to have any other alternative.* ‖ **2.** -se. Pararse. *To stop functioning.* ~De repente el motor se QUEDÓ. *The engine suddenly died on me.* ‖ **3.** •QUEDARSE para vestir santos. Quedar soltera. *To remain single.*

QUEJOSO, *adj.* Quejumbroso. *Complaining, whining.*

QUEMADO. *adj.* De color oscuro. *Dark-colored.*

QUEMADOR. *n.m.* Mechero. *Lighter.*

QUEMAZÓN. *n.f.* Incendio. *Fire.* ~Salvé estos libros de la QUEMAZÓN. *I saved these books from the fire.* ‖ **2.** Baratillo. *Second-hand shop.*

QUENA. *n.f.* (Acad.) Flauta con que los indios andinos acompañan sus cantos y especialmente el yaraví. *Reed flute used in Andean music.*

QUEQUE. *n.m.* Pastel, torta. *Cake.* ‖ **2.** Bizcocho. *Sponge cake.*

QUERENDÓN. *adj.* (Acad.) Muy cariñoso. *Affectionate, loving.* ‖ **2.** Enamoradizo. *Amorous, that falls in love easily.*

QUEROSÉN. *n.m.* (Acad.) Queroseno. *Kerosene.*

QUEROSÍN (variante de **querosén**).

QUERÚBICO. *adj.* Inocente. *Innocent.*

QUESADILLA. *n.f.* **Tortilla** doblada que lleva un relleno de queso. *Folded tortilla filled with cheese.*

QUILA. *n.f.* (Acad.) Especie de bambú. *Type of bamboo.*

QUILOMBO. *n.m.* Burdel. *Brothel.* ‖ **2.** Pelotera, bochinche. *Row, mess.*

QUIMBA. *n.f.* (Acad.) Especie de calzado rústico. *Rustic shoe.*

QUIÑAR. *v.* (Acad.) Dar golpes con la púa del trompo. *To hit, knock, bang (two spinning tops).*

QUIÑAZO. *n.m.* (Acad.) Cachada, golpe dado con la púa del trompo. *Hit (from a spining top to another).*

QUINCHA. *n.f.* (Acad.) Tejido o trama de junco con que se afianza un techo o pared de paja, totora, cañas, etc. *Laticework or wicker work*. || **2.** (Acad.) Pared hecha de cañas, varillas u otra materia semejante, que suele recubrirse de barro y se emplea en cercas, chozas, corrales, etc. *Wall of reeds and adobe*.

QUINCHAR. *v.* (Acad.) Cubrir o cercar con **quinchas**. *To cover or fence with reed and adobe, to thatch*.

QUINGOS. *n.m.* (Acad.) Líneas o direcciones que forman alternativamente ángulos entrantes y salientes, zigzag. *Zigzags*. || **2.** Vuelta, rodeo. *Turn, twist*.

QUIÑO. *n.m.* Puñetazo. *Punch*.

QUIRQUINCHO. *n.m.* (Acad.) Especie de armadillo, de cuyo carapacho se sirven los indios para hacer charangos. *Armadillo*.

QUITA. *n.f.* Rebaja, descuento. *Rebate*.

RABIA. *n.f.* •Con RABIA. Mucho, con exceso. Se dice especialmente de cualidades negativas. *Extremely, terribly.* ~Llueve con RABIA. *It's raining with a vengeance.*~Es fea con RABIA. *She's terribly ugly.*

RABIMOCHO. *adj.* De rabo cortado. *Short-tailed.*

RABO. *n.m.* || **1.** •RABO verde. Viejo enamoradizo, viejo verde. *Dirty old man.*

RABÓN. *adj.* Se dice de lo que es más corto o pequeño que lo ordinario. *Short, small.*

RABONA. *n.f.* (Acad.) Mujer libre que suele acompañar a los soldados en las marchas y en campaña. *Camp-follower.* || **2.** Mujer del soldado. *Soldier's wife.* || **3.** •Hacer RABONA. Hacer novillos, faltar a la clase los estudiantes. *To play truant, to miss classes.*

RADIAL. *adj.* Relativo a la radiodifusión. *Radio (used as an adjective).* Novelas RADIALES. *Radio serials.*

RADIAR. *v.* Eliminar a alguien de una lista. *To delete, cross off (from a list).* || **2.** Expulsar. *To expel.* || **3.** Suprimir. *To remove.*

RADIO. *n.m.* El RADIO. La radio. *The radio.* Escuchar el RADIO. *To listen to the radio.*

RADIODIFUSOR. -A. *n.f.* Relativo a la radio. *Pertaining to the radio.* || **2.** Emisora. *Radio station.*

RADIOOPERADOR. *n.m.* Técnico que maneja los aparatos de transmisión y recepción radial. *Radio operator.*

RADIOSO. *adj.* Radiante. *Radiant.*

RAICERO. *n.m.* Raigambre, conjunto de las raíces de una planta. *Roots.*

RAID. *n.m.* (dep.) Viaje atrevido y peligroso. *Ride.*

RAJAR. *v.* (Acad.) Hablar mal de uno, desacreditarlo. *To defame, slander.* || **2.** Huir, marcharse con precipitación. *To get away in a hurry. to split (coll.).* || **3.** -se. Gastar mucho dinero en regalos y fiestas. *To splurge.*

RAJO. *n.m.* Desgarrón, rotura. *Tear, rip.*

RAJÓN. *n.m.* Rasgadura. *Tear, rip.* || **2.** Valentón, fanfarrón. *Braggart.* || **3.** Ostentoso, liberal. *Generous, lavish, free-spending.*

RALEAR. *v.* Enrarecer, rarefacer. *To become rarified, to become scarce.*

RAMADA. *n.f.* Cobertizo hecho de ramas. *Shelter, covering (made of branches).*

RAMAZÓN. *n.f.* Cornamenta de animales, como la del ciervo. *Antler, horns.*

RAMBLAS. *n.f.* Paseo marítimo. *Esplanade, promenade.*

RANCHERA. *n.f.* Canción y danza popular de diversos países de Hispanoamérica. *Popular Latin American folksong.*

RANCHO. *n.m.* (Acad.) Granja donde se crían caballos y otros cuadrúpedos. *Ranch, large farm.* || **2.** Choza. *Hut.* || **3.** Casucha. *Hovel.*

RANCONTÁN. *n.m.* •Pagar (al) RANCONTÁN. Pagar al contado. *To pay cash.*

RANGO. *n.m.* (Acad.) Situación social elevada. *High social standing.* || **2.** (Acad.) Rumbo, esplendidez. *Pomp, spendor.* || **3.** Lujo. *Luxury.*

RANGOSO. *adj.* Generoso. *Generous.*

RAPADURA. *n.f.* Especie de caramelo. *Candy made of milk and syrup.*

RÁPIDO. *adj.* Campo o llanura extensos sin cultivar. *Fallow.* || **2.** Campo. *Open country.*

RASCA. *n.f.* Borrachera. *Drunkenness.* || **2.**

•Pegarse una RASCA. Emborracharse. *To get drunk, plastered (coll.).*

RASCABUCHAR. v. Curiosear. *To pry.*

RASCADO. *adj.* Borracho. *Drunk.* || **2.** Que tiene cabeza de chorlito. *Feather-brained.*

RASCARSE. *v.* Emborracharse. *To get drunk.* || **2.** •RASCARSE la barriga. Holgazanear. *To take it easy.*

RASGUÑADURA. *n.f.* Rasguño. *Scratch.*

RASGUÑÓN (variante de **rasguñadura**).

RASPA. *n.f.* (Acad.) Reproche, reprimenda. *Lecture, sermon, dressing-down.* || **2.** Burla. *Joke.*

RASPADURA. *n.f.* Azucar morena. *Brown sugar.*

RASPAR. *v.* Reprochar, reprender. *To reprimand.*

RASPÓN. *n.m.* Desolladura. *Scratch, graze, scrape.* || **2.** Reprimenda. *Severe reprimand.*

RASQUETA. *n.f.* (Acad.) Chapa dentada para limpiar el pelo de las caballerías, almohaza. *Currycomb.*

RASQUETEAR. *v.* (ACAD.) Limpiar el pelo de las caballerías con **rasqueta**. *To groom, brush down.*

RASQUIÑA. *n.f.* Picazón, prurito, comezón. *Itch.*

RASTACUERISMO. *n.m.* Condición de rastacuero. *Social climbing; ostentation, display.*

RASTACUERO. *n.m.* Persona inculta, adinerada y jactanciosa. *Upstart, parvenu, nouveau-riche.*

RASTRERISMO. *n.m.* Adulonería. *Flattering, fawning.*

RASTRILLAR. *v.* Disparar un arma de fuego. *To fire.* || **2.** Marrar un arma de fuego. *To misfire.*

RASTROJEAR. *v.* Recoger en los rastrojos los residuos de las cosechas. *To glean.* || **2.** Pastar los animales en los rastrojos. *To feed in the stubble.*

RASURADOR. *n.m.* Maquinilla de afeitar. *Electric razor or shaver.*

RASURAR. *v.* Afeitar. *To shave.* || **2.** -se. Afeitarse. *To shave (oneself).*

RATA. *n.f.* (Acad.) Porcentaje. *Percentage.*

RATING. *n.m.* Clasificación, puesto. *Rating.*

RATO. *n.m.* •A cada RATO. A cada momento. *Each five minutes, the whole time.* || **2.** •Hasta otro RATO. Hasta luego. *We'll see you later.*

RATONERA. *n.f.* Vivienda miserable, pocilga. *Hovel, slum; dive, hole (coll.).*

RAYA. n.f. •Llevar la RAYA al medio. Llevar la raya en medio. *To have one's hair parted in the middle.* || **2.** •Con la RAYA al costado. Con la raya al lado. *To have one's hair parted on one side.*

RAYADO. *adj.* Loco. *Crazy, cracked.*

RAYAR. *v.* Espolonear la cabalgadura. *To spur on (horse).* || **2.** Detener de improviso la cabalgadura. *To halt a horse suddenly.*

RAYARSE. *v.* Volverse loco. *To go crazy; to go off one's rocker, to crack up (coll.).*

RAYO. *n.m.* (de una rueda). Radio. *Spoke.*

REALENGO. *adj.* (Acad.) Desocupado, callejero, holgazán. *Idle.* || **2.** Sin dueño, en especial el ganado. *Stray, lost, ownerless.*

REATA. *n.f.* Cualquier cuerda o correa. *Strap.* || **2.** Arriate (de flores). *Flower-bed.*

REBALSAR. *v.* Sobrepasar las aguas embalsadas las paredes que las contienen. *To overflow.* ~Las últimas lluvias han REBALSADO el río. *The recent rains have caused the river to overflow.*

REBENQUE. *n.m.* (Acad.) Látigo recio de jinete. *Riding-crop, whip.*

REBENQUEAR. *v.* Azotar con el **rebenque**. *To whip.*

REBOZADO. *adj.* Se dice de lo que viene rebozado, listo para freír. *Meat dipped in batter for frying.*

REBOZO. *n.m.* Chal, pañoleta. *Shawl, wrap.*

REBUSCADO. *adj.* Atildado, afectado. *Affected, stuck-up.*

REBUSCARSE. *v.* Darse mañas la persona sin profesión ni oficio para encontrar una ocupación que le permita subsistir. *To get by.*

REBUSQUE. *n.m.* Acción de rebuscarse. *Work on the side.*

RECADO. *n.m.* Aperos, arreos más lujosos que los comunes. *Saddle and trappings, riding gear.*

RECALAR. *v.* Ir a parar. *To end up at.* || **2.** Recurrir a alguien para resolver algún problema. *To turn to someone for help.*

RECÁMARA. *n.f.* (Acad.) Dormitorio. *Bedroom.*

RECAUCHUTAR. *v.* Recauchar. *To retread.*

RECAUDO. *n.m.* Especias, condimentos. *Spices, condiments.* || **2.** Verduras y legumbres que se compran diariamente. *Daily supply of fresh vegetables.*

RECEPCIONAR. *v.* Recibir. *To receive, accept.*

RECESAR. *v.* (Acad.) Acción y efecto de retirarse o retroceder. *To recess, go into recess.*

RECESO. *n.m.* (Acad.) Vacación, suspensión temporal de actividades en los cuerpos colegiados, asambleas, etc. *Recess, adjournment.*

RECHINAR. *v.* Rabiar, ponerse furioso. *To rage, fume.* || **2. -se.** Requemarse la comida. *To burn.*

RECIBIRSE. *v.* Graduarse, licenciarse, diplomarse. *To graduate.*

RECIEN. *adv.* (Acad.) Apenas; sólo en. *Only.* ~Vicenta tiene RECIÉN una semana en casa. *Vicenta has hardly been at home a week.* || **2.** Acabar de. *Just.* ~RECIÉN me llamó. Acaba de llamarme. *He just called me (a moment ago).*

RECIPROCAR. *v.* (Acad.) Responder a una acción con otra semejante, corresponder. *To reciprocate.*

RECLAME. *n.m.* Publicidad. *Advertisement.*

RECLAMO. *n.m.* Aliciente. *Inducement, lure, attraction.* || **2.** Protesta, queja. *Complaint, protest.*

RECOGIDA. *n.f.* Acción de reunir y con-

ducir al **rodeo** el ganado disperso en el campo. *Round-up.*

RECOLECCIÓN. *n.f.* •RECOLECCIÓN de basura. Recogida de basura. *Rubbish collection.*

RECONFORTANTE. *n.m.* Tónico, estimulante. *Tonic, pick-me-up.*

RECONTRA. *adv.* En extremo. *Extremely, terribly.* RECONTRAcaro, bueno, etc. *Terribly expensive, extremely good, etc.*

RECORDAR. *v.* (Acad.) Despertar el que está dormido. *To wake up, awaken.* || **2.-se.** Despertarse. *To wake up.*

RECORTE. *n.m.* Noticia de periódico o revista que se recorta. *Clipping.*

RECOVA. *n.f.* Mercado de comestibles. *Market.*

RECULÓN. *n.m.* Reculada. *Backward movement.* || **2.** •Andar a RECULONES. *To go backwards.*

REDOMÓN. *adj.* (Acad.) Aplícase a la caballería no domada por completo. *Half-trained, not fully broken (horse).*

REDUCIDOR. *adj.* Se dice del que recibe objetos robados. *Receiver, fence.*

REDUCIR. *v.* Comerciar con objetos robados. *To receive, buy and dispose of stolen goods, to fence.*

REDUCTIBLE. *adj.* Reducible. *Reducible.*

REEDICIÓN. *n.f.* Acción de reeditar o reimprimir. *New edition or printing.*

REFACCIÓN. *n.f.* Compostura, reparación de un edificio. *Refurbishment.* || **2.** (agr.) Gastos de sostenimiento. *Running costs, upkeep expenses.*

REFACCIONAR. *v.* (Acad.) Restaurar o reparar, especialmente hablando de edificios. *To refurbish.* || **2.** Facilitar lo necesario para que prospere un negocio. *To finance, subsidize.*

REFALAR. *v.* Despojar a alguien de algo que tiene puesto. *To take something from someone.*

REFERÍ. *n.m.* Arbitro. *Referee, umpire.*

REFISTOLERÍA. *n.f.* Presunción, afectación, pedantería. *Vanity.*

REFISTOLERO. *n.m.* Presumido, vanidoso. *Vain, conceited.*

REFUNDIR. *v.* (Acad.) Perder, extraviar. *To loose, misplace.*

REGADERA. *n.f.* Ducha. *Shower.*

REGALADO. *adj.* Muy fácil. *Very easy.* ~El examen estuvo REGALADO. *The exam was very easy.* || **2.** Exactamente. *Exactly.* ~Hace su REGALADA gana. *He does exactly what he pleases.*

REGALÍA. *n.f.* (Acad.) Regalo, obsequio. *Gift, present.*

REGAÑADA. *n.f.* Regaño. *Reprimand, scolding.*

REGAÑAR. *v.* Reprender. *To scold, reprimand.*

REGARSE. *v.* Dispersarse (noticia). *To spread (news).*

REGATEADOR. *adj.* Que regatea. *Given to bargaining.*

REGIO. *interj.* ¡Fabuloso! ¡Fantástico! *Great! Terrific!*

REGIR. *v.* •El mes que RIGE, el año que RIGE. El mes actual, el año presente. *The current month, year.*

REGRESAR. *v.* (Acad.) Devolver o restituir algo a su poseedor. *To return.* ~REGRESAR un libro. *To return a book.* || **2. -se.** Regresar, volver. *To return.* ~Nos REGRESAREMOS hoy mismo. *We'll return this very day.*

REGRESO. *n.m.* Devolución. *Return.*

REINVINDICARSE. *v.* Recuperar una persona su buena reputación. *To vindicate oneself.*

REJA. *n.f.* Enrejado. *Railing.*

REJO. *n.m.* (Acad.) Azote, látigo. *Whip.* || **2.** •Dar REJO. *To whip.*

REJUGADO. *adj.* Taimado, astuto. *Sly, crafty.*

REJUNTA. *n.f.* Rodeo. *Round-up.*

REJUNTAR. *v.* Recoger cosas que andan dispersas. *To collect, gather.* || **2.** Recoger el ganado. *To round up.* || **3.** Sumar. *To add.* || **4. -se.** Amancebarse. *To live together.*

RELACIONADO. *adj.* Se dice de la persona que cuenta con personas influyentes. *Well-connected.*

RELACIONARSE. *v.* Trabar relaciones de amistad, negocios, etc. *To make contacts.*

RELAJAR. *v.* Causar repugnancia algún alimento. *To sicken, disgust.*

RELAJO. *n.m.* (Acad.) Broma pesada. *Rude joke, practical joke.* || **2.** Depravación en las costumbres. *Laxity, dissipation, depravity.* || **3.** Desorden, confusión. *Bedlam, mayhem, disorder.* ~Las calles están hechas un RELAJO. *It's absolute chaos out there in the streets.* || **4.** •Armar RELAJO. Hacer el payaso. *To clown around.*

RELAMIDO. *adj.* (Acad.) Descarado, jactancioso, desfachatado. *Shameless.*

RELIEVE. *n.m.* •Poner de RELIEVE. Subrayar, destacar. *To emphasize.*

RELLENA. *n.f.* Morcilla. *Blood pudding.*

REMADURO. *adj.* Excesivamente maduro. *Overripe.*

REMALLAR. *v.* Zurcir. *To darn.*

REMALO. *adj.* Muy malo. *Really bad.*

REMATADOR. *n.m.* Subastador. *Auctioneer.*

REMATAR. *v.* (Acad.) Comprar o vender en subasta pública. *To auction or buy at an auction.* ~Se REMATÓ en $80.000. *It went for $80.000.* || **2.** Saldar. *To liquidate, sell off cheaply.* .

REMATE. *n.m.* (Acad.) Subasta pública. *Sale (by auction).*

REMEDIO. *n.m.* Preparado, medicina. *Medicine.* ~¿Has tomado el REMEDIO? *Did you take your medicine?* || **2.** •Santo REMEDIO. Recurso o procedimiento definitivo. *God and behold, as if by magic.* ~Les pegó cuatro gritos y santo REMEDIO se callaron en seguida. *She yelled at them and, God and behold, they immediately kept quiet.*

REMEZÓN. *n.m.* (Acad.) Terremoto ligero o sacudimiento breve de la tierra. *Earth tremor, slight earthquake.*

REMILGÓN (variante de **remilgoso**).

REMILGOSO. *adj.* Remilgado, melindroso. *Fussy, fastidious, particular.*

REMISIÓN. *n.f.* Remesa, envío. *Consignment, shipment.*

REMISOR. *n.m.* Remitente. *Sender.*

REMOJO. *n.m.* Regalo. *Gift, present.* || **2.** Propina. *Tip, gratuity.*

RENDIDOR. *adj.* Que produce o rinde mucho. *Highly productive, highly profitable (fin.)*

RENDIR. *v.* Durar una cosa más de lo regular. *To last longer, keep going.* || **2.** Aumentar de tamaño alguna cosa al remojarse o cocerse; henchirse. *To swell up (in cooking).*

RENEGAR. *v.* || **1.** Rabiar, enfurecerse. *To shout, rage.* || **2.** Disgustarse, enojarse, ponerse de mal humor. *To get angry, get upset.* || **3.** Prostestar. *To protest.*

RENEGRIDO. *adj.* Muy negro, negruzco, ennegrecido. *Very black, very dark, blackened.*

RENGLÓN. *n.m.* (com.) Conjunto de artículos de un mismo ramo comercial. *Line of goods.*

RENGO. *n.m.* Patojo, lisiado. *Lame, cripple.*

RENGUEAR. *v.* Cojear, requear. *To limp.*

RENGUERA. *n.f.* (Acad.) Renquera, cojera. *Limp, limping, lameness.*

REÑIDERO. *n.m.* Sitio donde riñen los gallos. *Cockpit.*

RENQUERA. *n.f.* (Acad.) Cojera especial del renco. *Limp, limping, lameness.*

REPARO. *n.m.* Respingo del caballo. *Shy, start.* || **2.** •Dar un REPARO. Respingar. *To shy, start.*

REPARTICIÓN. *n.f.* (Acad.) Cada una de las dependencias que, en organización administrativa, está destinada a despachar determinadas clases de asuntos. *Government department, administrative section.*

REPASAR. *v.* Quitar el polvo. *To dust.*

REPATINGARSE. *v.* Repanchigarse. *To lounge, sprawl out.*

REPELA. *n.f.* Recolección de los últimos granos de café después de la cosecha. *Gleaning of coffee crop.*

REPELARSE. *v.* Darse con la cabeza contra la pared, darse de patadas. *To be mad at oneself.* ~Me REPELÉ de no haberlo comprado. *I could have kicked myself for not buying it.*

REPLANTIGARSE. *v.* Repanchigarse. *To lounge, sprawl.*

REPOLLITO. *n.m.* •REPOLLO de Bruselas. Col de Bruselas. *Brussels sprout.*

REPORTAJE. *n.m.* Entrevista. *Interview.* ~Le hicieron un REPORTAJE para la televisión. *They did an interview with him for television.*

REPORTAR. *v.* Dar parte, denunciar (robo, pérdida). *To report, denounce.* || **2.** Informar, notificar, comunicar. *To report.* ~Agradeceremos REPORTAR cualquier queja al teléfono 658 1111. *To communicate, report.* || **3.** Anunciar, dar a conocer. *Report.* || **4.-se.** Presentarse. *To show up, to report (for duty).*

REPORTEAR. *v.* (Acad.) Entrevistar un periodista a una persona importante para hacer un **reportaje**. *To interview for the purpose of writing an article.* || **2.** (Acad.) Tomar fotografías para realizar un reportaje gráfico. *To photograph for the press.* || **3.** Informar sobre algo, presentar un informe. *To cover, report on.*

REPOSTADA. *n.f.* (Acad.) Repuesta desabrida o grosera. *Rude reply, sharp answer.*

REPRISAR. *v.* Repetir el estreno de una obra. *To revive, put on again.*

REPRISE. *n.f.* Presentación de una obra teatral anteriormente estrenada. *Revival.*

REPROBAR. *v.* Aplazar, dar calabazas. *To fail, flunk.*

REPUNTAR. *v.* (Acad.) Empezar a manifestarse alguna cosa, como enfermedad, cambio del tiempo, etc. *To begin to appear or to be visible, give the first signs.* || **2.** (Acad.) Volver a subir las aguas del río. *To rise suddenly (river).* || **3.** (Acad.) Aparece alguien de improviso. *To turn up unexpectedly.* || **4.** Reunir a los animales que están dispersos en un campo para dirigirlos hacia algún lugar. *To round up.* || **5.** (dep.) Mejorar, reponerse. *To improve, recover, pick up.*

REQUINTAR. *v.* (Acad.) Poner tirante una cuerda. *To tighten.*

REQUISICIÓN. *n.f.* Incautación, registro. *Search.*

REQUISITORIA. *n.f.* Interrogatorio. *Examination, interrogation.*

RESABIOSO. *adj.* (Acad.) Resabiado. *Cunning, crafty; that has learned his lesson.*

RESACA. *n.f.* Aguardiente de la mejor calidad. *Quality liquor.* || **2.** Residuos que quedan depositados en la playa al retirarse la marea. *Silt.* || **3.** Le escoria de la sociedad. *Riffraff, the dregs of society.*

RESACAR. *v.* Destilar por segunda vez un líquido. *To distill (a second time).*

RESALTANTE. *adj.* Que se distingue o sobresale. *Outstanding.*

RESAQUERO. *adj.* Remolón, terco. *Stubborn.*

RESBALADA. *n.f.* Resbalamiento. *Slip.* || **2.** •Darse o pegarse una RESBALADA. Resbalarse. *To slip.*

RESBALOZO. *adj.* Resbaladizo. *Slippery.*

RESERVACIÓN. *n.f.* Reserva de habitaciones, de localidades para un espectáculo, etc. *Reservation (hotels, restaurants, etc.).*

RESERVORIO. *n.m.* (Acad.) Depósito, estanque. *Tank, reservoir.*

RESFRÍO. *n.m.* Resfriado. *Cold.* ~Pesqué un RESFRÍO. *I caught a cold.*

RESIDENCIA. *n.f.* Internado. *Internship.*

RESOLANA. *n.f.* Irradiación de los rayos del sol. *Sunlight.*

RESORTE. *n.m.* Incumbencia, competencia, atribución. *Jurisdiction, concern, responsability.* ~No es de mi RESORTE. *It's not my concern.* || **2.** Autoridad, juridicción. *Authority, jurisdiction.* || **3.** Gomita. *Elastic band, rubber band.*

RESPINGO. *n.m.* (Acad.) Frunce, arruga. *Crease (in clothing).*

RESPLANDOR. *n.m.* Irradiación de los rayos del sol. *Sunlight.*

RESUELLO. *n.m.* Descanso, pausa, respiro. *Rest, breathing space, breather.* || **2.** •Tomar un RESUELLO. *To take a breather.* || **3.** •Sumir (cortar) el RESUELLO a uno. Matar. *To kill, bump off (coll.).*

RESUMIDERO. *n.m.* (Acad.) Sumidero, alcantarilla. *Drain.*

RETACÓN. *adj.* (Acad.) Retaco, dícese de la persona de baja estatura. *Short and fat, squat.*

RETADOR. *n.m.* (dep.) Contendiente, aspirante. *Challenger.*

RETAJAR. *v.* Castrar (animal). *Castrate, geld.*

RETALIACIÓN. *n.f.* Desquite, represalia. *Retaliation.*

RETAMO. *n.m.* Retama, escoba. *Broom.*

RETAZO. *n.m.* Despojos, achuras. *Offal.*

RETEMPLAR. *v.* Reanimar, reavivar. *To cheer up, revive.*

RETIRO. *n.m.* Retirada (tropas, empleados, apoyo, fondos). *Withdrawal.*

RETOBADO. *adj.* (Acad.) Respondón, rezongón. *Given to grumbling or answering back.* || **2.** (Acad.) Indómito, obstinado. *Unruly, rebellious.* || **3.** (animal) Salvaje, indómito. *Wild, untamed.* || **4.** (Acad.) Enojado, airado, enconado. *Offended.* || **5.** Taimado, socarrón, mañero. *Sly, crafty.*

RETOBAR. *v.* Cubrir o forrar con cuero. *To line or cover with leather.* || **2.** Encapricharse, porfiar. *To be stubborn, dig one's heels in.* || **3.** Rezongar, protestar. *To grumble, protest.*

RETOBO. *n.m.* Forro. *Lining.* || **2.** Terquedad. *Stubbornness.* || **3.** Protesta, rezongo. *Grumbling, moan.* || **4.** Capricho. *Whim.*

RETORCIJÓN. *n.m.* Retortijón. *Stomach cramp.*

RETRANCA. *n.f.* Freno de un vehículo. *Brake.* || **2.** •Echarse a la RETRANCA. Volverse atrás. *To back out.*

RETRANCAR. *v.* Frenar un vehículo. *To brake, apply the brakes.*

RETRECHERO. *adj.* Malicioso, receloso. *Suspicious.* || **2.** Tramposo. *Deceitful, unreliable.* || **3.** Tacaño. *Mean, stingy.*

RETRETA. *n.f.* Concierto al aire libre. *Open-air concert.* || **2.** Tanda, serie, retahila.

Series, string.

RETRIBUIR. *v.* Corresponder. *To return, repay (a favor).*

RETRUCAR. *v.* (Acad.) Replicar con acierto y energía. *To retort.*

RETRUQUE. *n.m.* Réplica áspera y firme. *Sharp retort.* || **2.** •De RETRUQUE. De rebote; como consecuencia. *As a rebound; as a consequence, as a result.*

REUBICACACIÓN. *n.f.* Traslado (trabajadores, empresas). *Relocation, redeployment.* || **2.** (pobladores) restablecimiento, repoblación, nueva colonización.*Resettlement.*

REUBICAR. *v.* Trasladar (trabajadores, empresas). *To relocate, redeploy.* || **2.** Repoblar (pobladores), restablecer. *To resettle.*

REVALUACIÓN. *n.f.* Revalorización. *Revaluation.*

REVALUAR. *v.* Revalorizar. *To revaluate.*

REVENTAR. *v.* •¡Mira, llegas tarde y te REVIENTO! ~¡Mira, llegas tarde y te acogoto! *You come late and I'll break your neck.*

REVERBERO. *n.m.* (Acad.) Cocinilla, infiernillo. *Small spirit stove.*

REVERENDO. *adj.* (pey.)Total, completo, absoluto. *Tremendous, awful, utter, perfect (iron.).* ~Lo que acabas de decir es un REVERENDO disparate. *What you just said is utter nonsense.* ~Es un REVERENDO imbécil. *He's a perfect moron.*

REVISADA. *n.f.* Revisión, acción de revisar. *Check, review, inspection, revision.*

REVISAR. *v.* Registrar (equipaje, bolsillos). *To search, go through.* ~Alguien me estuvo REVISANDO los cajones. *Someone's been going through my drawers.* || **2.** Reconocer, examinar. *To examine (a patient), check (someone's teeth).* ~Cada seis meses se hacer REVISAR la dentadura. *He has his teeth checked every six months.*

REVISIÓN. *n.f.* Inspección. *Inspection.*

REVOCATORIA. *n.f.* Anulación dada por un juez o autoridad competente, de una ley, edicto, etc. *Revocation, repeal.*

REVOLEAR. *v.* Hacer girar con la mano una correa, ejecutar molinetes con cualquier objeto. *To whirl, twirl.*

REVOLOTEAR. *v.* Ir de un lado a otro, de aquí para allá. *To run to and fro, to dash around.*

REVOLOTEO. *n.m.* Movimiento continuo. *Constant movement.* ~El REVOLOTEO de los niños en el parque. *The children running to and fro in the park.*

REVOLTURA. *n.f.* Confusión, mezcla. *Confusion, jumble.*

REVOLVEDORA. *n.f.* Hormigonera. *Concrete mixer.*

REVUELO. *n.m.* (Acad.) Salto que da el gallo en la pelea asestando el espolón al adversario y sin usar el pico. *Spur trust of fighting cock.* || **2.** •Dar (hacer, echar) una REVUELO. Revisar. *To inspect, check, review.*

REZAGA. *n.f.* Zaga. *Rear.*

REZAGADO. *adj.* Atrasado. *Late.*

REZONGAR. *v.* Reñir, reprender. *To tell off, scold.*

REZONGO. *n.m.* Reprimenda. *Scolding.*

RIBERA. *n.f.* Vecindad o caserío en tierra cercana a los ríos. *Riverside community.* || **2.** Arrabal de ciudad mayor formado de viviendas pobres. *Slum quarters.*

RIBERANO. *adj.* Ribereño. *Coastal.*

RICO. *adj.* Agradable. *Lovely, wonderful.* ~¡Qué RICO estar en la playa ahora! *Wouldn't it be wonderful to be on the beach now!.* ||**2.** •¡Qué RICO! *How lovely!* ~¡Te vas a Acapulco? ¡Ay, qué RICO! *You're going to Acapulco? How lovely?*

RICURA. *n.f.* Voz de expresión cariñosa, especialmente aplicada a niños. *Charm, cuteness.*

RIEGOSO. *adj.* Aventurado, peligroso, que entraña contingencia o proximidad de un daño. *Risky.*

RIFLERO. *n.m.* Soldado provisto de rifle. *Rifleman.* || **2.** Persona hábil en el manejo del rifle. *Marksman, crack shot.*

RIÑA. *n.f.* •RIÑA de gallos. Pelea de gallos. *Cockfight.*

RINCONADA. *n.f.* (Acad.) Porción de terreno, con límites naturales o artificiales, destinada a ciertos usos de la hacienda. *Stretch of land set aside on a ranch for certain purposes.*

RINQUELETE. *n.m.* Persona inquieta y ligera. *Rolling stone.*

RIPIO. *n.m.* Casquijo que se usa para pavimentar. *Hard core, gravel.*

RIZADOR. *n.m.* Tenacillas para rizar el pelo. *Curler.*

ROCAMBOR. *n.m.* (Acad.) Juego de naipes muy parecido al tresillo. *Ombre (card game).*

ROCIADOR. *n.m.* Pulverizador. *Spray, sprayer.*

ROCOLA. *n.f.* Máquina de discos. *Jukebox.*

ROCOTE. *n.m.* Pimiento de gran tamaño y poco picante. *Large pepper.*

ROCOTO (variante de **rocote**).

RODADA. *n.f.* Caída del caballo o del jinete. *Fall from a horse.*

RODAR. *v.* Caer el caballo hacia adelante al correr. *To stumble, fall (horse).*

RODARSE. *v.* Estropearse, gastarse (rosca). *To strip.* ~Se RODÓ el tornillo. *I/you/he stripped the thread on the screw.*

RODEAR. *v.* (Acad.) Reunir el ganado mayor en un sitio determinado, arreándolo desde los distintos lugares en donde pace. *To round up.*

ROGATORIA. *n.f.* Rogativa. *Request, plea.*

ROLAR. *v.* Tocar un tema en una conversación. *To touch on, mention (in a conversation).* ~La conversación ROLÓ la religión. *The conversation touched on religion.* ||**2.** Tener trato, tener relaciones con alguien. *To associate with.*

ROMPEHUELGAS. *n.f.* Esquirol. *Strikebreaker.*

ROMPENUECES. *n.m.* (Acad.) Instrumento para romper o cascar nueces, cascanueces. *Nutcracker.*

ROMPLÓN. *adv.* •De ROMPLÓN. De improviso, de golpe. *Off the cuff, on the spur of the moment.*

ROMPOPE. *n.m.* Bebida que se prepara con yemas de huevo batidas, leche y azúcar. *Eggnog.*

ROMPOPO (variante de **rompope**).

RONCADORA. *n.f.* (Acad.) Espuela de rodaja muy grande. *Large spur.*

RONCEAR. *v.* Voltear, ronzar, mover una cosa pesada ladeándola a un lado y otro con las manos o por medio de palancas. *To move with levers, lever along.* ||**2.** Rondar, acechar, espiar. *To keep watch on, spy on.*

RONDANA. *n.f.* Roldana o rodaja, en especial la que se emplea para sacar el agua de los pozos. *Pulley, winch (used in drawing water from a well).*

ROPAVIEJA. *n.f.* Guiso de carne, deshebrada con chile, cebolla, y tomate. *Meat stew with chile, onions and tomato.*

ROPÓN. *n.m.* Traje que usan las mujeres para montar a caballo. *Woman's horse-riding apparel.*

ROSADO. *adj.* Se dice del pelo del caballo entre castaño y blanco. *Roan (livestock).*

ROSCA. *n.f.* Grupo político o social que obra en beneficio propio, camarilla. *Clique.* ~Es imposible conseguir un trabajo sin conocer alguien en la ROSCA. *It's impossible to get a job unless you know the right people.*

ROSEDAL. *n.m.* Rosaleda. *Rose garden.*

ROSITA. *n.f.* •Andar de ROSITA. Andar desocupado, estar sin trabajo. *To be out of work.*

ROTO. *n.m.* Apodo con que se designa al chileno. *Chilean (derog.).*

ROTOSO. *adj.* Roto, desharrapado. *Ragged, shabby.*

ROZAGANTE. *adj.* Rebozante. *Brimming with health.* •Una criatura ROZAGANTE. *A healthy baby.*

RUBIA. *n.f.* •RUBIA platinada. Rubia platino. *Platinum blond.*

RUBRO. *n.m.* (Acad.) Título, rótulo. *Heading.* ||**2.** (com.) Sección de un comercio. *Category, line (of products).* ||**3.** Renglón. *Item.* ~El segundo RUBRO de exportación del país. *The country's most important export item.*

RUEDO. *n.m.* Dobladillo. *Hem.*

RUMA. *n.f.* (Acad.) Montón, rimero. *Pile, heap.*

RUMBAR. *v.* Orientarse, seguir un rumbo. *To get one's bearings.*

RUMBEAR. *v.* (Acad.) Orientarse, tomar el rumbo; encaminarse, dirigirse hacia un lugar. *To make one's way, to head for.* ‖ **2.** Andar de parranda. *To go out on a spree, go out on the town.* ‖ **3.** Bailar la rumba. *To dance the rumba.*

RUMORAR. *v.* (Acad.) Correr un rumor entre la gente, rumorearse. ~Se RUMORA que va a dimitir. *It is rumored that he's going to resign.*

RUÑIR. *v.* Roer. *To nibble, gnaw.*

RUNRÚN. *n.m.* (Acad.) Juguete que se hace girar y produce un zumbido. *Purring, whirring.*

SABANA. *n.f.* Llanura extensa. *Savannah.*

SABANDIJA. *n.m.* Pícaro. *Little monkey, rascal.*

SABANEAR. *v.* (Acad.) Recorrer la sabana donde se ha establecido un hato, para buscar y reunir el ganado, o para vigilarlo. *To scour the plain for cattle, round up cattle on the savannah.*

SABANERO. *n.f.* Hombre encargado de **sabanear.** *Plainsman.* ‖ **2.** Perteneciente o relativo a la **sabana.** *Of or from the plain or sabana.*

SABER. *v.* Soler, acostumbrar. *To be in the habit of, be accustomed to.* ~Mario no SABE venir por acá. *He doesn't usually come this way.*

SABROSERA. *n.f.* Cosa muy grande y sabrosa. *Tasty thing of large proportion.*

SABROSO. *adj.* Se dice de todo lo bueno y agradable. *Pleasant, nice, wonderful.* ~Es una música SABROSA. *It's wonderful music.* ‖ **2.** Se dice de la persona simpática, habladora y murmurona. *Talkative, chatty.*

SABROSÓN. *adj.* Sabroso. *Tasty, delicious.* ‖ **2.** Templado (clima). *Mild.* ‖ **3.** Guapa. *Beautiful, attractive (woman).* ‖ **4.** Agradable (música). *Pleasant.* ‖ **5.** Hablador. *Talkative, chatty.*

SABROSURA. *n.f.* (Acad.) Dulzura, fruición, deleite. *Tastiness (food), (fig.) pleasantness, delightfulness, sweetness; delight, enjoyment.*

SACA. *n.m.* Mobilización del ganado. *Moving (herd of cattle).* ‖ **2.** Grupo de ganado que se conduce de una parte a otra. *Cattle being moved.*

SACAR. *v.* Quitar. *To take off, remove.* ~SÁCATE los zapatos antes de entrar. *Take your shoes off before entering.* ‖ **2.** Hacer desaparecer. ~SACAR el polvo, una mancha. *To remove.* ‖ **3.** Aliviar. *Relieve.* ~Esta aspirina te va a SACAR el dolor de cabeza. *This aspirine will relieve your headache.* ‖ **4.** Restar. *Substract, take away.* ~SACAR uno de tres. *To take one from three.* ‖ **5.** Extraer. *Extract.* SACAR las impurezas a un mineral. *To extract the impurities from a mineral.* ‖ **6.** Robar. *To take, steal.* ~Me han SACADO el bolso. Me han quitado el bolso. *They have taken my bag.*

SACHA. *n.m.* Presunto. *So-called.* ~Un SACHA médico. *A so-called doctor, a quack.* ‖ **2.** Desmañado. *Unskilled, bungling.* ~Un SACHA carpintero. *A clumsy carpenter.*

SACO. *n.m.* (Acad.) Chaqueta, americana. *Coat, jacket.* ‖ **2.** •SACO sport. *Sport jacket.* ‖ **3.** •Ser un SACO de huesos. Ser muy flaco. *To be a bag of bones.*

SACÓN. *n.m.* Adulador. *Flatterer.* ‖ **2.** *adj.* Lisonjero, adulador. *Flattering.* ‖ **3.** Soplón, delator. *Telltale, informer.*

SACONERÍA. *n.f.* Adulación, zalamería. *Flattery.*

SACUDIR. Limpiar, quitar (el polvo). *To dust.*

SACUDÓN. *n.m.* (Acad.) Sacudida rápida y brusca. *Violent shake, severe jolt.* ~Me agarró del brazo y me dio un SACUDÓN. *He grabbed me by the arm and shook me.*

SAFACOCA. *n.f.* Barahunda. *Hullaballoo, racket, din, row.*

SAL. *n.f.* (Acad.) Mala suerte, desgracia, infortunio. *Misfortune, piece of bad luck.*

SALADO. *adj.* (Acad.) Desgraciado, infortunado, que tiene mala suerte. *Unlucky, unfortunate, jinxed (coll.)* || **2.** (Acad.) Caro, costoso. *Dear, expensive, high-priced.*

SALAME. *n.m.* (Acad.) Salami. *Salami.*

SALAR. *v.* (Acad.) Manchar, deshonrar. *To dishonor.* || **2.** (Acad.) Desgraciar, echar a perder. *To ruin, spoil.*

SALAZÓN. *n.f.* Mala suerte. *Bad luck.*

SALCOCHO. *n.m.* (Acad.) Preparación de un alimento cociéndolo en agua y sal para después condimentarlo. *Stew, boiled dinner.*

SALIDOR. *adj.* Andariego. *Gadabout, fond of going out.* ~Estás muy SALIDOR últimamente. *You're always out on the town lately.*

SALIVADERA. *n.f.* (Acad.) Pequeño recipiente para echar la saliva, escupidera. *Spittoon, cuspidor.*

SALIVAR. *v.* Escupir. *To spit.*

SALÓN. *n.m.* •SALÓN de fiestas. *Function room, reception room.*

SALPICADO. *adj.* Se dice del caballo de pelaje oscuro sembrado de puntitos blancos muy pequeños. *Spotted, dappled, mottled.*

SALSA. *n.f.* •Salsa golf. *Cocktail sauce.*

SALTO. n.m. •SALTO (en) alto. Salto de altura. *High jump.* || **2.** •SALTO (en) largo. Salto de longitud. *Long jump.*

SALTÓN. *adj.* Medio crudo. *Undercooked, half-cooked.*

SALUD. *n.m.* •¡SALUD! (al estornudar). ¡Jesús! *Bless you!*

SALUDES. *n.f.* (Acad.) Saludos, fórmula de salutación. *Regards, greetings.*

SALVADA. *n.f.* Salvación. *Salvation.*

SANCOCHO. *n.m.* (Acad.) Olla compuesta de carne, yuca, plátano y otros ingredientes, y que se toma en el almuerzo. *Stew of meat, yucca and other ingredients.* || **2.** Lío, confusión, embrollo. *Fuss; confusion; row.*

SANDUNGA. *n.f.* (Acad.) Jarana, jolgorio, parranda. *Party, binge.*

SANDWICH. *n.m.* Emparedado. *Sandwich.*

SANFASÓN. *n.f.* •A la SANFASÓN. Sin ceremonia o protocolo. *Unceremoniously, informally.*

SANGRADERA. *n.f.* Sangría del brazo. *Bleeding, bloodletting.*

SANGRE. *n.f.* (Acad.) •SANGRE ligera. Dícese de la persona simpática. *To be easygoing.*

SANGRILIGERO. *adj.* Simpático. *Pleasant, nice, congenial.*

SANGRIPESADO. *adj.* Antipático. *Unpleasant, nasty.*

SANGUARAÑA. *n.f.* Circunloquio, rodeo de palabras. *Circumlocutions, evasions.*

SANITARIO. *n.m.* Excusado, retrete. *Toilet, lavatory.*

SANTERÍA. *n.f.* (Acad.) Tienda en que se venden imágenes de santos y otros objetos religiosos. *Shop selling religious articles.*

SANTERO. *n.m.* Persona que vende artículos religiosos en una **santería**. *Maker or seller of religious articles.*

SANTIGUAR. *v.* Curar santiguando. *To heal by blessing.*

SANTO. *n.m.* Cumpleaños. *Birthday.*

SANTULARIO. *n.m.* Santurrón. *Sanctimonious, hypocritical.*

SAPALLO. *n.m.* (Acad.) Zapallo. *Pumpkin.*

SAPILLO. *n.m.* Especie de alfa que padecen en la boca algunos niños de pecho. *Ulcer, sore.*

SAPO. *n.m.* (Acad.) Juego de la rana. *Game consisting of throwing coins into the mouth of an iron toad.* || **2.** *adj.* Astuto. *Cunning, sly.*

SAPORRO. *adj.* Rechoncho. *Tubby, chubby.*

SARAZO. *adj.* (Acad.) Aplícase al fruto que empieza a madurar. *Underripe.*

SARDÓNICO. *adj.* Irónico, sarcástico. *Ironical, sarcastic.*

SARGENTEAR. *v.* Mandonear, mangonear. *To boss around.*

SARTÉN. *n.f.* (Acad.) •El SARTÉN. La sartén. *Frying pan, skillet.*

SARTENEJA. *n.f.* (Acad.) Grieta que se forma con la sequía en algunos terrenos. *Cracked soil, parched soil.* || **2.** Acad.) En los terrenos lodosos, huella que deja el ganado. *Tracks left by cattle on marshy land.*

SATÍN. *n.m.* Satén. *Satin.*

SAZÓN. *adj.* Sazonado. *Ripe.* || **2.** •Tener buena SAZÓN. Ser buena cocinera. *To be a good cook.*

SECADOR. *n.m.* (Acad.) Enjugador de ropa. *Clothes dryer.*

SECO. *adj.* •Tener SECO a alguien. Tener harto a alguien. *To be fed up with.*

SECRETARÍA. *n.f.* (Acad.) Ministerio. *Department.* SECRETARÍA de Educación. Ministerio de Educación. *The Department of Education.* SECRETARÍA de Defensa. Ministerio de Defensa. *The Defense Department.*

SECRETARIADO. *n.m.* Curso que capacita para desempeñar el puesto de secretario. *Secretarial course.* || **2.** Carrera de secretario. *Career as a secretary, profession of secretary.*

SECRETARIO. *n.m.* (Acad.) Ministro. *Minister.*

SECRETEAR. *v.* Hablar en voz baja. *To wisper.*

SECRETEO. *n.m.* Acción de hablar en secreto. *Whisper.*

SEDALINA. *n.f.* Tela fina de algodón de aparencia de seda, usada para vestidos femeninos. *Silkaline, silkalene.*

SEGUIDO. *adj.* A menudo. *Often.* ~Viene por aquí muy SEGUIDO. *He comes by very often.*

SEGUNDARIA. *n.f.* Enseñanza media. *Secondary education, high school.*

SEGURO. *adj.* Se dice de una persona de confianza, honesta. *Honest, straight.* || **2.** •Irse uno del SEGURO. Encolerizarse. *To get furious.*

SEGURO. *adv.* Seguramente. *Of course, you bet (coll.).*

SEIBÓ. *n.m.* Aparador donde se guarda lo necesario para el servicio de mesa. *Sideboard.*

SELECCIONADO. *n.m.* Selección nacional. *National team.*

SELLO. *n.m.* (Acad.) Cruz o reverso de las monedas. *Reverse, tail.* || **2.** •¿Cara O SELLO? *Heads or tails?*

SEMANERO. *n.m.* Trabajador que recibe el sueldo semanalmente. *Weekly-paid worker.* || **2.** Trabajador a quien le toca hacer un trabajo especial en una determinada semana. *Worker specially engaged for a week's work.*

SEMBLANTEAR. *v.* (Acad.) Mirar a uno cara a cara para penetrar en sus sentimientos o intenciones. *To look straight in the face.*

SEMBRÍO. *n.m.* Sembrado. *Land prepared for sowing.*

SEMEJANTE. *adj.* Enorme, desproporcionado, fuera de lo común. *Huge, enormous.* ~Me picó un SEMEJANTE mosquito. *This big, huge mosquito bit me.*

SEMILLA. *n.f.* •Quedar para SEMILLA. Ser muy viejo y tener salud. *To be old but healthy.*

SEÑAL. *n.f.* Marca del ganado que consiste en hacerle algunas cisuras en las orejas. *Earmark (on cattle).*

SEÑALAR. *v.* Hacer una señal en la oreja de las reses. *To brand, earmark (cattle).*

SENCILLO. *n.m.* (Acad.) Calderilla, dinero suelto. *Small change, loose change.*

SENTADERA. *n.f.* Parte de los asientos donde descansan y se apoyan las nalgas. *Seat of a chair.*

SENTADOR. *adj.* Se dice de la prenda de vestir que **sienta** o cae bien. *Becoming, well-fitting (clothes).*

SENTAR. *v.* (Acad.) Sofrenar bruscamente al caballo, haciendo que levante las manos y se apoye sobre los cuartos traseros. *To rein in, to pull up sharply.* || **2.** Quedar bien a alguien una prenda de vestir. *To become, fit.*

SENTENCIAR. *v.* Amenazar con tomar una venganza. *To swear revenge on someone.*

SENTIR. *v.* Percibir. *To smell; to taste.* ~SIENTO olor a quemado. *I smell something burning.* ~Le SIENTO gusto a ajo. *This has a garlic taste.*

SENTIRSE. *v.* Resentirse, enojarse. *To get*

cross, get angry.

SERRUCHAR. *v.* Aserrar con el serrucho. *To saw.* || **2.** •SERRUCHARLE el piso a alguien. *Undermine someone's position.*

SESTEAR. *v.* Tomar una siesta. *To have a siesta, take a nap.*

SESTEO. *n.m.* Siesta. *Siesta, nap.*

SIEMPRE. *adv.* Todavía. *Still.* ~¿SIEMPRE vives en Palermo?. *Do you still live in Palermo?* || **2.** Positivamente, seguramente. *Certainly, definitely.*

SIETECUEROS. *n.m.* Flemón que se forma en el talón del pie. *Gumboil, whitlow.*

SILBATINA. *n.f.* (Acad.) Silba, rechifla prolongada. *Whistling, booing, hissing (in disapproval).*

SILLA. *n.f.* •SILLA de hamaca. Mecedora. *Rocking chair.*

SILLETA. *n.f.* (Acad.) Silla de montar. *Saddle.* || **2.** Taburete de patas cortas. *Low stool.*

SILLÓN. *n.m.* Mecedora. *Rocking chair.*

SIMULTÁNEA. *n.f.* Simultáneamente. *Simultaneously.*

SINDICACIÓN. *n.f.* Acusación, cargo. *Accusation, charge.*

SINDICADO. *adj.* (Acad.) Dícese de la persona acusada de infracción de las leyes penales. *Defendant, accused.*

SINDICAR. *v.* Acusar. *To accuse, charge.*

SINGLES. *n.m.* Individuales. *Singles.*

SINVERGÜENZADA. *n.f.* Acción propia del sinvergüenza. *Villainous trick, rotten thing to do.*

SIQUIERA. *adj.* Por lo menos. *At least.* ~SIQUIERA come un poquito. *At least eat a little.*

SIQUITRAQUE. *n.m.* (Acad.) Triquitraque. *Clatter.*

SIROPE. *n.m.* Jarabe, almíbar. *Syrup.*

SLIP. *n.m.* Pequeño pantalón de baño para hombre. *Swimming trunk,*

SMOG. *n.m.* Contaminación con niebla. *Smog.*

SO. *interj.* Voz insultante para imponer silencio, ~¡Silencio! *Quiet!, shut up!*

SOBAJEAR. *v.* Sobar, manosear. *Handle, grope.*

SOBAQUERA. *n.f.* Sobaquina. *Underarm odor.*

SOBAR. *v.* Concertar los huesos dislocados. *To set (bone).* || **2.** Adular. *Flatter.* || **3.** •SOBARLE la mano a uno. Sobornar a una persona. *To grease someone's palm, to bribe someone.*

SOBERADO. *n.m.* Desván, sobrado. *Attic, garret.*

SOBORNO. *n.m.* Sobrecarga. *Overload.*

SOBRE. *n.m.* Cartera. *Clutch bag.*

SOBREBOTA. *n.f.* (Acad.) Polaina de cuero surtido. *Leather legging.*

SOBRECAMA. *n.f.* Colcha. *Bedspread.*

SOBRECOSTILLA. *n.f.* Carne del vacuno que esta junto al lomo sobre los costillares. *Rib roast.*

SOBREPASO. *n.m.* Paso de andadura peculiar del caballo **andador**. *Amble, gait (of a walking horse).*

SOBREPESO. *n.m.* Exceso de equipaje. *Excess baggage.*

SOBRERRIENDA. *n.f.* La falsa rienda. *Checkrein.*

SOCA. *n.f.* (Acad.) Ultimo retoño de la caña de azúcar. *Ratoon (of sugar cane).*

SOCAPAR. *v.* (Acad.) Encubrir faltas ajenas. *To cover up for someone.*

SOCOLAR. *v.* (Acad.) Desmontar, rozar un terreno. *To clear, clear of scrub.*

SOCOLLÓN. *n.m.* Sacudida violenta. *Shake, jolt, jerk.*

SOCUCHO. *n.m.* Acad.) Rincón, chiribitil, tabuco. *Little room, den.* || **2.** Casa muy pequeña y arruinada. *Slum, hovel.*

SOMBRA. *n.f.* Sombrilla, quitasol. *Sunshade.*

SOMBRERO. *n.m.* •Sacarle el SOMBRERO a uno. Admirar a una persona. *To take off one's hat to.* ~A esta persona tiene que sacarle el

SOMBRERO. *You really have to admire this person.* || **2.** •SOMBRERO de pelo. Sombrero de copa. *Top hat.*

SONADO. *adj.* En dificultades. *In trouble.* ~Si no hay nadie en casa, estoy SONADO. *If there's nobody at home, I've had it.*

SOÑADO. *adj.* •Que ni SOÑADO. *Heavenly, divine.* ~Hemos encontrado una casa que ni SOÑADO. *We have found the perfect house.*

SONAR. *v.* Fracasar. ~SONÉ en el examen. *I blew the exam.* || **2.** Estar en apuros. *To be in trouble.* ~SONAMOS, perdimos el autobús. *We missed the bus, we've had it!*

SONSERA. *n.f.* Tontería. *Nonsense.*

SOPLAR. *v.* Vencer. *To beat.* || **2.** Matar. *To kill, bump off (coll.).* || **3.** •Figurarse que no hay más que SOPLAR y hacer botellas. Imaginarse que todo es muy fácil. *To underestimate the feasibility of an undertaking.* ~No todo es SOPLAR y hacer botellas. *It's not quite easy as you make it.*

SOQUETE. *n.m.* Tonto. *Fool, idiot.* || **2.** Escarpín, calcetín corto. *Ankle sock.*

SOROCHARSE. *v.* Padecer **soroche**. *To get altitude or mountain sickness.*

SOROCHE. *n.m.* Mal de montaña. *Mountain sickness, altitude sickness.*

SORPRESIVO. *adj.* (Acad.) Que sorprende, que se produce por sorpresa, inesperado. *Surprising, sudden, unexpected.*

SOTACURA. *n.m.* Coadjutor eclesiástico. *Assistant priest.*

SUDÓN. *adj.* Sudoroso. *Sweaty.*

SUELA. *n.f.* Arandela. *Washer.*

SUELAZO. *n.m.* Batacazo. *Heavy fall.*

SUELTISTA. *n.m.* Periodista que escribe sueltos en los periódicos. *Freelance journalist.*

SUEÑERA. *n.f.* Sueño, modorra. *Sleepiness, drowsiness.*

SUERTERO. *adj.* (Acad.) Afortunado, dichoso. *Lucky, fortunate.*

SUERTUDO. *adj.* Afortunado, dichoso. *Lucky, fortunate.*

SUÉTER. *n.m.* Jersey. *Sweater.*

SUFRAGAR. *v.* Votar a un candidato o una propuesta, dictamen, etc. *To vote for.*

SUIZA. *n.f.* Paliza. *Beating, thrashing.*

SUMIRSE. *v.* •SUMIRSE el sombrero. Encasquetarse el sombrero hasta las cejas. *To pull one's hat over one's eyes.*

SUSPENDER. *v.* Separar, apartar. *To suspend (from).*

SUSPENSO. *n.m.* (libro, cine) Expectación impaciente o ansiosa por el desarrollo de una acción o suceso. *Suspense.*

SUSPENSORES. *n.m.* Tirantes. *Suspenders.*

SWITCH. *n.m.* Conmutador electrico. *Switch.*

T

TABACO. *n.m.* Puro. Cigar. || **2.** •Fumarse un TABACO. *To smoke a cigar.*

TABANCO. *n.m.* Desván, sobrado. *Attic.*

TABAQUERA. *n.f.* Bolsa para llevar tabaco picado, cigarros o cigarrillos, petaca. *Tobacco pouch.*

TABAQUERÍA. *n.f.* Fábrica de tabaco. *Tobacco factory.*

TABAQUERO. *adj.* Relacionado o perteneciente al tobaco. *Pertaining to tobacco.* ~El comercio TABAQUERO. *The tobacco industry.*

TABAQUITO. *n.m.* Puro pequeño. *Small cigar.*

TABLERO. *n.m.* Pizarrón. *Blackboard.*

TABLOIDE. *n.m.* (Acad.) Periódico de dimensiones menores que las ordinarias, con fotograbados informativos. *Tabloid (newspaper format).*

TABLÓN. *n.m.* Terreno para sembrar, o sembrado, de una medida determinada y con un solo tipo de vegetal. *Plot, patch, bed.* ~Tenemos tres TABLONES de tomates y dos de cebollas. *We have three patches of tomatoes and two of onions.*

TACANA. *n.f.* Mano del mortero. *Pestle.*

TACHA. *n.f.* (Acad.) En la fabricación del azúcar, aparato donde se evapora en vacío el jarabe hasta obtener una masa cristalizada. *Crystallizing pan or vat used in sugar refining.*

TACHERO. *n.m.* (Acad.) Operario que maneja los tachos en la fabricación del azúcar. *Worker in charge of sugar pans in a refinery.*

TACHO. *n.m.* (Acad.) Paila grande en que se acaba de cocer el melado y se le da el punto de azúcar. *Sugar pan or vat, evapo-*

rator. || **2.** (Acad.) Recipiente para calentar agua y otros usos culinarios. *Boiler, large boiling pan.* || **3.** (Acad.) •TACHO de basura. Cubo de la basura. *Garbage or refuse can.* || **4.** Papelera. *Wastebacket.*

TACHUELA. *n.f.* Rechoncho, grueso y de poca altura. *Short stocky person.* || **2.** Taza de metal que se tiene en el tinajero para beber agua. *Metal cup.*

TACLE. *n.m.* Entrada fuerte, placaje (fútbol americano). *Tackle.*

TACLEAR. *v.* Entrarle a, placar (fútbol americano). *To tackle.*

TACO. *n.m.* (Acad.) Tacón. *Heel.* || **2.** Miedo, preocupación. *Worry, anxiety, fear.* || **3.** Atasco, obstrucción. *Obstruction, blockage.*

TAFETA. *n.f.* Tafetán. *Taffeta.*

TAFIA. *n.f.* Aguardiente de caña. *Low-grade rum.*

TAGARNINA. *n.f.* Borrachera. *Drunkenness.*

TAITA. *n.m.* (Acad.) Nombre familiar y infantil con que se alude al padre y a las personas que merecen respeto. *Child's term of endearment for a loved one (father, mother, nurse).*

TAJAMAR. *n.m.* (Acad.) Malecón, dique. *Breakwater, dike.*

TAJEADURA. *n.f.* Cicatriz grande de herida cortante. *Long scar.*

TAJEAR. *v.* Cortar en tajos, tajar. *To cut up, chop.* || **2.** Acuchillar. *To slash.*

TALAJE. *n.m.* Lugar destinado al pasto. *Grazing land.*

TALCO. *n.m.* Polvos de talco. *Talco powder.*

TALERO. *n.m.* Látigo de jinete. *Crop, riding whip.*

TALLA. *n.f.* Repartición (en naipes). *Deal.*

TALLADOR. *n.m.* Mano (en naipes). *Dealer.*

TALÓN. *n.m.* Matriz. *Stub.*

TALONEAR. *v.* (Acad.) Incitar el jinete a la caballería, picándola con los talones. *To spur one's horse on.*

TAMAL. *n.m.* (Acad.) Especie de empanada de masa de harina de maíz, envuelta en hojas de plátano o de la mazorca del maíz y cocida al vapor o en horno. *Tamale.* || **2.** (Acad.) Lío, embrollo, pastel, intriga. *Fraud, hoax, intrigue, trick.* || **3.** Bulto, atado, envoltorio. *Clumsy bundle or package.*

TAMALERO. *adj.* (Acad.) Persona que vende tamales. *Person who makes or sells* **tamales.**

TAMANGO. *n.m.* Calzado rústico de cuero. *Rustic leather shoe.* || **2.** (Acad.) Calzado viejo y deformado. *Old shoe or sandal.* || **3.** (Acad.) Cualquier calzado. *Footwear.*

TAMAÑO. *adj.* Tremendo, descomunal. *Huge, collosal.* ~No permitiremos que se cometa TAMAÑO error. *We will not allow such terrible mistake to be committed.*

TAMBARRIA. *n.f.* (Acad.) Holgorio, parranda. *Spree, party, night out.*

TAMBERO. *adj.* (Acad.) Perteneciente al **tambo.** *Pertaining to an inn.* || **2.** (Acad.) Persona que tiene un tambo o está encargada de él. *Innkeeper.*

TAMBO. *n.m.* Venta, posada, parador. *Roadside hostelry, inn.*

TAMBOR. *n.m.* Barril, bidón. *Drum.*

TAMPAX. *n.m.* Tampón, tapón. *Tampon.*

TAN/TANTO. *adj.* ¿Cuanto...? *How...?* ¡Qué TAN ancho es? ¿Cuánto mide (tiene de ancho)? *How wide is it?* ¿Qué TAN largo lo quieres? ¿Cómo lo quieres de largo? (¿Qué de largo lo quieres?). *How long do you want it?* ¿Qué TAN graves son los daños? ¿De qué gravedad son los daños? *How bad is the damage?* ¿Qué TAN buen cocinero eres? ¿Qué tal eres como cocinero? *How good a cook*

are you?

TANATE. *n.m.* (Acad.) Mochila, zurrón de cuero o de palma. *Bag, knapsack, haversack.* || **2.** (Acad.) Lío, fardo, envoltorio. *Bundle, parcel.* || **3.** •Cargar uno con los TANATES. Mudarse, marcharse. *To move away.* || **4.** -s. Cachivaches, trastos. *Odds and ends.*

TANDA. *n.f.* Sección de una representación teatral. *Performance.*

TANGUEAR. *v.* Bailar el tango. *To dance the tango.*

TAPADO. *n.m.* (Acad.) Dícese del personaje o candidato político cuyo nombre se mantiene en secreto hasta el momento propicio. *Officially-backed candidate.* || **2.** (Acad.) Abrigo o capa de señora o de niño. *Winter coat, coat.* || **3.** (Acad.) Tesoro enterrado. *Buried treasure.* || **4.** Se dice del animal de un solo color de pelo. *Unspotted, without mark.*

TAPANCA. *n.f.* Gualdrapa del caballo. *Saddle blanket.*

TAPAOJO. *n.m.* Quitapón. *Blindfold, bandage over the eyes (cattle).*

TAPAR. *v.* Atascar, bloquear (escusado, caño). *To block.* || **2.** -se. Atascarse, bloquearse. *To get or become clogged (plumbing).* || **3.** Empastar muelas o dientes. *To fill.*

TAPERA. *n.f.* (Acad.) Ruinas de un pueblo. *Abandoned village.* || **2.** (Acad.) Habitación ruinosa y abandonada. *Ruined house.*

TAPESCO. *n.m.* (Acad.) Especie de zarzo que sirve de cama, y otras veces, colocado en alto, de vasar. *Kind of wattle used as a bed, bedframe, camp bed.*

TAPISCA. *n.f.* (Acad.) Recolección del maíz. *Corn harvest.*

TAPISCAR. *v.* (Acad.) Cocechar el maíz, desgranando la mazorca. *To harvest corn.*

TAPONAMIENTO. *n.m.* Embotellamiento. *Traffic jam, holdup.*

TAQUEAR. *v.* Atacar con un arma de fuego. *To fire.* || **2.** Jugar al billar. *To play billiards.*

TARABITA. *n.f.* (Acad.) Maroma por la cual corre la cesta u oroya del andarivel.

Cable of a rope bridge (with hanging basket for carrying passengers across ravines).

TARANTÍN. *n.m.* (Acad.) Cachivache, trasto. *Odds and ends.*

TARASCÓN. *n.m.* (Acad.) Tarascada, mordedura. *Bite.*

TARASQUEAR. *v.* Dar un mordisco, arrancando un pedazo de algo. *To bite off.*

TARDE. *n.m.* •En la TARDE. Por la tarde. *In the evening.*

TARECO. *n.m.* (Acad.) Trasto, trebejo, tereque. *(plur.) Things, gear, odds and ends.*

TARJA. *n.f.* (Acad.) Tarjeta de visita. *Card, visiting card.*

TARJETERA. *n.f.* Tarjetero. *Credit card holder or wallet.*

TARRAYA. *n.f.* Red redonda para pescar. *Fishing net.*

TARRAYAZO. *n.m.* Redada. *Cast of a net.*

TARRO. *n.m.* Asta o cuerno de algunos cuadrúpedos. *Horn.* || **2.** Sombrero de copa. *Top hat.* || **3.** Lata para aceite, petróleo o cualquier otro producto. *Can, tin.*

TARUGO. *adj.* Ignorante, tonto. *Chump, blockhead.*

TASAJEAR. *v.* Atasajar. *To cut into slices.*

TASAJUDO. *adj.* Flaco y alto. *Tall and thin.*

TATA. *n.m.* (Acad.) Padre, papá. *Dad, daddy.* || **2.** •Tata Dios. *The Lord, God.* || **3.** Abuelo. *Grandpa (coll.).*

TATITA. *n.f.* Padre. *Father.*

TATÚ. *n.m.* Armadillo. *Armadillo.*

TÉ. *n.m.* Reunión. *Tea party.*

TEATRO. *n.m.* Cine. *Movies.*

TECLEAR. *v.* Tocar el piano o escribir a máquina con poca pericia. *To play the piano or type in a clumsy manner.* || **2.** Andar muy mal un negocio. *To be doing very badly (business).*

TECOMATE. *n.m.* Vasija de barro en forma de jícara para beber. *Earthware cup.* || **2.** Calabaza. *Gourd, calabash.*

TEJAMANÍ. *n.m.* Tabla delgada que se coloca como teja en los techos de las casas.

Roofing board, shingle.

TEJAMANIL (variante de **tejamaní**).

TEJAVÁN. *n.m.* Cobertizo. *Shed.* || **2.** Casa rústica con techo de tejas. *Rustic dwelling.*

TEJIDO. *n.m.* Punto. *Knitting.* || **2.** Ganchillo. *Crochet.*

TEMBLADERA (variante de **tembladeral**).

TEMBLADERAL. *n.m.* Tremedal. *Quaking bog, quagmire.*

TEMBLOR. *n.m.* Terremoto. *Earthquake.*

TEMPERADO. *adj.* Templado (clima). *Mild, temperate.*

TEMPERANTE. *adj.* (Acad.) Que no bebe vino ni otros licores, abstemio. *Teetotaller, abstainer.*

TEMPERAR. *v.* (Acad.) Mudar temporalmente de clima una persona por razones de placer o de salud. *To have a change of climate, to change climates.*

TEMPLADO. *adj.* Enamorado. *In love.* || **2.** Medio borracho. *Tipsy.* || **3.** Listo, competente. *Able, competent.*

TEMPLO. *n.m.* •Como un TEMPLO. Grande, excelente. *Huge; first-rate, excellent.*

TEMPORARIAMENTE. *adv.* Temporalmente. *Temporarily.*

TEMPORARIO. *adj.* Temporal. *Temporary.*

TEMPRANEAR. *v.* Madrugar. *To get up early.*

TENAMASTE. *n.m.* (Acad.) Cada una de les tres piedras que forman el fogón y sobre las que se coloca la olla para cocinar. *Cooking stone.* || **2.** Testarudo. *Stubborn.*

TENDAL. *n.m.* Patio solado para secar el café al sol. *Sunny place for drying coffee.* || **2.** Conjunto de personas o cosas que por causa violenta han quedado tendidas desordenadamente en el suelo. *Group of things or persons scattered on the ground.*

TENDALADA (variante de **tendal**).

TENDER. *v.* •TENDER la cama. Hacer la cama. *To make the bed.* || **2.** •TENDER la mesa. Poner la mesa. *To set the table.*

TENDIDO. *n.m.* Ropa de cama. *Bedclothes*.

TENDIENTE. *adj.* Que tiende a. *Aimed at, designed to.* ~Medidas TENDIENTES a la creación de empleo. *Measures aimed at creating jobs.*

TENER. *v.* (En expresiones de tiempo) Hacer. *To have been doing something for a certain lenght of time.* ~TENGO cuatro años de vivir en esta ciudad. *I have been living in this city for four years.* ~TIENE tres meses de no cobrar. *He hasn't been paid for three months.*

TENIDA. *n.f.* Reunión de masones. *Meeting of a masonic lodge.* || **2.** Reunión. *Get-together.*

TEQUIO. *n.m.* (Acad.) Molestia, perjuicio. *Trouble, burden, harm, damage.* || **2.** (Acad.) Porción de mineral que forma el destajo de un barretero. *Amount of ore dug by one man.*

TEQUIOSO. *adj.* Cargante, molesto. *Annoying, bothersome.*

TERAPIA. *n.f.* TERAPIA intensiva. Cuidados intensivos. *Intensive care.*

TERCIADA. *n.f.* Contrachapado. *Plywood.*

TERCIAR. *v.* (Acad.) Cargar a la espalda una cosa. *To carry on one's shoulder.* || **2.** (Acad.) Mezclar líquidos, especialmente con el vino y la leche, para aldulterarlos. *To water down.*

TERCIO. *n.m.* Fardo, lío, bulto. *Package, bale, pack.*

TEREQUES. *n.m.* Trastos, trebejos, cachivaches. *Junk, odds and ends, things, gear.*

TERMINAL. *n.m.* Estación terminal. *Terminal.*

TERRAL. *n.m.* Polvareda. *Cloud of dust.*

TERTULIAR. *v.* Estar de tertulia, conversar. *To attend a social gathering; to get together, meet informaly and talk.*

TESONERO. *adj.* Tenaz, perseverante. *Tenacious, persevering.*

TESTEAR. *v.* Someter a alguien a una prueba. *To test someone.*

TETELQUE. *adj.* Amargo, desabrido. *Sharp, bitter.*

TETERA. *n.f.* (Acad.) Tetilla, mamadera. *Feeding bottle.* || **2.** Pava. *Kettle.*

TIBIARSE. *v.* Irritarse, molestarse. *To get cross.*

TIBIO. *adj.* Enojado. *Cross, angry.*

TICO. *adj.& n.m.* Costarriqueño. *Costa Rican.*

TIENDA. *n.f.* Lugar en que se vende ropas y telas. *Dry goods store.* || **2.** •TIENDA de abarrotes. *Grocery store.*

TIENTO. *n.m.* Tela delgada de cuero sin curtir. *Thong of raw leather.* || **2.** •Tener la vida en un TIENTO. Tener la vida pendiente de un hilo. *To have one's life hanging by a thread.*

TIERRA. *n.f.* Polvo. *Dust.* || **2.** •Echar TIERRA a uno. Hablar mal de alguien. *To speak ill of someone.* || **2.** •TIERRA adentro. *Interior, remote area.*

TIERRAL. *n.m.* Polvareda. *Cloud of dust.*

TIERRERO. *n.m.* Polvareda. *Cloud of dust.*

TIGRA. *n.f.* (Acad.) Jaguar hembra. *Female jaguar.*

TIGRE. *n.m.* Jaguar. *Jaguar.* || **2.** •Hijo de TIGRE, overo ha de ser. De tal palo, tal astilla. *A chip off the old block.* || **3.** •Ser un TIGRE. Ser valiente y arriesgado. *To be brave, daring.*

TIGRERO. *n.m.* Cazador de tigres. *Jaguar hunter.*

TIJERETEAR. *v.* (Acad.) Murmurar, criticar. *To gossip.*

TIJERETEO. *n.m.* Chismorreo, murmuración. *Gossiping.*

TILCHERO. *n.m.* (Acad.) Vendedor de **tiliches**. *Hawker, peddler.*

TILICHE. *n.m.* (Acad.) Baratija, cachivache, bujería. *Odds and ends, bits and pieces, trinkets.*

TILÍN. *n.m.* (Acad.) •En un TILÍN. En un iris. *In a flash.*

TILINGADA (variante de **tilinguería**).

TILINGO. *adj.* (Acad.) Dícese de la persona insustancial, que dice tonterías y suele comportarse con afectación. *Empty-headed, foolish, silly.* || **2.** *n.m.* Persona tonta. *Fool.*

TILINGUERÍA. *n.f.* Dichos y acciones propios de un **tilingo**. *Silliness, stupidity, nonsense.*

TIMBA. *n.f.* (Acad.) Barriga, vientre. *Potbelly.*

TIMBRE. *n.m.* (Acad.) Sello postal. *Postage stamp.* || **2.** Señas personales o comerciales que se estampan en papeles para la correspondencia. *Personal description; description of goods.*

TIMONEAR. *v.* Manejar o gobernar un negocio. *To direct, manage.* || **2.** Dirigir a una persona. *To guide.*

TINACO. *n.f.* (Acad.) Depósito de metal, de gran capacidad que se usa para almacenar agua en las casas. *Water tank.*

TINER. *n.m.* Disolvente, diluyente. *Paint thinner.*

TINTERILLADA. *n.f.* (Acad.) Embuste, trapisonada, acción propia de un **tinterillo**. *Chicanery, trickery; pettifogging.*

TINTERILLO. *n.m.* (Acad.) Picapleitos, abogado de secano, rábula. *Pettifogger, shyster, unqualified lawyer.*

TIPEAR. *v.* Escribir a máquina. *To type.*

TIQUE. *n.m.* (Acad.) Billete, boleto. *Ticket.*

TIQUET (variante de **tique**).

TIQUETE. *n.m.* (Acad.) Billete, boleto. *Ticket.*

TIRA. *n.m.* Detective infiltrado. *Police plant, undercover cop.*

TIRADA. *n.m.* Discurso largo y tedioso, rollo. *Boring speech, tedious discourse.*

TIRADERA. *n.f.* Cinta con que las mujeres se sujetan las faldas a la cintura. *Sash, belt, strap.*

TIRAJE. *n.m.* (Acad.) Tiro de la chimenea. *Damper.* || **2.** Tirada. *Printing run.*

TIRAR. *v.* •TIRAR al arco. Tirar a puerta. *To shoot at goal.* || **2.-se.** Tumbarse. *To lie down.* Estoy agotado, me voy a TIRAR en el sofá. *I'm exhausted, I'm going to lie down on the sofa.*

TIRO. *n.m.* •Como un TIRO. A la(s) disparada(s). ~La motocicleta pasó como un TIRO. *The motorbike just wizzed by.* ~Salió de casa como un TIRO. Salió disparado. *He shot out of the house.* || **2.** Ser un TIRO al aire. Ser un despistado, un atolondrado. *To be a scatterbrain.* || **3.** •Tiro al arco. Tiro a puerta. *Shot at goal.* || **4.** Canica, bolita. *Marble.* || **5.** (Acad.) •Al TIRO. En el acto, inmediatamente. *At once, right away.*

TIRONEAR. *v.* Dar tirones, arrastrar, tirar de. *To pull, tug.* ~TIRONEABA del vestido de la mamá. *He was pulling (tugging) at his mother's dress.*

TOBANCO. *n.m.* (Acad.) Desván, sobrado. *Attic, loft, garret.*

TOCUYO. *n.m.* (Acad.) Tela burda de algodón. *Calico.*

TOLETE. *n.m.* (Acad.) Garrote corte. *Short club.*

TOMA. *n.f.* Acequia, cauce. *Irrigation channel.*

TOMACORRIENTE. *n.m.* (Acad.) Toma de corriente eléctrica. *Socket, outlet.*

TOMADO. *adj.* Embriagado, borracho. *Drunk.*

TOMADOR. *n.m.* Bebedor, aficionado a la bebida. *Drunkard, drinker.*

TOMAR. *v.* Beber alcohol. *To drink.* || **2.** Torcer. *To turn.* ~TOME a la izquierda. Tuerza a la izquierda. *Turn, go left.* || **3.-se.** Mandar hacer. *To have someone do something.* ~Me TOMÉ dos fotos para el pasaporte. *I had two pictures taken for my passport.*

TONADA. *n.f.* (Acad.) Dejo, modo de acentuar las palabras al final. *Accent, local peculiarity, typical intonation.*

TONGONEARSE. *v.* Contonearse. *To swing one's hips.*

TONGONEO. *n.m.* Contoneo. *Swaying of the hips.*

TONTERA. *n.f.* Tontería. *Silliness, foolishness.*

TONY. *n.m.* Payaso de circo. *Clown.*

TOPAR. *v.* (Acad.) Echar a pelear los gallos por vía de ensayo. *To try (two cocks in a* *fight).*

TÓPICO. *n.m.* Tema de conversación en general. *Topic.*

TOPO. *n.m.* (Acad.) Alfiler grande con que las indias se prenden el mantón. *Large cloak pin.*

TOQUETEAR. *v.* Manosear, sobar. *To fondle.*

TOQUETEO. *n.m.* Acción de **toquetear**. *Fondling.*

TOREAR. *v.* Provocar. *To provoke, enrage (animal), infuriate (person).*

TORONJA. *n.f.* Pomelo. *Grapefruit.*

TORREJA. *n.f.* Torrija. *French toast.*

TORRENTOSO. *adj.* (Acad.) Dícese de los ríos o arroyos de curso rápido e impetuoso. *Fast-flowing.*

TORTILLA. *n.f.* (Acad.) Alimento en forma circular y aplanada, para acompañar la comida, que se hace con masa de maíz en agua con sal, y se cuece en comal. *Tortilla.*

TOSEDERA. *n.f.* Tos continuada. *Persistent coughing.*

TOTOPOSTE. *n.m.* (Acad.) Torta o rosquilla de harina de maíz, muy tostada. *Corn pancake, tortilla.*

TOTORA. *n.f.* Especie de junco. *Reed.*

TOTORAL. *n.m.* Sitio donde abunda la **totora**. *Patch of cattails or bulrushes.*

TRABAJOSO. *adj.* Poco complaciente, exigente. *Exacting, demanding.*

TRABARSE. *v.* (Acad.) Entorpecérsele a uno la lengua al hablar, tartamudear. *To get tongue-tied, stammer.*

TRACALADA. *n.m.* (Acad.) Matracalada, cáfila, multitud. *A lot of, a huge amount of, a great number of.* Una TRACALADA de coches. *A whole bunch of cars.* || **2.** •A TRACALADAS. A montón. *By the hundreds.*

TRAGO. *n.m.* Bebida alcohólica. *Drink.*

TRAGUEARSE. *v.* Emborracharse. *To get drunk.*

TRAÍLER. *n.m.* Casa rodante. *Trailer.*

TRAMOJO. *n.m.* (Acad.) Especie de trangalo que se pone a un animal para que no haga daño en los cercados. *Yoke.*

TRANCA. *n.f.* Borrachera. *Drunken spree.*

TRANCARSE. *v.* Estreñirse. *To be constipated.*

TRANCO. *n.m.* •Al TRANCO. A paso largo. *With long steps, with long strides.*

TRANQUEAR. *v.* Recorrer o frecuentar la gente un sitio o camino. *To frequent a place.* || **2.** Dejar huellas. *To make deep tracks on.*

TRANQUERA. *n.f.* Especie de puerta rústica en un alumbrado, hecha generalmente de trancas. *Cattle-gate.*

TRANSAR. *v.* (Acad.) Transigir, ceder, llegar a una transacción o acuerdo. *To give way, to compromise.* || **2.** Comprar y vender. *To buy and sell, to deal, to trade.*

TRÁNSFUGA. *n.m.* Sinvergüenza. *Rogue.*

TRAPEADOR. *n.m.* Trapo para limpiar suelos. *Mop.*

TRAPEAR. *v.* Fregar o limpiar el suelo con estropajo. *To mop.* || **2.** Dar una paliza. *To trash, give a beating.*

TRAPERO. *n.m.* Jerga. *Floorcloth.*

TRASNOCHARSE. *v.* Trasnochar. *To stay up late, to go to bed late.*

TRASPATIO. *n.m.* Segundo patio de las casas de vecindad que suele estar detrás del principal. *Backyard.*

TRASQUE. *conj.* Además de que... *In addition to the fact that...*

TRASTABILLÓN. *n.m.* Tropezón, traspie. *Trip, stumble.*

TRASTE. *n.m.* (Acad.) Trasto. *Junk.*

TREMENDO. *adj.* Terrible. *Dreadful.* ~Están en una situación TREMENDA. Están en una situación terrible. *They're in a dreadful situation.* || **2.** Travieso. *Naughty, mischievous.*

TREN. *n.m.* Proceso o trabajos que se están haciendo para ciertos fines. *In the process of.* Estamos en TREN de solicitar un préstamo. *We're in the process of applying for a loan.*

TRENZARSE. *v.* Enzarzarse, liarse dos

personas a golpes o de palabra. *To get involved (in an argument).*

TREPADOR. *n.m.* Arribista. *Social climber.*

TREPIDAR. *v.* (Acad.) Vacilar, dudar. *To hesitate.*

TRICHINA. *n.f.* Triquina. *Trichina.*

TRICÓFERO. *n.m.* Medicamento que sirve para conservar el pelo. *Hair restorer.*

TRILLO. *n.m.* (Acad.) Senda formada comúnmente por el tránsito. *Path, track.*

TRINCAR. *v.* (Acad.) Apretar, oprimir. *To press, squeeze.* || 2. •TRINCARSE a. Ponerse a. *To set about.* ~Se TRINCÓ a llorar. Se puso a llorar. *He began to cry.*

TRINCHE. *n.m.* Trinchero o mesa para trinchar. *Side table, sideboard.* || **2.** *n.m.* (Acad.) Tenedor de mesa. *Fork.*

TRINCHERA. *n.f.* Vallado en general. *Fence, stockade.*

TRISTE. *adj.* Pobre de espíritu, apocado. *Shy, timid.* || **2.** Pobre, de poco valor. *Poor, valueless, wretched.* || **3.** *n.m.* Cantar melancólico al son de la guitarra. *Sad love song.*

TROCHA. *n.f.* Ancho del tren ferrocarrilero de rueda a rueda. *Gage.* ~Trenes de TROCHA angosta. *Narrow-gauge trains*

TROJA. *n.f.* Troje. *Granary, barn.*

TROMPA. *n.f.* Boca de labios salientes y gruesos. *Thick prominent lips.* || **2.** Boca (hum.). *Smacker (coll.).* ~Cierra la TROMPA. *Shut your trap.* || **3.** Gesto de disgusto por el cual ciertas personas alargan los labios. *Long face (fig.).* ~¿Qué le pasa que anda con TROMPA? *Why is he walking around with such a long face?*

TROMPEADURA (variante de **trompada**).

TROMPEAR. *v.* Dar trompadas o puñetazos. *To punch, to thump.*

TROMPEZAR. *v.* Tropezar (vulg.). *To trip, tumble.*

TROMPEZÓN. *n.m.* Tropezón. *Trip, tumble.*

TROMPO. *n.m.* •Bailar como un TROMPO. Ser buen bailador. *To be a good dancer.*

TROMPUDO. *adj.* Jetudo. *Thick-lipped.*

TRONCHA. *n.f.* Tajada, porción cortada de alguna cosa, especialmente comestible. *Slice, chunk, piece.* || **2.** Acomodo. *Sinecure, soft job.*

TRONCO. *n.m.* Persona inepta. *Useless person.* ~Esta niña es un TRONCO. *That girl is a complete bonehead (blockhead).* ~Es un TRONCO para los idiomas. *He's useless at languages.* || **2.** Tocón. *Tree stump.*

TROPA. *n.f.* (Acad.) Recua de ganado. *Herd.*

TROZAR. *v.* Cortar en pedazos. *To cut into pieces, cut up.*

TRUCHA. *n.f.* (Acad.) Puesto o tenducha de mercería. *Stall, booth.*

TRUPIAL. *n.m.* (Acad.) Turpial. *Troupial.*

TUALÉ. *n.f.* Tocado o arreglo femenino. *Toilette (feminine).* || **2.** Retrete, baño. *Bathroom.*

TUCO. *n.m.* Muñón. *Stump.* || **2.** Salsa de tomate. *Tomato sacue.* || **3.** Persona que carece de un miembro o lo tiene inútil. *Cripple (person).* || **4.** *adj.* Mutilado. *Maimed, limbless.*

TUMBA. *n.f.* Corta, tala de árboles. *Felling of timber.*

TUMBAR. *v.* Talar árboles. *To fell.*

TÚNICO. *n.m.* (Acad.) Túnica que usan las mujeres. *Woman's robe.*

TUPICIÓN. *n.f.* (Acad.) Confusión, turbación, empacho. *Bewilderment, confusion.*

TUPIDO. *adj.* Obstruido. *Blocked.* || **2.** Con constancia y mucho tesón. *Persistently, steadily.* ~Le dio TUPIDO al estudio. *He studied intensely.*

TURCO. *n.m.* Sirio o libanés de habla árabe. *Arab, Syrian.*

TUSA. *n.f.* (Acad.) Espata o farfolla de la mazorca del maíz. *Corncob (stripped of its kernels)* || **2.** (Acad.) Mujer despreciable. *Despicable woman.*

TUSAR. *v.* (Acad.) Atusar el pelo. *To smooth (hair).* || **2.** (Acad.) Trasquilar. *To cut, clip, shear.* || **3.** Cortar mal el pelo dando cortes desparejos. *To cut roughly, cut badly.*

TÚTANO. *n.m.* Tuétano. *Marrow.*

TUTELAJA. *n.m.* Tutela. *Guardianship.*

TUTILIMUNDI. *n.m.* Todo el mundo. *Everybody.*

TUTURUTO. *adj.* Lelo, turulato. *Dazed, stunned.* || **2.** Achispado. *Tipsy.*

U

UBICACIÓN. *n.f.* Situación, posición. *Location*. El nuevo centro tiene UBICACIÓN privilegiada. *The new center is in a prime location.* || **2.** Localización. *Location*. ~Están poniendo todos sus esfuerzos en la UBICACIÓN del avión. *They're doing everything in their power to locate the airplane.*

UBICADO. *adj.* Situado. *Situated, located.* ~Una casa muy bien UBICADA. *A house in a very desirable location.* || **2.**•Estar bien UBICADA (una persona). Tener buen empleo. *To be well set up in a job.*

UBICAR. *v.* (Acad.) Situar o instalar en determinado espacio o lugar. ~Me UBICARON al lado del festejado. *They placed (seated) me next to the guest of honor.* || **2.** Localizar. *To find.* ~No consigo UBICAR el párrafo. *I can't seem to find the paragraph.* ~UBICARON el avión perdido. *They located the missing plane.* || **3.** Identificar. *To recognize.* ~Me suena el nombre, pero no lo UBICO. *The name rings a bell, but I can't quite place him.* ||**4.** -se. Situarse, colocarse. *To occupy a place.* ~Se UBICARON en la primera fila. *They seated themselves in the front row.* || **5.** Orientarse. *To find one's way around.* ~No me UBICO todavía en esta ciudad. *I still have trouble finding my way around this city.* || **6.** Estar situado. *To be situated.* ~La catedral se UBICA al norte de la ciudad. *The cathedral is located (situated) in the north side of the city.* || **7.** Establecerse. *To settle in, establish oneself.* || **8.** Colocarse en un empleo. *To find employment, fix oneself up with a job.* || **9.** Clasificar. *To rank.* ~El equipo se UBICA en los primeros puestos de la clasificación. *The team is at the top of the division.*

UJUJUY. *interj.* Voz de admiración y sorpresa. *Yippee!, Hahoo!*

ULTIMADOR. *n.m.* Asesino. *Killer, murderer.*

ULTIMAR. *v.* (Acad.) Matar. *To kill, murder, bump off (coll.).*

UMBRALADO. *n.m.* (Acad.) Umbral. *Threshold.*

UNTO. *n.m.* Ungüento. *Ointment.*

UÑA. *n.f.* (Acad.) •No tener uñas para guitarrero. Carecer una persona de las cualidades necesarias para llevar a cabo una tarea. *To be unqualified for a job or task.* || **2.** •Comerse las uñas. Ser muy pobre. *To be very poor.*

USAR. *v.* Manipular, explotar. *To use.* ~Me sentí USADO. *I felt used, I felt that someone was taking advantage of me.*

USINA. *n.f.* (Acad.) Instalación industrial importante. *Factory, plant.* || 2.•USINA eléctrica. Planta de producción de energía eléctrica. *Power station.*

USUTA. n.f. Ojota. *Sandal.*

UTILERÍA. *n.f.* Utiles y trastos que se usan en los teatros para decorar el escenario. *Stage props.*

UTILERO. *n.m.* Persona encargada de guardar y conservar la **utilería** de los teatros. *Person in charge of stage props.*

ÚTILES. *n.m.* •ÚTILES escolares. Artículos escolares. *Pens, pencils, rulers, etc., for school.*

UTILIDADES. *n.f.* Ganancia, beneficio. *Profits.*

VACA. *n.f.* || **1.** Contrato entre varias personas para entrar en un negocio cuyas ganancias han de repartirse de acuerdo con lo invertido. *Enterprise with profits on a pro rata basis.* || **2.** •Hacer VACA. Asociarse para cualquier negocio pasajero. *To go into a temporary business partnership.* || **3.** •Hacer una VACA (vaquita). Hacer una colecta. *To make a collection.* || **4.** •Volvérsele a uno la VACA toro. Dar más trabajo un negocio de lo que se esperaba. *To be more difficult than one anticipated.*

VACILAR. *v.* Divertirse. *To have fun, to have a good time.*

VACILÓN. *n.m.* Juerga, diversión. *Party, good time, fun.* || **2.** Tomadura de pelo. *Joke.*

VACUNA. *n.f.* Vacunación. *Vaccination.*

VAGAMUNDERÍA. *n.f.* Vagancia, holgazanería. *Idleness, lazyness.* || **2.** Descaro, poca vergüenza. *Brazenness, insolence.*

VAINA. *n.f.* (Acad.) Contrariedad, molestia, cosa no bien conocida o recordada. *Nuisance, bother.* ~¡Qué VAINA! *What a nuisance!* || **2.** •Salirse de la VAINA. Impacientarse por decir o hacer algo. *To be dying to say or do something.* || **3.** *adj.* Molesto, inoportuno. *Annoying.*

VAJEAR. *v.* Ganarle a alguien la voluntad con lisonjas. *To win over by flattery.*

VALE. *n.m.* Compañero, camarada, compinche. *Pal, chum, buddy.*

VALEDOR (variante de **vale**).

VALLISTO. *adj.* Vallero. *Relative or pertaining to a valley.* Vino VALLISTO. *Wine from the valley.*

VALONA. *n.f.* (Acad.) Crines convenientemente recortadas que cubren el cuello de las caballerías. *Artistically trimmed mane.*

VALONAR. *v.* Esquilar. *To trim, cut, shear.*

VALORIZACIÓN. *n.f.* Aumento en el precio de un producto. *Increase in value, appreciation.*

VALORIZAR. *v.* Aumentar el valor de una cosa. *To increase in value.*

VALSE. *n.m.* Vals. *Waltz.*

VALSEAR. *v.* Bailar el vals. *To waltz*

VALUAR. *v.* Valorar. *To value.*

VANARSE. *v.* Echarse a perder un fruto, sin llegar a sazonarse. *To spoil.* || **2.** Malograrse. *To fall through, come to nothing, produce no results.*

VAQUERÍA. *n.f.* Oficio del vaquero. *The craft of the cowboy.*

VAQUETA. *n.f.* Cuero de vacuno curtido y adobado. *Calfskin, leather, cowhide.*

VAQUILLA (variante de **vaquillona**).

VAQUILLONA. *n.f.* (Acad.) Vaca de uno o dos años aún no servida. *Heifer, calf.*

VARADO. *adj.* •Estar VARADO. Se dice de la persona que no tiene recursos económicos. *To be broke.*

VARAR. *v.* (Acad.) Quedarse detenido un vehículo por avería. *To break down (aut.).* || **2.** Quedar inmobilizado. *To be stranded.* ~Miles de turistas quedaron VARADOS. *Thousands of tourists were left stranded.*

VARAZÓN. *n.m.* Conjunto de varas. *Sticks, bunch of sticks.*

VAREJÓN. *n.m.* (Acad.) Verdasca, vergueta. *Green twig.*

VEJARANO. *adj.* Vejarrón, vejancón. *Ancient, decrepit.*

VEJESTORIO. *n.m.* Reliquia. *Old relic.*

VELADOR. *n.m.* (Acad.) Mesa de noche. *Night table, bedside table.* ‖ **2.** (Acad.) Lámpara o luz portátil que suele colocarse en la mesita de noche. *Night light.*

VELADORA. *n.f.* Lámpara de mesa de noche de luz tenue. *Bedside lamp.*

VELAR. *v.* Pedir con la mirada y con cierto alejamiento, principalmente comida. *To look covetously at (food).*

VELÓN. *n.m.* Vela de sebo muy gruesa y corta. *Thick tallow candle.*

VELORIO. *n.m.* Fiesta muy poco concurrida, desanimada. *Dull party, flat affair.*

VENCERSE. *v.* Gastarse por el uso una cosa. *To wear out, get worn out.*

VENDAJE. *n.m.* Yapa o adehala. *Perk, bonus.*

VENDUTA. *n.f.* Subasta. *Auction, public sale.*

VENDUTERO. *n.m.* Subastador. *Auctioneer.*

VENIA. *n.f.* Saludo que se da inclinando la cabeza. *Bow.* ‖ **2.** Saludo militar. *Military salute.*

VENTAJEAR. *v.* (Acad.) Aventajar, obtener ventaja. *To excel, surpass, to outsrip, be superior to.* ~ AVENTAJA a todos en los deportes. *He surpasses everyone in sports.* ‖ **2.** Ganar. *To beat.* ‖ **3.** Llevar ventaja. *To lead, come (finish) ahead (in front) of.* ~Le VENTAJEÓ en la carrera. *He came ahead of him in the race.* ‖ **4.** Mejorar. *To improve, give advantage to.* ‖ **5.** Preferir. *To prefer, put before.*

VENTAJERO. *adj.* Aprovechador. *Opportunistic, self-seeking.*

VENTAJISMO. *n.m.* Calidad del ventajista. *Opportunism.*

VENTAJOSO (variante de **ventajero**).

VENTEAR. *v.* Poner el hierro del comprador al ganado que se vende. *To brand the buyer's name on cattle.* ‖ **2.** Andar mucho tiempo fuera de casa una persona. *To be outdoors a great deal.* ‖ **3.** Engreirse, enva-

necerse. *To grow vain, get conceited.*

VENTOLINA. *n.f.* Ventolera. S*udden gust of wind.*

VENTORRILLO. *n.m.* Tenducho. *Small shop.*

VER. *v.* •VIERA... You should have seen... ~¡VIERAS como se asustaron...! *You should have seen the fright they got!* ‖ **2.** Hacerse VER. *To see (consult) someone.* ~¿Por qué no te haces VER por un médico? *Why don't you see (consult) a doctor?* ‖ **3.** •Estar una cosa en VEREMOS. Estar lejos de cumplirse una cosa. *To be undecided, pending, unresolved (matter, affair).* ~Todavía está en VEREMOS. *The matter has not yet been resolved (is still pending).* ‖ **4.** Parecer. *To look.* ~Me VEO muy gorda con este vestido. *I really look fat in thi*s *dress.* ‖ **5.** •Nos VEREMOS. *I'll be seeing you.* ‖ **6.** •Si te VI (he VISTO), no me acuerdo. Refrán que manifiesta el despego con que los ingratos suelen pagar los favores recibidos. *To have a short memory, to be ungrateful.*

VERAGUARSE. *v.* Mancharse la ropa por causa de humedad, llenarse de veraguas. *To become stained with mildew.*

VEREDA. *n.v.* Acera. *Sidewalk.*

VERIJA. *n.f.* Ingle, Ijar. *Flank.*

VERSACIÓN. *n.f.* Conocimiento de una materia. *Expertise, skill.*

VERSADA. *n.f.* Composición en verso de mucha extensión y poco interés.*Long tedious poem.*

VERTIENTE. *n.m.* Manantial, fuente. *Spring, fountain.*

VEZ. *n.f.* •Cada VEZ más. Día a día. *Increasingly, more and more.* ~Está cada VEZ más enfermo. *He's getting worse by the day.*

VIAJE. *n.m.* •Agarrar VIAJE. (Acad.) Aceptar una proposición o invitación. *To accept an offer or an invitation.* ‖ **2.** •De un VIAJE. De una sola vez, de un solo golpe, a un tiempo. *All in one go, all at once, at one blow.*

VIARAZA. *n.f.* Acceso de mal humor. *Fit of anger.* ‖ **2.** •Estar con la VIRAZA. *To be in a bad mood.*

VIBOREO. *n.m.* Murmuración. *Gossip.*

VICTIMAR. *v.* Matar. *To kill.*

VICTIMARIO. *n.m.* Asesino. *Killer, murderer.*

VIDRIERA. *n.f.* Escaparate. *Show window, shop window.*

VIDRIERISMO. *n.m.* Escaparatismo. *Window dressing.*

VIDRIERISTA. *n.m.* Escaparatista. *Window dresser.*

VIDRIO. *n.m.* Cristal. *Window pane.*

VIEJO. *n.m.* Voz de cariño que usan entre sí los cónyuges o amigos fraternales. *Love, darling (spouse), buddy, chap (friend).* ‖ **2.** Manera de referirse a los padres por parte de los muchachos en conversaciones amistosas. *Old man.* ~Mi VIEJO está de vacaciones. *My old man is on vacation.*

VIEJÓN. *adj.* Algo viejo, avejentado. *Elderly.*

VINAGRERA. *n.f.* (Acad.) Acedía. *Heartburn, acidity.*

VIÑATERO. *n.m.* Viñador. *Vine-grower.* ‖ **2.** Que guarda relación al viñedo. *Pertaining to vine-growing.*

VINCHA. *n.f.* (Acad.) Cinta, elástico grueso o acesorio con que se sujeta el pelo sobre la frente. *Hairband.*

VINERÍA. *n.f.* Tienda de vinos. *Wine shop.*

VINOTERÍA. *n.f.* Tienda donde se vende vino. *Wine shop.*

VIROLA. *n.f.* Rodaja de plata con que se adornan los arreos del caballo. *Silver circlet or nail head for decorating harnesses.*

VISA. *n.f.* Visado. *Visa.*

VISITADOR. *n.m.* •VISITADOR social. Asistente social. *Social worker.*

VISITADORA. *n.f.* (Acad.) Ayuda, lavativa. *Enema.*

VISÓN. *n.m.* Abrigo de visón. *Mink coat.*

VITRINA. *n.f.* Escaparate. *Shop window.*

VITRINISMO. *n.m.* Acción de andar mirando escaparates. *Window-shopping.*

VITRINISTA. *n.m.* El que mira escaparates.

Window-shopper.

VITROLA. *n.m.* Fonógrafo. *Phonograph.*

VIUDEDAD. *n.f.* Viudez. *Widowhood.*

VIVAR. *v.* (Acad.) Vitorear, dar vivas. *To cheer.*

VÍVERES. *n.m.* •Cortarle los VÍVERES a alguien. Suspender el pago gratuito que se acostumbra entregar periodicamente a una persona. *To cut off someone's allowance (subsidy).*

VIVEZA. *n.f.* •VIVEZA criolla. Astucia que se atribuye al natural del país y que consiste en ser hábil en percatarse de lo que le conviene para aprovecharse de las oportunidades. *Native wit and cunning.*

VOCERO. *n.m.* El que habla en nombre de otro, llevando su voz y representación. *Spokesman.*

VOLADA. *n.f.* •En una VOLADA. En un dos por tres. *In no time, in a jiffy.* ‖ **2.** Falsa noticia, rumor, cuento. *Rumor.*

VOLADO. *n.m.* Volante, faralá de los vestidos. *Pleated ruffle or flounce.* ‖ **2.** De genio violento. *Quick-tempered.*

VOLANTE. *n.m.* Folleto (publicitario). *Leaflet, flier.* ‖ **2.** Timón. *Rudder, helm.*

VOLANTÍN. *n.m.* Cometa que se echa al aire como juguete. *Kite.* ‖ **2.** Voltereta. *Somersault.*

VOLANTUSA. *n.f.* Mujer callejera. *Prostitute.*

VOLAR. *v.* Fugarse. *To flee, disappear.* ‖ **2.** Encolerizarse. *To get angry, lose one's temper.* ‖ **3.** •Tener una fiebre que VUELA. Tener mucha fiebre. *To have a really high temperature.*

VOLCÁN. *n.m.* Torrente de verano, aludes de agua, barro, árboles y cantos rodados. *Summer torrent.*

VOLIBOL. *n.m.* Balón volea. *Volleyball.*

VOLTEADA. *n.f.* Accion de pasar de un partido político a otro. *Defection.*

VOLTEAR. *v.* (Acad.) Cambiar de partido político. *To defect, to change one's allegiance.* ‖ **2.** Invertir, dar la vuelta (tortilla, disco). *To turn over, flip over.* || **3.** Poner boca arriba (abajo). *Turn the right way up (upside down).* || **4.** Poner del revés (manga, media). *To turn inside out.* ~El viento me VOLTEÓ el paraguas. *The wind blew my umbrella inside out.* || **5.** Volver. *To turn.* ~Les VOLTEÓ la espalda. *She turn her back on them.* || **6.** Dar la vuelta. *To turn around.* ~Al oir su nombre se VOLTEÓ. *Upon hearing her name she turned around.* ||**7.** Volcar, derramar. *To knock down, knock over, spill.* ~VOLTEÓ todo el contenido de la valija en el suelo. *He threw all the content of the suitcase on the floor.* || **8.** Hacer que una persona cambie de parecer. *To force someone to change his mind.* || **9.** Torcer, doblar. *To turn (in a certain direction).* ~Siga todo derecho hasta la calle Princesa y VOLTEE a la izquierda. *Go straight to Princesa street and then turn left.* || **10.** -se. (pol.) Pasar a otro partido. *To defect.*

VUELTA. *n.f.* •Buscar la VUELTA a una cosa. Buscar la manera de solucionar un problema. *To look for a way to solve a problem.* || **3.** Vez. *Time.* ~Esta VUELTA les ganamos. *This time we won.*

VUELTO. Cambio. *Change.* ~Quédese con el VUELTO. Quédese con el cambio. *Keep the change.*

Y

YA. *adj.* •YA mismo. Ahora mismo. *Right away.* || **2.** interj. •YA está. De acuerdo. *Agreed, it's a deal (coll.).* || **3.** •Desde YA. Por anticipado. *Right now.* ~Desde YA te digo que lo veo muy difícil. Le digo por anticipado (le anticipo) que lo veo muy difícil. *I can tell you right now that I think it's not going to be easy.*

YACARÉ. *n.m.* (Acad.) Caimán, reptil. *Alligator.*

YAGUAL. *n.m.* (Acad.) Rodete para llevar pesos sobre la cabeza. *Padded ring for carrying loads on top of one's head.*

YAGUANÉ. *n.m.* Mofeta. *Skunk.* || **2.** *adj.* (Acad.) Dícese del animal vacuno, y ocasionalmente del caballar, que tiene el pescuezo y los costillares de color diferente al del lomo, barriga y parte de las ancas. *Having throat and flanks of a different color than the rest of the body (said of cattle).*

YANACÓN. *n.m.* Indio arrendatario o aparcero. *Indian tenant farmer, Indian sharecropper.*

YAPA. *n.f.* (Acad.) Añadidura, adehala, refacción. *Small amount of extra good given free.* ~Me dio una manzana de YAPA. *She threw in an apple for good measure.* || **2.** Azogue que se añade al mineral argentífero. para trabajarlo más fácilmente *Mercury added to silver ore.*

YAPADA (variante de **yapa**).

YAPAR. *v.* (Acad.) Añadir la **yapa**. *To add something as a bonus, add as an extra.*

YARARÁ. *n.f.* Serpiente de gran tamaño, muy venenosa. *Rattlesnake, pit viper.*

YAYÁ. *n.f.* Dolor insignificante. *Slight pain.* || **2.** Herida pequeña, cicatriz. *Small scar, slight wound.*

YERBATERO. *n.m.* (Acad.) Dícese del médico o curandero que cura con hierbas. *Herb doctor.* || **2.** Vendedor de hierbas medicinales. *Herbalist.*

YERRA. *n.f.* Acto de marcar el ganado con un hierro. *Branding.*

YÉRSEY. *n.m.* (Acad.) Tejido fino de punto. *Jersey.*

YESQUERO. *n.m.* Encendedor que utiliza la yesca como materia combustible. *Cigarette lighter.*

YETA. *n.f.* Mala suerte. *Bad luck.*

YUCA. *n.f.* Nombre vulgar de algunas especies de mandioca. *Cassava.*

YUNGAS. *n.f.* Valles calientes. *Hot valleys.*

YUYO. *n.m.* Mala hierba. *Weed.*

Z

ZACATAL. *n.m.* (Acad.) Terreno de abundante pasto, pastizal. *Pasture.*

ZACATE. *n.m.* (Acad.) Hierba, pasto, forraje. *Grass, pasture.*

ZACATÓN. *n.m.* (Acad.) Hierba alta de pasto. *Tall grass.*

ZAFACOCA. *n.f.* Riña, pendencia, alboroto. *Row, quarrel, brawl.*

ZAFADO. *adj.* Atrevido, descarado. *Brazen, shameless, insolent.*

ZAFADURA. *n.f.* Dislocación de los huesos. *Dislocation, sprain.*

ZAFADURÍA. *n.f.* Descaro. *Cheek, nerve.*

ZAFAR. *v.* (Acad.) Dislocarse, desconyuntarse un hueso. *To dislocate a bone.* || **2.** -se. Escaparse, evadirse. *To escape, run away.* || **3.** Excluir. *To exclude.*

ZAFRA. *n.f.* Cosecha de caña de azúcar. *Sugar cane harvest.*

ZALAMEAR. *v.* Usar de zalamerías. *To flatter.*

ZAMBO. *n.m.* Se dice del hijo de negro e india. *Half-breed (of Negro and Indian parentage).*

ZAMBULLÓN. *n.m.* Zambullida. *Dive, plunge.*

ZAMPAR. *v.* (Acad.) Arrojar, impeler con violencia una cosa. *To hurl.* ~Lo zampó en el suelo. *He threw it on the floor.* ~Le zamparon en la cárcel. *He was thrown in jail.* || **2.** Poner. *Put, stick.* ~Zampó el pie en el barro. *He stuck his foot in the mud.* || **4.** Pegar. *To hit.* ~Le zampó una patada. *He kicked him.* || **5.** Decir. *To tell.* ~Le zampó que de ninguna manera iba a ir. *She told him straight out that under no circumstance would she go.* ||

6. Tirarse, lanzarse. *To throw oneself, to leap.*

ZANCÓN. *adj.* (Acad.) Aplícase al traje demasiado corto. *Too short (dress, trousers).* ~El pantalón le queda zancón. *His trousers are too short for him.*

ZANCUDERO. *n.m.* Nube de mosquitos. *Swarm of mosquitos.*

ZANCUDO. *n.m.* (Acad.) Mosquito. *Mosquito.*

ZANGUANGO. *n.m.* Tonto, imbécil. *Fool, idiot.*

ZANJA. *n.f.* (Acad.) Arroyada producida por el agua corriente. *Gully, watercourse.*

ZANJÓN. *n.m.* Despeñadero. *Cliff.* || **2.** Barranco. *Gully, ravine.*

ZAPALLADA. *n.f.* Acierto involuntario, chiripa. *Fluke, lucky break.*

ZAPALLO. *n.m.* (Acad.) Cierta calabaza comestible. *Pumpkin.*

ZAPATÓN. *n.m.* Zapato de goma para la lluvia. *Overshoe, galosh.*

ZARAGATE. *n.m.* (Acad.) Persona despreciable. *Rogue, rascal.*

ZARANDEAR. *v.* Contonearse. *To swing one's hips, to strut about.* || **2.** Bambolear. *To shake violently to and fro, toss about, jostle.* ~El barco se zarandeó mucho durante la travesía. *The boat rocked (tossed, pitched) about a lot during the crossing.* || **3.** Maltratar públicamente de palabra a una persona. *To speak publicly against someone.*

ZARANDEO. *n.m.* Trajín. *Hustle and bustle, commotion, coming and going.*

ZARAZO. *adj.* Medio borracho. *Tight, typsy.* || **2.** Se dice del fruto a medio madurar. *Underripe*.

ZARCILLO. *n.m.* Marca del ganado que consiste en un corte en la oreja. *Earmark*.

ZARPEAR. *v.* Salpicar de barro. *To splash with mud*.

ZIPER (angl.). *n.m.* Cierre relámpago. *Zipper*.

ZOCOTROCO. *n.m.* Pedazo grande e informe de algo. *Chunk, big lump*. || **2.** Persona grande y pesada. *Hefty man*.

ZONA. *n.f.* •Zona de tolerancia (zona roja). Barrio chino. *Red-light district*.

ZONCEAR. *v.* Tontear, sonsear. T*o behave stupidly*.

ZONCERA. *n.f.* (Acad.) Tontera, simpleza. ~Discutieron por una ZONCERA. Discutieron por una bobada. *They argued over a trifle*.

ZONZO. *adj.* Tonto. *Silly, stupid*.

ZOPILOTE. *n.m.* Halcón. *Buzzard*.

ZOQUETADA. *n.f.* (Acad.) Necedad, simpleza. *Stupidity*.

ZOQUETAZO. *n.m.* (Acad.) Golpe, guantazo, sopapo. *Punch, smack in the face*.

ZOQUETE. *n.m.* Mentecato. *Dimwit, blockhead*.

ZOQUETEAR. *v.* (Acad.) Comportarse como un **zoquete** o mentecato. *To act like a blockhead, to act like a dimwit*.

ZORRILLO. *n.m.* Mofeta. *Skunk*.

ZUMBA. (Acad.) *n.m.* (Acad.) Tunda, zurra. *Beating*.

ZUMBAR. *v.* Arrojar, lanzar. *To throw*.

ZURDEAR. *v.* (Acad.) Hacer con la mano izquierda lo que generalmente se hace con la derecha. *To do with the left hand what is normally done with the right hand. to be ambidextrous*.

Basic Biography

Americanismos. Diccionario ilustrado Sopena. Sopena, Barcelona, Barcelona, 1983

Collins Spanish English, English Dictionary. Unabridged edition. HarperCollins Publishers. 1993.

Diccionario actual de la lengua española. Biblograf, Barcelona, 1993.

Diccionario General Ilustrado de la Lengua Española. Barcelona, 1989.

Moliner, María de. *Diccionario del uso del español.* Gredos, Madrid, 1992.

Morínigo, Marcos A. *Diccionario del español de América.* Anaya & Mario Muchnik, Madrid, 1994.

Neves, Afredo N. *Diccionario de americanismos.* Sopena Argentina, Buenos Aires, 1973.

Real Academia Española. *Diccionario manual e ilustrado de la lengua española.* Espasa Calpe, Madrid, 1989.

Real Academia Española. *Diccionario de la lengua española.* Espasa Calpe, Madrid, 1992.

Santamaría, Francisco J. *Diccionario General de Americanismos.* 3 vols. Editorial Pedro Robredo, Mexico, 1942.

Simon & Schuster's International Dictionary. English/Spanish, Spanish/English. Simon & Schuster, New York, 1974.

Steel, Brian. *Diccionario de americanismos/ABC of Latin American Spanish.* SGEL. Madrid, 1990.

The Oxford Spanish Dictionary. Oxford University Press, 1994.

ORDER FORM

BILINGUAL BOOK PRESS
Quality Bilingual Publications

BILINGUAL BOOK PRESS
10977 Santa Monica Blvd.
Los Angeles, CA 90024

Date _____

P.O. _____

Fax # _____

COPIES	DESCRIPTION	ISBN	PRICE	TOTAL
	Bilingual Dictionary of Mexican Spanish. 2nd Ed. Trade paperback.	1-886835-01-2	$16.95	
	The Best of Latin American Short Stories. Paper.	1-886835-02-0	$10.95	
	Bilingual Dictionary of Latin American Spanish. Trade paperback.	1-886835-03-9	$14.95	
	Two Holiday Folktales from Mexico.	1-886835-04-7	$7.95	
	Forthcoming: *California Missions* (Bilingual Edition)			
	Forthcoming: *Bilingual Dictionary of Spanish False Cognates*			
	Message:			

SUBTOTAL	
CALIFORNIA STATE TAX (8.25%)	
SUBTOTAL	
SHIPPING & HANDLING. 8% of Subtotal ($3.00 min.)	
TOTAL	

SEND TO

ATTN: _____

INSTITUTION: _____

ADDRESS: _____

CITY: _____ STATE _____ ZIP _____

 Tel. (310) 475-0453 Or   Fax (310) 473-6132